Adobe® LiveCycle® Designer

Creating Dynamic PDF and HTML5 Forms
for Desktop and Mobile Applications

SECOND EDITION

J.P. Terry
and SmartDoc Technologies

Adobe

Adobe® LiveCycle® Designer, Second Edition
J.P. Terry and SmartDoc Technologies

Adobe Press books are published by Peachpit, a division of Pearson Education.
For the latest on Adobe Press books, go to www.adobepress.com.
To report errors, please send a note to errata@peachpit.com.
Copyright © 2014 by J.P. Terry

Adobe Press Editor: Victor Gavenda
Project Editor: Nancy Peterson
Development Editor: Robyn G. Thomas
Technical Editors: Adam Jay, Rajesh R. Kandasamy, Yanhui Wang
Copyeditor: Liz Welch
Compositor: Danielle Foster
Indexer: Karin Arrigoni
Cover Design: Aren Straiger
Interior Design: Charlene Charles-Will, Mimi Heft
Illustrations: J.P. Terry and Elizabeth Hughes

Printed and bound in the United States of America

ISBN 13: 978-0-321-94199-2
ISBN 10:   0-321-94199-3

9 8 7 6 5 4 3 2 1

Dedication

To Shannon, Patrick, Rollins,
and Eva—you make my life dynamic
and interactive.

To my father, the engineer, and my mother, the teacher—
this book is a testament to your influence, encouragement,
and love.

To the incredible SmartDoc Technologies team—
thank you for all your hard work on this book.

— J.P. Terry

Acknowledgments

I'd like to thank my colleagues at SmartDoc Technologies. You have all contributed greatly to this book, and our team effort has made it complete. A special thanks to the core team of Yanhui Wang, Adam Jay, Rajesh R. Kandasamy, and Meghan Pipher, who worked many hours on the hands-on exercises. Thanks also to Kevin Guterl, Ming Luo, Elizabeth Hughes, Gowthami Sagi, Xiaojuan Zhu, Fei Zhong, and Yuling Zhu, who all supported the core team with valuable research and reviews.

Thanks to the Adobe LiveCycle Business team, including Dave Welch, Jeff Stanier, Vamsi K. Vutukuru, Steve Monroe, Girish Bedekar, and Gary Robbins. A special thanks to Jeff Stanier, who has been extremely helpful on both editions of this book. Thanks to LiveCycle Engineering, including Rajiv Mangla, Suvrat Chaturvedi, Arvind Heda, Raghavendra K. Pandey, Deepak Kumar, Kamlesh Bahedia, Saket Sidana, Sudhanshu Singh, Dinesh Pandey, and Akshit Jain. A special thanks to Suvrat Chaturvedi and Arvind Heda, who have helped me and the SmartDoc team understand the new HTML technologies. Thanks to the LiveCycle partner team, including Tony Sanders, Bill McCulloch, Howard Zemel, and Lakshmi Anumolu. Thanks also to others at Adobe who I have had the pleasure to work with over the past year, including Joe Coughlin, Neal Wadhwani, Jason Barnett, Matt Rodgers, Michael Jackson, and Mark Johnson. Adobe has developed a great foundation for us to build automated desktop and mobile business solutions.

Thanks to Nancy Peterson and the team at Peachpit, including but not limited to Robyn Thomas, Damon Hampson, Danielle Foster, Liz Welch, and Scout Festa. Their professional efforts and friendship have greatly helped this book.

On a personal note, thanks to my siblings, Kevin, Mary Beth, and Dodd, and our extended family and friends for the encouragement you have all given me through the years.

About the Author

 J.P. Terry is the CEO of SmartDoc Technologies (www. smartdoctech.com), a leading provider of solutions with Adobe LiveCycle and Adobe Experience Manager (AEM) document services. SmartDoc has developed paperless systems for Fidelity Investments and Merrill Lynch and is an Adobe Business Partner. SmartDoc has offices in New York; New Jersey; and Beijing, China.

J.P. is an ACI (Adobe Certified Instructor) and an ACE (Adobe Certified Expert) in Adobe LiveCycle technology. He often writes and speaks about technology solutions for business and is the author of *Creating Dynamic Forms with Adobe LiveCycle Designer* (Adobe Press, 2007) and *Paperless: Real-World Solutions with Adobe Technology* (Adobe Press, 2009).

J.P. is a graduate of the Rhode Island School of Design. He has programming certificates from Microsoft and Novell, and a certificate in financial management from the Wharton School of the University of Pennsylvania. He has recently completed coursework in Java and Android programming at New York University. He has participated in international mission trips to build housing with local teams and families.

Prior to founding SmartDoc Technologies, J.P. founded BrandWizard Technologies in 1996. BrandWizard was an early pioneer in MRM (Marketing Resource Management) and is now part of the Omnicom Group (OMC). He was the CEO of BrandWizard from 2000 to 2005.

Contents

PART 2 PDF FORMS

PART 3   HTML FORMS

PART 4   AUTOMATING BUSINESS

Introduction

Did you fill out a form to purchase this book?

If not, are you going to fill out a form to expense it to your company?

In the information age, the primary way that we provide information to computer systems is through forms. Computers can communicate with each other easily. However, when we need to provide information to a computer system, we have to fill out some type of form (**Figure I.1**).

Figure I.1 Some forms that might have been used to purchase this book.

Forms are everywhere today. We're presented with forms when a system or an organization wants some type of information from us. For example, the government uses forms to ask us for income information for tax purposes; youth soccer teams use forms to ask us about our children's health before the start of the season. And with the rise of e-commerce, we're seeing an increase in interactive forms for opening accounts and for purchasing products and services. Paper forms and online forms are part of our daily lives in the information age.

It's interesting to note that computers don't need forms as we think of them. Most computer programs require data in much smaller and simpler structures. The graphic and layout elements in our forms like rules; shapes and images are usually disregarded by the computers that process them. For instance, in a typical address change, the most pertinent information for the computer to know can be contained within a simple and compact file like this one:

```
<addressChange>
    <individual>
        <firstName>James</firstName>
        <lastName>Shannon</lastName>
        <oldAddress>
            <address>1 Main Street</address>
            <city>Springfield</city>
            <state>IL</state>
            <zipCode>62701</zipCode>
        </oldAddress>
        <newAddress>
            <address>101 Main Street</address>
            <city>Springfield</city>
            <state>IL</state>
            <zipCode>62701</zipCode>
        </newAddress>
    </individual>
</addressChange>
```

People are the ones who need clearly designed forms (**Figure I.2**). We need a graphically clear presentation of data to understand it and process it. We need to comprehend the context of the information exchange. We don't want to simply provide and access data. We want to know why we're providing data and what benefits we're deriving from our data provision. Forms should be designed for us and be human compatible.

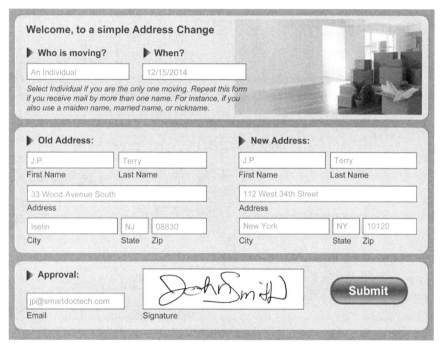

Figure I.2 A well-designed form helps users understand the required information and how to supply it to complete the transaction.

The trouble is that too many forms are difficult to use and fill out properly. According to a survey by Compete Inc., over 70 percent of online account opening forms are abandoned before completion. The cost to business in lost opportunity and increased customer call center traffic is so substantial that it requires us to make a renewed effort to create engaging and effective forms.

If only there were a program with features and tools to help us create engaging and effective forms and link them with data. It would be even better if this program were developed and supported by the unquestioned worldwide leader in graphics software. Well, your dreams have come true, and it gets even better.

Adobe LiveCycle Designer, the premier form development tool for the last 10 years, can now create HTML forms as well as PDF forms. The same LiveCycle Designer source files can be used for both. You can create your interactive and dynamic fully featured forms and deploy them as HTML forms to mobile devices like the Apple iPad and Google Android tablets.

Adobe LiveCycle Designer

LiveCycle Designer (Designer for short) is a Microsoft Windows–based program that provides all the tools you need to create basic or sophisticated forms. You can use Designer in either of the following ways:

- As a standalone program to create forms and documents
- As part of Adobe LiveCycle Enterprise Suite (**Figure I.3**)

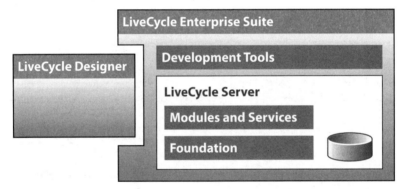

Figure I.3 Designer can be used independently and as part of LiveCycle Enterprise Suite.

LiveCycle Enterprise Suite consists of additional development tools and a Live-Cycle Server. You'll learn more about LiveCycle Enterprise Suite in Chapter 9. When it's relevant, I'll mention server tools and features and refer to them simply as "LiveCycle Server" to differentiate them from LiveCycle Designer.

However, the focus of this book is Designer. You'll learn all about Designer's tools and how you can use them to create and manage interactive forms and dynamic documents. There are many step-by-step exercises so you can get hands-on and learn the best practices for creating PDF and HTML forms. After you learn the techniques, the last part of this book will show you how your Designer documents are used in the real world to automate business.

Who This Book Is For

This book is designed for people who want effective and efficient customer engagement with their form systems. You may want to create a new form system or improve an existing one. In either case, the following types of professionals will benefit from this book.

Form Developers

Whether you are new to Designer or you're a seasoned professional, you'll find valuable information and examples in these pages to help you with your craft. As you probably know, today's form developers need to be multi-talented, and this book will help you in these areas:

- Developing your graphic layout and data pattern skills to meet form requirements

- Developing new advanced scripting skills for form automation

- Understanding how your forms fit into your workflow automation

- Understanding the new world of mobile forms

Programmers and IT Professionals

Forms and documents provide the input and output for the computer systems you create and manage. Many of your data goals, including validation and formatting, can be accomplished with well-designed interactive forms. This book will show you how to

- Take advantage of Designer's out-of-the box tools and features to improve your systems right away.

- Enhance Designer's standard tools with custom scripting.

- Integrate Designer's forms and documents into your existing enterprise systems, including databases, workflow tools, websites, and document management systems.

Business Professionals

Business has changed greatly in the last 20 years. B2C (business-to-consumer) and B2B (business-to-business) e-commerce is an increasingly important aspect of your job. This book will show you how effective forms and workflow automation will help you deliver the following:

- Improved customer engagement with your forms and electronic communications

- Greater conversion of prospects into customers by simplifying the data-gathering process

- Fewer costs and greater speed by converting previously paper-based processes to electronic workflows

 Part 4 of this book is designed to show how your paperless and mobile goals will be achieved. You'll learn how Designer and other Adobe LiveCycle modules will save you time and money while improving the quality of your customer communications. You can see a demonstration of these tools on the book's companion site: www.smartdoctech.com/support. You can run this demo on your PC, Macintosh, or mobile tablet (**Figure I.4**).

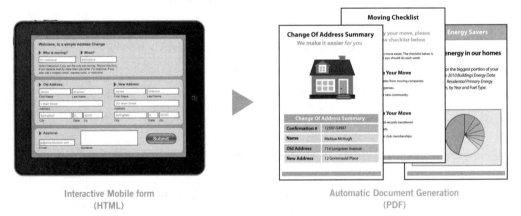

Interactive Mobile form
(HTML)

Automatic Document Generation
(PDF)

Figure I.4 The book's companion site includes a demo of an automated Address Change workflow that includes an interactive form and dynamic document generation.

What This Book Covers

You'll learn what Designer is, how you can use it to create PDF and HTML forms, and why this is important for your organization.

The Designer Tool

Part 1 is a thoroughly updated version of the first edition of this book. As in the first edition, this section covers the tools and features of Designer. However, it also includes the new features of Designer like style sheets and has additional advanced scripting techniques that were not part of the first edition. Part 1 ends with a comprehensive step-by-step exercise where you can put your new knowledge to the test. You'll create a complete interactive and dynamic form from scratch.

PDF Forms

Part 2 focuses specifically on PDF forms, documents, and best practices. You'll learn about the various types of PDFs and the different readers that people use to view them. Chapter 4 includes important information about the differences between Adobe Acrobat and the free Adobe Reader and shows you how to Reader extend your files to overcome the limits of the free version. Chapter 5 covers best practices, including form fragments, localization, accessibility, and performance optimization.

HTML Forms

Part 3 covers Designer's new HTML capabilities and details the similarities and differences between Designer's HTML and PDF forms. You'll learn how to iron out some of the differences so you can develop Designer forms that can be used to render whichever form type is needed in your workflow. Like Part 1, this part ends with step-by-step exercises where you'll create interactive and dynamic forms. However, this time they'll be HTML forms.

Automating Business

The last part of the book shows how your Designer forms and documents will be used to automate your business. You'll learn about Adobe's other LiveCycle tools and modules and how they can be used to manage your forms and streamline your workflows. The last chapter of the book covers the new world of mobile forms and compares and contrasts different strategies for competing in this world.

What You Need to Begin

As mentioned, there are many hands-on exercises in this book. Therefore, you'll need the following items to enhance your learning experience.

The Software

You need both LiveCycle Designer and Adobe Acrobat installed on your computer. You'll develop your forms and documents in Designer and preview them with Acrobat. You'll also need a relatively new web browser to view your forms as HTML. Chapter 6 includes a list of supported web browsers.

LiveCycle Designer

You need the Designer program. You may already have it if either of the following is true:

■ Your company has a license for Adobe LiveCycle Enterprise Suite.

■ You have a version of Adobe Acrobat earlier than 11. Designer shipped with earlier versions of Acrobat, but beginning with Acrobat 11, Designer is sold as a separate product on the Adobe website. Please note that the versions of Designer that shipped with Acrobat prior to Acrobat 11 do not fully support the HTML capabilities described in this book. If you want to develop HTML forms, you must have Designer ES4 (version 11) or later.

If you don't have LiveCycle Designer, you can either buy it or download a trial version from www.adobe.com. As of this writing, Adobe is offering a 60-day free trial at www.adobe.com/products/livecycle/tools/designer.html.

If this link gets changed, simply do a Google search for LiveCycle Designer trial download. You'll need an Adobe ID, and you can select your language version prior to downloading (**Figure I.5**).

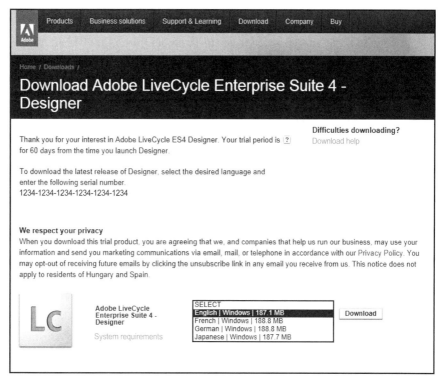

Figure I.5 You can download a free trial version of Designer from the Adobe website.

There are various ways to configure your LiveCycle Designer workspace. To easily follow the exercises in this book, open the following palettes in your Designer workspace. If you don't see any of the palettes listed, you can open them from Designer's Window menu.

- The Script Editor palette

- The Hierarchy palette

- The Data View palette

- The Tab Order palette

- The Object and Fragment Library palettes

- The Style Catalog palette

- The Layout, Border, Object, and Accessibility palettes

- The Font and Paragraph palettes

Adobe Acrobat

In addition to previewing your Designer forms, you'll need Acrobat for some of the exercises in Part 2, "PDF Forms." If you don't have Acrobat, you can either buy it or download a free trial version from www.adobe.com.

The Companion Site

Throughout the book, you'll see this globe icon next to a topic with more information on the book's companion site: www.smartdoctech.com/support.

You'll find support materials on this site, including the following:

- Additional bonus articles and exercises for LiveCycle Designer.

- Links to important information in the Adobe Help System, Knowledge Base, and Developer Connection.

- FAQ (Frequently Asked Questions) about the book.

- Errata: The exercises in this book have been reviewed many times by several technical editors. However, as with all human endeavors, it's possible that something is incorrect. If you find an incompatibility with one of the sample files, please report it to support@smartdoctech.com.

The Sample Files

You can also download the sample files from the book's companion site. You need these files to work through the hands-on exercises in this book.

Moving On

Now that you know what to expect, let's get started by learning the features and functions of Adobe LiveCycle Designer.

The Designer Tool

Part 1 focuses on the LiveCycle Designer program and the important tools and features you'll find in it. This section is meant for beginner to intermediate form developers; it's been updated for the current version of Designer.

1

The Basics

After a game in which his team performed very poorly, Vince Lombardi, the legendary coach of the Green Bay Packers, held up a football in front of the team and said, "Men, this is a football."

One of his players looked up and said, "Slow down, Coach, you're going too fast."

This chapter introduces you to the LiveCycle Designer interface and then covers the important fundamentals you need to get started. I'll walk you through the more difficult-to-understand concepts like using subforms, organizing flow, and working with data. With a solid grasp of the basics, you'll then be able to move on to more advanced topics in Chapter 2, "Scripting and Advanced Techniques," and create a complete form in Chapter 3, "Creating the SmartDoc Expense Report."

Understanding LiveCycle Designer

LiveCycle Designer (Designer for short) is a Microsoft Windows–based program that provides all the tools you need to create basic or sophisticated forms. Designer is a multifaceted tool that supports the four most important requirements of smart forms:

■ **Multiple format and device support:** With the new version of Designer, you can create one Designer file and render it in all the formats you need for your business. These formats include HTML, interactive and dynamic PDF forms, and read-only PDF documents. Your Designer forms and documents can be used on traditional PCs and Macintoshes and also on tablets and smartphones.

■ **Data handling:** Designer makes it easy to get data structures into your forms and to output properly formatted data from your forms. Powerful tools are provided for data validation, data formatting, and data binding.

■ **Scriptable interactivity:** Designer's scriptable interactivity goes way beyond what is available in Acroforms and other form technologies. Virtually every form object is scriptable at any step in your process. Designer has a sophisticated object model, which you can use to add powerful interactivity to your forms.

■ **Graphic precision and fidelity:** The three preceding features would usually be enough for an interactive forms tool, but Designer also offers the graphic precision and quality of an Adobe solution. For the last 30 years, Adobe has been the unquestioned leader in computer graphics with industry leading products in graphic design, marketing, and digital publishing tools. You don't need to compromise on typography, layout, or graphic quality with Designer forms, and your one form can be used for all your business needs.

Working in the Designer Workspace

If you're ready to start working with LiveCycle Designer, launch the program by clicking the Windows Start button and locating the Designer icon. Follow these steps to create a new form:

1. Select File > New, and Designer launches the New Form Assistant.

2. Select Use A Blank Form, and click Next to continue.

3. Keep the defaults, and click Finish to create your new form.

The Designer workspace appears (**Figure 1.1**), which is the interface you'll use to create your dynamic forms and documents. The workspace consists of many editors, views, and palettes that can float or be docked. You can configure your workspace in many different ways, but Figure 1.1 shows a typical configuration.

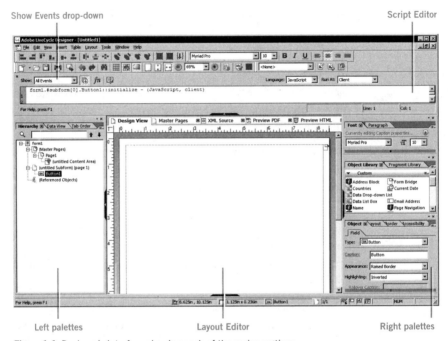

Figure 1.1 Designer's interface showing each of the major sections.

Using the Layout Editor

The Layout Editor is in the middle of the workspace, and it contains five main views: Design View, Master Pages, XML Source, Preview PDF, and Preview HTML. You'll see the Layout Editor when you have a document opened. The following is a brief introduction to each of the Layout Editor views:

■ **Design View:** Design View is the main view in the Layout Editor and the one that you'll use the most. This view displays a WYSIWYG view of your form and allows you to edit many of the visual properties of your form objects directly.

- **Master Pages:** The Master Pages tab shows an independent view of your master pages without any body page content. Master pages contain content areas that define the outer boundaries for body page objects.

- **XML Source:** If you don't see the XML Source tab, you can select it in the View menu. This is your form in XML format. The structure of Designer forms is all XML, and as you make additions and edits to your form in Design View, this XML is updated in the background. You can quickly locate the XML source code for any of your form objects by selecting the object in the Hierarchy palette while the XML Source view is open. You'll immediately see the XML Source view update, and your selected form object will be highlighted in the XML Source view.

- **Preview PDF:** You can preview your forms directly in Designer by switching to the Preview PDF tab. This tab uses your computer's default PDF viewer, so if you have Acrobat, you'll notice part of the familiar Acrobat interface wrapping around your form when you view it in this tab. You can see more of Acrobat by pressing Alt+F8.

- **Preview HTML:** If you don't see the Preview HTML tab, you can select it in the View menu. If it doesn't appear in your View menu, you're likely using a version of Designer prior to Designer ES4. You'll learn how to configure and use this view in Part 3, "HTML Forms."

Using the Script Editor

By default, the Script Editor is located directly above the Layout Editor and below the menu bar (Figure 1.1). You use this tool to create and edit scripts, and it's usually docked at the top of the Designer workspace. Scripts are an important part of smart forms because they enable you to customize the functionality of your forms at both the client and the server level. You'll learn more about this later in the book.

Using the Left Palettes

The area on the left in Figure 1.1 includes palettes you'll use to organize the structure of your form:

- **Hierarchy:** You'll spend a lot of time using this palette to view and organize the objects and structure of your form. When you select an object on your form, it's also selected in the Hierarchy palette, and vice versa. The Hierarchy palette displays your form's objects in a tree view, which is a great way to examine and edit your form's structure. Understanding this structure becomes particularly important when you start adding script to your form. The Hierarchy palette also displays referenced objects under the Referenced Objects node. A *referenced object* is an object that's added to a form only when it's required. Overflow leader and trailer subforms are examples of referenced objects. Whenever data flows across multiple pages or content areas, the overflow leader and trailer subforms are inserted into the form in the appropriate places.

■ **PDF Structure:** This palette does not appear in Figure 1.1 but is available in Designer. It isn't usually relevant for the XML Forms Architecture (XFA) PDF forms you'll create with Designer. It's more relevant for Acroforms and PDF documents because it displays a hierarchical view of the accessibility tags in these types of PDFs. You'll use this feature in Designer if you're working with PDF forms with fixed pages and fixed background artwork. You add accessibility features to XFA PDFs with the Accessibility palette, which is described in Part 2, "PDF Forms."

■ **Data View:** When you open a form that's connected to a data source, the Data View palette shows you a graphical representation of your form's data elements (**Figure 1.2**). You can associate your forms with data sources through a process called data binding. You can bind your form objects to an XML Schema, a Sample XML Data file, an Adobe Data Model, a WSDL (Web Services Description Language) file, or an OLEDB (Object Linking and Embedding Database).

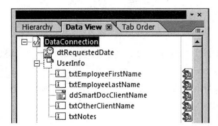

Figure 1.2 The Data View palette showing the schema binding on the SmartDoc Expense Report form that you'll create in Chapter 3.

■ **Tab Order:** The Tab Order palette shows all your form objects in a list that corresponds to the order that a user will see when tabbing through the form. You can change your form's tab order with this tool. The default tab order for Designer forms is left to right and top to bottom. If you don't see this palette, choose Window > Tab Order. You'll find more information about tabbing at the end of the next chapter.

Using the Right Palettes

The area on the right in Figure 1.1 includes palettes you'll use to create and edit your form objects:

- **Font:** The Font palette enables you to edit the font family, size, and style of text in your objects. Many interactive form objects like Text Fields have both a caption and a value font property that can be set independently.

- **Paragraph:** The Paragraph palette enables you to edit the alignment, indents, and line spacing of your text.

- **Object Library:** The Object Library palette provides a collection of all available form objects. You can easily drag and drop form objects from this palette onto your form layout.

- **Fragment Library:** The Fragment Library palette provides a collection of your form fragments. Form fragments are reusable form parts that are saved as separate files. These fragments are ideal if you're creating or managing numerous forms that use the same form parts. You'll learn more about this in Part 2.

- **Object:** You use the Object palette to modify the properties of your form's interface objects. As you work with this palette, you'll learn that it's very useful and very adaptive. It enables you to edit and customize the most important aspects of your objects without having to provide any custom JavaScript. It's flexible because it reconfigures its options based on the object you select. For instance, if you select a master page object, you'll see the Master Page and Pagination tabs on the Object palette.

- **Layout:** The Layout palette works hand in hand with the Layout Editor. As you make changes to your object in the Layout Editor, they are reflected here, and vice versa.

- **Border:** Most of the information in the Border palette is self-explanatory. However, it's important to note that these border properties affect the entire object, not just the editable portion of the field. The entire area surrounding your field and caption will be outlined with a border that you set with this palette (**Figure 1.3**). If you want to edit the border around your field, use the Appearance property on the Field tab of the Object palette.

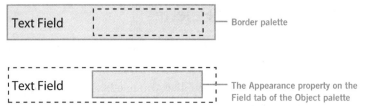

Figure 1.3 The Border palette settings outline the entire object, but the Appearance property in the Object palette enables you to outline just the field.

■ **Accessibility:** You can use the Accessibility palette to set Screen Reader properties for your forms. You can set several different options for each field on your form; you'll learn more about this in Part 2.

Options for Saving Your Form

When you save your Designer file, you need to consider how it will be used. The following is a list of file format options available in Designer. You'll learn how and when to use these formats throughout the subsequent chapters of this book.

■ **Adobe Static PDF Form (*.pdf):** Saves forms as static PDFs based on the Acrobat and Adobe Reader target version specified in the form properties. Even if you specify a dynamic, flowable layout, this type of PDF form will still be static and will not rerender in response to user action. The fields on this form type can be interactive or non-interactive.

■ **Adobe Dynamic XML Form (*.pdf):** Saves forms as dynamic PDFs based on the Acrobat and Adobe Reader target version in the form properties. In this case, a dynamic, flowable layout will rerender in response to user action. A user can add or remove table rows and even entire form sections with this type of PDF.

■ **Adobe XML Form (*.xdp):** Saves forms in the native XML-based file format created by LiveCycle Designer. Use this option if you'll be using a LiveCycle Server to render PDF or HTML forms. The form design can contain dynamic and interactive elements.

■ **Adobe LiveCycle Designer Template (*.tds):** Saves the basic structure for a form as a template. It can contain components and settings, such as fonts, page layout, formatting, and scripts. Use it as a starting point for a new form.

■ **Adobe LiveCycle Designer Style Sheet (*.xfs):** Saves the internal style sheet in the form as an external style sheet. Style sheets can be used to provide consistent formatting to all your forms. Style sheets can control the look of caption and field value text, the appearance of object borders and background colors, as well as the size and style of Radio Buttons and Check Box objects.

Understanding Important Designer Concepts

Now that you know where everything is, let's review some important concepts about dynamic forms: master and body pages, subforms, tables, and data. These are usually the concepts that trip people up when they start creating Designer forms. By mastering these ideas, you'll avoid many pitfalls when designing and implementing your forms. Open the expenseReportCompleted. xdp file from the Samples folder as you read through this section.

Working with Master and Body Pages

Designer documents consist of master pages and body pages. Master pages define the layout and background elements of your form. You should put common page items like page numbers, repeating logos, and date/time stamps on your master pages when designing PDF forms (HTML forms will differ). Body pages should contain all the form objects that are unique to a particular page.

When you're working with multipage forms, it's quite possible that you'll need a different look and feel on different pages. For instance, an account opening form may require three pages of interactive objects and six pages of legal text in columns. In this case, it makes sense to define two different master pages: one for the body pages with the interactive objects and one for the body pages with the legal text.

Master pages

You edit your master pages in the Master Pages tab in the Layout Editor. If you don't see this tab, choose View > Master Pages. You don't need to create a master page; Designer creates a default master page for you. You can design a complete form with this default master page. If several pages in your form have the same layout and need the same objects (like page numbers and footers), it's more efficient to put these items on the master page. Updating a master page automatically updates all the body pages associated with the master page.

The SmartDoc Expense Report (expenseReportCompleted.xdp, which you opened from the Samples folder) has two master pages (**Figure 1.4**). They contain a few important objects that you typically find on master pages.

■ **Automatic page numbering:** There's an automatic page numbering object on masterPage2 that calculates the current page number and the current number of pages.

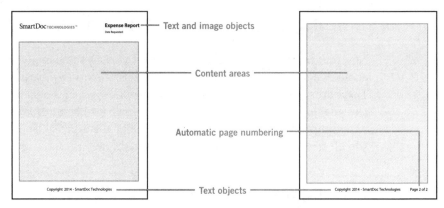

Figure 1.4 Master pages in the SmartDoc Expense Report: masterPage1 (left) and masterPage2 (right).

■ **Content areas:** These objects define the outer bounds of your layout area for the body pages that are associated with the master page. Content areas are particularly important for dynamic forms with flowing content. In the SmartDoc Expense Report form, the content area on masterPage2 is larger than the content area on masterPage1. This larger content area means that all body pages that reference masterPage2 can display more information than the body page that references masterPage1. Content areas are regular Designer objects and are found in the Object Library palette.

■ **Static objects:** The copyright statement at the bottom of each master page is a static text object that repeats on all body pages.

The SmartDoc Expense Report is a dynamic form, so there's no limit to the number of pages a user can create when entering expense items. This PDF form can result in one page with one expense, or it can be 1000 pages with 20,000 expenses. In all cases, it will have one instance of masterPage1, and in some cases it will have one or more instances of masterPage2. You can achieve this by setting the Restrict Page Occurrence property on masterPage1.

In this example, the property is set with a minimum count of 1 and a maximum count of 1 (**Figure 1.5**, left), which is why masterPage1 with the logo and header only appears as the first page of the rendered PDF. However, masterPage2 doesn't have any page restrictions (Figure 1.5, right). Since there's no maximum occurrence restraint for this master page, it's used for every subsequent page in the rendered PDF. Each succeeding page also has an incrementing page number in the lower-right corner because the automatic page numbering control is on masterPage2.

Figure 1.5 The Restrict Page Occurrence option is selected in masterPage1 (left) but not selected in masterPage2 (right).

Body pages

Most of your form objects will be placed on body pages. Each body page will reference a master page. You can view your body page objects by switching from the Master Pages tab to the Design View tab on the SmartDoc Expense Report.

Body pages are subform objects in Designer and as such are treated just like any other subform. The SmartDoc Expense Report has one body page subform titled "page1." This body page subform has three child subforms that define different sections of the dynamic form. Your forms will be made up of body page subforms and standard subforms; you'll learn how these two types of subforms relate in the next section.

Working with Subforms and Flow

A *subform* is a logical grouping of form objects. Subforms define the structure of your form, and you can nest a child subform inside a parent subform (**Figure 1.6**). In fact, there's no limit to the nesting you can do with subforms. But too much nesting will slow down the rendering and performance of your form at runtime.

Figure 1.6 Subforms can be nested in a tree structure.

Subforms work in conjunction with the content areas that you learned about earlier. Content areas control where objects are located, and subforms control how objects are placed as the form is rendered. By grouping certain objects together in a subform, you can be assured that they'll be consistently positioned relative to each other as the form is rendered.

Depending on the incoming data or the user interaction, subforms can be repeated, expanded, or hidden. Repeating and expanding subforms are ideal for forms with repeating data like the SmartDoc Expense Report. Repeating subforms are child subforms that are placed inside an expanding parent subform. Because subforms are separate, independent sections of a form, they can be hidden or shown based on the needs of the user or other business logic.

Subforms can be challenging and complex, but they are what make dynamic documents dynamic. Without subforms and tables, which are just a type of subform, you wouldn't be able to create dynamic documents that grow and shrink based on data or user interaction.

Pagination and Subform Flow Is Different in HTML Forms

Pagination and subform flow work differently in the HTML renderings of your Designer files than they do in the PDF renderings. For instance, the repeating expense rows of the SmartDoc Expense Report will flow from page to page in a PDF rendering of the form. However, in the HTML rendering, these repeating rows will simply repeat on the same HTML page without flowing to a secondary page.

For more information and to see how pagination and subform flow works in HTML forms, please see Part 3.

How subforms work

As with other Designer features, subforms are easy to understand if you look at an example. Open the basicSubform.xdp file (**Figure 1.7**) from your Sample folder. This basic example shows you most of the important options that subforms offer:

■ **The Body Page subform:** The parent subform (bodyPageSubform) acts as a wrapper for subforms A, B, C, and D. Select bodyPageSubform in the Hierarchy palette and view the settings in the Subform tab of the Object palette. The Content property is set to Flowed, and the flow direction is set to Top To Bottom. These parent subform settings are significant, as you'll see in the next section on hidden and invisible subforms.

Figure 1.7 The basicSubform.xdp file in your Samples folder shows you how subforms work.

■ **subform A:** Select subformA in the Hierarchy palette and view its settings in the Subform tab of the Object palette. The Content property is set to Positioned, which means that all objects on this subform will be positioned exactly where you place them in Design View. Each object on subform A will maintain its X and Y position relative to subform A regardless of where subform A appears on the rendered form.

■ **subform B:** Select subformB in the Hierarchy palette and view its settings in the Subform tab of the Object palette. This time the Content property is set to Flowed, and the flow direction is set to Top To Bottom. As you can see in Figure 1.7, this causes the objects to stack on top of each other regardless of where you originally positioned them in Design View.

■ **subform C:** subformC is similar to B except the flow direction is set to Western Text, which displays the objects left to right and wraps them onto the next line if more space is required.

■ **subform D:** subformD is similar to B and C except the flow direction is set to Right To Left, which displays the objects right to left and wraps them onto the next line if more space is required.

Hidden and invisible subforms

As mentioned previously, you can hide subforms in your dynamic forms. You accomplish this by setting the Presence property on the subform. Depending on the option you choose for the Presence property and the Content property of the parent subform, different effects will result, as illustrated in **Figure 1.8**.

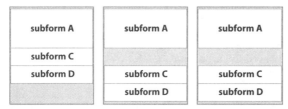

Figure 1.8 The Presence property of a child subform and the Content property of the parent subform determine how your form is rendered.

■ **Hidden subform in a flowed parent (left form):** This is the usual structure for dynamic forms and is ideal for customizing your forms based on user choices. For instance, if you present your users with a series of options at the beginning of your form and they select a subset, the remainder of the form is automatically adjusted to the subset they chose. You achieve this effect by setting the Presence property of the child subform. Select subform B in the basicSubform.xdp example. Set the Presence property to Hidden (Exclude From Layout). Subforms C and D automatically move up in the form to occupy the position previously held by subform B.

■ **Invisible subform in a flowed parent (center form):** The Invisible Presence property works differently than the Hidden property. Change the Presence property of subform B to Invisible, and you'll see that it disappears but subforms C and D don't move up. Use the Invisible property when you want to hide something from view, but you don't want to alter the layout of the form.

■ **Hidden subform in a positioned parent (right form):** Recall that the Content property of the parent subform is significant. Let's change this property to Positioned to see what effect it has on the form. Start by setting subform B back to Visible. You should now see all four of the child subforms. Select bodyPageSubform in the Hierarchy palette and change the Content property from Flowed to Positioned (you can find this in the Subform tab of the Object palette). Set the Presence property of subform B to Hidden (Exclude From Layout) like you did previously. This time subforms C and D don't move up because the parent subform is set to Positioned. Just as you saw with form objects, setting a parent subform to Positioned keeps all of its child subforms in the same relative X and Y position.

When you're working with subforms and other dynamic content, you should save your file as a dynamic PDF and not a static PDF. Now that you understand some subform basics, the dynamic features in the SmartDoc Expense Report will make more sense.

Working with Tables

Tables in Designer are a lot like tables in a word processing program. You can use tables to organize data into a structured grid of related objects. But in Designer, tables are also complex container objects, so you can work with them just like you worked with subforms in the previous section.

The Table object

You can add a simple table to your form by dragging and dropping a Table object from the Library palette onto your form. Designer then automatically launches the Insert Table dialog box (**Figure 1.9**).

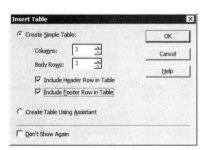

Figure 1.9 The Insert Table dialog box can be used to create a simple table.

You can specify the number of columns and rows that you want for your table. You can also choose to add a header row or a footer row to your table. This method enables you to enter a maximum of 20 columns and 50 rows. If needed, you can add more columns and rows later by using the Insert commands on the Table menu.

Designer automatically adds a table to your form, and it constructs a table hierarchy in your Hierarchy palette. The hierarchy of a table is similar to the hierarchy that you saw with subforms. The top-level object, called Table, is the parent object, and each row is a child object. Each row contains a Text object for each cell. Depending on your needs, you can change this Text object to a Text Field object, a Date/Time object, or any other object from the Standard tab of your palette. You can even nest a Table object inside the cell of another Table object.

The Table Assistant and Table menu

The Table Assistant is an alternative to the Insert Table dialog box. It is a multipage wizard tool, and it provides more features and additional information about tables. To create a table with the Table Assistant, select Table > Insert Table > Create Table Using Assistant. One of the additional tools in the Table Assistant is the Row Shading page (**Figure 1.10**), which enables you to set different colors for alternating rows. This is a useful design method to use on your forms. Changing the colors on alternating rows makes it easier for your users to read and comprehend table-based data.

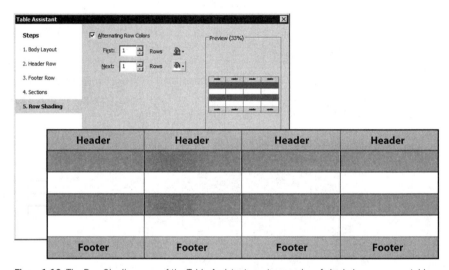

Figure 1.10 The Row Shading page of the Table Assistant creates a series of shaded rows on your table.

The Table menu is on the main menu of Designer, and it provides many tools for working with tables, including

- **Insert Table:** Launches the Insert Table dialog box that appeared when you dropped a Table object onto your form.

- **Merge Cells:** Select any two adjacent cells in a row and merge them into one by selecting Merge Cells.

- **Distribute Rows Evenly:** Distributes the selected rows in a table evenly, based on the height of the tallest row in the selection. This is a good way to ensure consistency in your table layout.

- **Distribute Columns Evenly:** Distributes the selected columns in a table evenly, based on the total width divided by the number of columns in the selection. This is a good way to ensure consistency in your table layout.

Dynamic tables

As mentioned earlier, tables are complex container objects, and you can work with them as you did with subforms to build dynamic forms. Tables can be dynamic, and table rows can repeat just like repeating subforms.

A good example of a dynamic table is the purchaseOrder.xdp form in the Samples folder. Follow these steps to see how a dynamic table is similar to the dynamic subforms in the SmartDoc Expense Report:

1. Open the purchaseOrder.xdp form in Designer.

2. Select Preview PDF, and navigate down to the middle of the form where you enter your items.

3. Click the Add Item button. A new instance of a Body Row object will be added to the table.

4. Click the X button. An existing instance of a Body Row object will be deleted from the table.

5. Select Design View, and notice that the hierarchy of a table looks like the hierarchy of nested subforms (**Figure 1.11**). A Body Row object (detail) is nested inside a Table object (details).

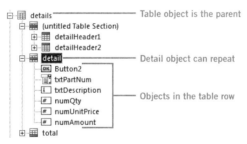

Figure 1.11 The hierarchy of a table is similar to the hierarchy of a parent subform with multiple child subforms.

6. Select the detail Body Row object and look at the Binding tab of the Object palette. You'll see that Repeat Row For Each Data Item is selected. Right below this property on the Binding tab is the Initial Count property, which is set to 3. This is why the form begins with three instances of the detail body row.

7. Select the addItem button in the Table Header (detailHeader1).

8. Expand the Script Editor and select the `click` event. You'll see the JavaScript that is called when the user clicks the button. You'll learn more about scripting in the next chapter.

```
// Invoke the instance manager to add one instance of the detail
// subform.
details._detail.addInstance(1);
// Invoke the recalculate method to include the added values in
// calculations.
xfa.form.recalculate(1);
```

Working with Data

The last important Designer concept to review is form data. Designer enables you to integrate your forms with data by binding your form objects to a data source or schema, formatting your data fields with patterns, and validating your user's data directly in the form.

Data binding

Data binding is the process of mapping your form objects to elements in a data file. Typically, you'll bind your form objects to elements in an XML schema or an XML data file. The different data binding techniques illustrated in this book can be set using the Binding tab of the Object palette. All the techniques fall into one of the following data binding approaches:

- **Use Name:** Your form will have implicit data binding if you merely drag and drop standard Designer form fields onto a blank form; Designer will create an implicit data binding, and the XML data associated with your form will be structured according to the form hierarchy. Designer refers to *implicit binding* as Use name in the Binding tab of the Object palette.

- **Use Global Data:** If you set a form object's binding property to Use Global Data, all other form objects with the same name will have the same value. For example, if you have four Text Field objects with identical names and one of the objects is set to Use Global Data, they'll all be set to Use Global Data. This is referred to as *global binding*, and if you change the data in any one of the fields, the data in all the others will be mirrored automatically.

■ **Data Connection:** Binding your form fields directly to a data connection can be used when you have an external XML schema or other data source. All imported and exported data going to and from fields that are bound to a data connection will have the same structure as the data source. This type of binding is often called *explicit binding* because you're explicitly connecting a field to an external data source.

■ **No Data Binding:** When a field is set to No Data Binding, it doesn't participate in any data binding; data will not flow into the field, and data will not flow out. All fields and subforms that don't need to have data imported or exported should be set to No Data Binding to improve the performance of importing and exporting data.

NOTE In addition to these typical binding methods, you can also use JavaScript to import data and bind it to your form objects. This is helpful when you need to perform some scripting logic on the data in addition to binding it to the form objects.

Data formatting

The Designer tools enable you to control how data is displayed in your form and how it's formatted when it's exported from your form. The methods you use to control these two data states are similar, but their execution is slightly different. If you're new to data formatting, look at the U.S. Social Security Number form object in the Custom tab of the Object Library palette. Follow these steps to learn more about data formatting in Designer:

1. Create a new blank form by choosing File > New. Designer launches the New Form Assistant.

2. Select Use A Blank Form, and click Next to continue.

3. Keep the defaults, and click the Finish button to create your new form.

4. Drag and drop the U.S. Social Security Number object from the Custom tab of the Object Library palette to the Design View.

5. With the U.S. Social Security Number (SSN) object selected, select the Field tab of the Object palette.

6. Click the Patterns button. The Patterns dialog box appears (**Figure 1.12**). The Display tab shows the pattern that will be assigned to the nine digits that are entered into this field at runtime. Click OK to close this dialog box.

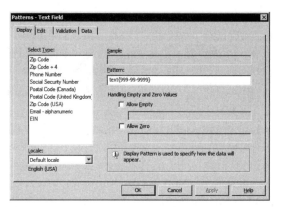

Figure 1.12 The Patterns dialog box showing the Display tab.

7. Click Preview PDF and enter nine digits into the SSN field. Upon field exit, the display of your nine digits will match the data format that was set in the Patterns dialog box.

8. Return to the Patterns dialog box and investigate some of the other tabs.

The Built-in Patterns in HTML Forms

The built-in Designer patterns work fine in PDF forms and documents, but not all of them work when you render your form as HTML. For instance, the Edit patterns on Date Field objects weren't supported in the first release, but Adobe may support more features in Service Pack (SP) releases.

For more information and to see how you can add patterns to HTML forms, please see Part 3.

Data validation

Data binding and data formatting are closely related to data validation in Designer. Data validation is the process of checking the data on an interactive PDF form, and Designer provides many ways to validate form data. The data can be checked in various ways, including format, type, and completeness.

Data validation is one of the major advantages of smart forms. Even if the penmanship on a paper form is legible (and that's a big *if*), there's no capability for data validation until the information is painstakingly keyed into a computer system. To add insult to injury, data errors on paper forms are usually found late in a business process, when they can be very costly to correct.

But with smart forms, you can perform data validation at runtime as users are filling in the form. To help avoid data errors, you can use scripting to provide information and solutions so that users can correct their mistakes during the data-entry process. The two standard validation strategies are

- **Field validation:** You can put your data validation script in the exit or validate events of form objects to provide field-level validation. You can apply three different data validation methods to a field in Designer:

  - You can test to see if the field has any data.

  - You can test to see if the field's data matches a pattern.

  - You can write customized JavaScript to perform a test on the data.

- **Form validation:** You can validate the entire form when a user tries to submit the form. You'll learn how to do this in the next chapter.

You can use either strategy, both strategies, or a combination of elements of each to support your design and data goals (**Figure 1.13**).

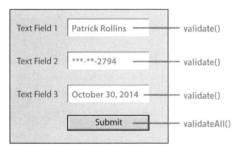

Figure 1.13 You can validate data as a user works through the form, or all at once when a user submits the form.

If you bind your form to an XML schema with explicit binding, Designer will perform some of the data validation for you automatically.

Binding to an XML schema

If you're new to Designer, this is a simple but effective demonstration of the remarkable integration that Designer has with data files. In a corporate environment, this is important because your forms will produce data that meets all the stringent requirements of your enterprise systems and databases. Follow these steps to bind a new blank form to an XML schema:

9. Create a new blank form by choosing File > New. Designer opens the New Form Assistant.

10. Select Use A Blank Form, and click Next to continue.

11. Keep the defaults on all subsequent screens, and keep clicking Next until you get to the Finish button. Click Finish to create your new form.

12. Switch from the Hierarchy palette to the Data View palette on the left side of your workspace. If you don't see the Data View tab, choose Window > Data View.

13. The Data View palette should be empty. Right-click this empty window, and choose New Data Connection. Designer launches the New Data Connection wizard (**Figure 1.14**).

14. Enter **sampleSchema** as the name of your connection, select the XML Schema option, and click Next.

15. Locate and select the sampleSchema.xsd file in the Samples folder. Set its properties to match those shown in **Figure 1.15**, and click Finish to create your connection.

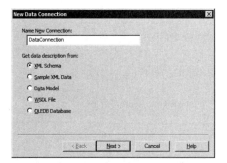

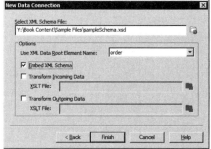

Figure 1.14 The New Data Connection wizard showing the XML Schema option selected.

Figure 1.15 Although you won't use these options in this exercise, you can transform the XML data your Designer forms use at runtime with an XSLT file.

16. Your Data View palette will be populated with the data objects illustrated in **Figure 1.16**. Drag and drop the data connection onto the upper-left corner of your form. Designer automatically creates the data-bound form fields for you.

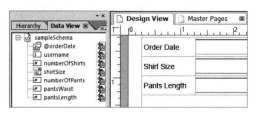

Figure 1.16 When you drag and drop a data connection onto a form, Designer automatically creates data-bound form fields.

17. Save your file as **mySampleSchemaForm.xdp**.

18. Select Preview PDF in the Layout Editor to see that attributes from the schema are now in your form.

19. Click the Shirt Size drop-down list. The three available choices—Small, Medium, and Large—came directly from the XML schema file. These values are an enumeration in the schema, and this example shows you one way your forms can benefit from explicit data binding.

20. Enter a length of **27** in the Pants Length Text Field and press Enter. You'll receive a "The value you entered for Pants Length is invalid." message. This data validation JavaScript was automatically generated by Designer based on a restriction in the schema file.

21. Switch back to Design View and select the Order Date field. This is an example of a Designer Date field, and it contains a data pattern. Click the Pattern button on the Field tab of the Object palette to bring up the Patterns dialog box. Select the Data tab to see the data pattern date{YYYY-MM-DD}. The XML data that's output from this field will correspond to this pattern.

With the fundamental Designer concepts under your belt, you're ready to learn how to customize your environment to make it easier to create consistent and professional forms and documents.

New Date and Time fields

The Date field and the Time field are new additions to the Object Library. The modification of the Date/Time field, found in older versions of Designer, into separate fields allows the creator of the form to be specific about the required user entry.

The new Date field presents the user with a calendar drop-down in both PDF and HTML forms. The new Time field displays and validates times in a variety of time patterns without presenting the user with a calendar drop-down. Time fields have a default display pattern that expects a two-digit hour input at a minimum. For example, 05 will automatically display as 05:00:00 AM. A Time field will display a time pattern consistent with the locale selected in the Field tab of the Object palette. You can overwrite the default settings by setting specific display patterns.

Date/Time fields

With the introduction of separate Date and Time fields, the Date/Time form object has changed. Date/Time fields are now used to accommodate both a date and a time in the same field. This field no longer presents a drop-down calendar in PDF or HTML forms. The display and validation patterns expect the user to enter a date and then a time into the same field.

Customizing Your Environment

The Help system has a good section on customizing your workspace that includes

- How to customize your script and layout editors
- How to show or hide different palettes
- How to customize your toolbars

This section will build on this information by describing features in Designer that enable you to customize your environment for the graphic and functional standards of your company's forms and documents.

Setting Default Fonts

You can set default fonts in general for your Designer program, or you can set them specifically for your current form.

Default fonts for Designer

You set Designer's default fonts in the Options dialog box.

1. Select Tools > Options > Default Fonts.

2. Select the default caption and value fonts that you want for all new forms, and click OK.

3. Select File > New, and create a blank form.

4. Drag and drop a Text Field object from the Object Library onto your form. You'll notice that it uses your new default fonts.

Default fonts for your current form

You set your current form's default fonts in the Form Properties dialog box.

5. Open your mySampleSchemaForm.xdp file if it's not already open. If you don't have this file, open the smartdocSampleSchemaForm.xdp file.

6. Select File > Form Properties > Default Fonts (**Figure 1.17**).

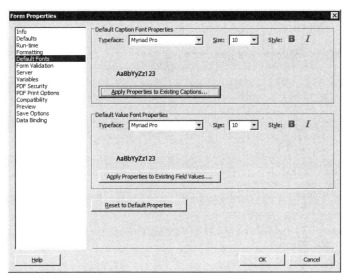

Figure 1.17 The Default Fonts dialog box showing a default font of Myriad Pro.

7. Select the Georgia font from the Default Caption Font Properties Typeface drop-down. Click Apply Properties To Existing Captions, and the Apply Default Caption Font Properties dialog will appear.

8. Select all the properties and the Apply To All Captions radio button, and click OK. You'll see the captions in your form change to the Georgia font.

9. Repeat steps 7 and 8, but this time select the Georgia font from the Default Value Font Properties Typeface drop-down, and click Apply Properties To Existing Field Values. You'll see the font change in your field values.

10. Click OK to close the Default Fonts dialog box.

11. Drag and drop a Text Field object from your Object Library to your form. The default fonts for this new object are now Georgia.

These default form fonts will override Designer's default font settings, so if you send this form to a different user, they'll see these same default fonts when working with this form.

Using Style Sheets

You can now create and manage style sheets to provide consistent formatting in all your forms. For example, you can control the look of caption and field value text, the appearance of object borders and background colors, and the size and style of Radio Buttons and Check Box objects. You create and work with style sheets with Designer's Style Catalog palette (**Figure 1.18**). If you don't see this palette, select Window > Style Catalog. You can create both internal and external style sheets.

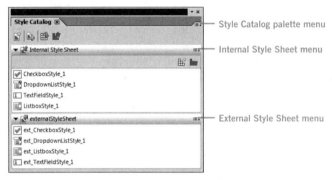

Figure 1.18 The Style Catalog palette showing an internal and an external style sheet.

Internal style sheets

An internal style sheet is useful when you're creating a single form and you want an easy way to apply consistent styles to different form objects. You can also change a style in an internal style sheet, and all the form fields referencing that style will update automatically.

1. Open the formWithInternalSS.xdp file from your Samples folder.

2. Select the Check Box form object.

3. Right-click CheckboxStyle_1 in your Internal Style Sheet, and select Apply Style. Your check box will now look like the check box in **Figure 1.19**.

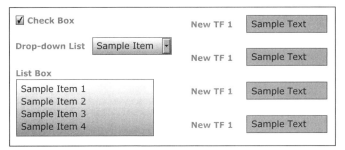

Figure 1.19 Your form with the styles applied.

4. Repeat steps 2 and 3, but this time select the Drop-Down List object and apply DropdownListStyle_1.

5. Repeat steps 2 and 3, but this time select the List Box object and apply ListboxStyle_1.

6. You can also apply styles to multiple objects at once. Select all of the Text Field objects and apply TextFieldStyle_1.

7. Right-click TextFieldStyle_1 in the Style Catalog, and select Edit Style.

8. Select Appearance > Custom, and change the Background Fill option to a solid gray. Click OK twice to close the dialog boxes. Your form will now look like Figure 1.19.

   Notice that all the text fields that referenced your internal style were updated when you updated the style. You can also add a new style to your internal style sheet.

9. Right-click one of the Text Fields with the gray background, and select Styles > Create New Style From Object. The Style Editor will open.

10. Change the name of your new style to **TextFieldStyle_2**, and review some of the other graphic styling options you have in this dialog box. When you're satisfied with your choices, click OK to add this new style to your internal style sheet.

External style sheets

If you are creating more than one form and need to maintain a consistent design, you can create an external style sheet and add it to each form. Multiple designers can access the same external style sheet from a shared folder on a network.

11. Click the Style Catalog palette menu (Figure 1.18), and select Add Style Sheet.

12. Select the externalStyleSheet.xfs file in the Samples folder, and click Open. Your external style sheet will now appear in your Style Catalog. You can now use these styles just like you used the internal styles to update the graphics on your form.

Internal and external style sheets are interchangeable. You can extract the styles from an internal style sheet to create a new external style sheet for use in other forms. You can also add the styles from various external style sheets to an internal style sheet by embedding the external style sheets within the form design. Follow these steps to learn more about style sheets.

13. Click the Internal Style Sheet menu, and select Extract Style Sheets To New Style Sheet. The Extract Style Sheet dialog box will open.

14. Name your new external style sheet **myExternalSS.xfs** and save it as an XFS file.

15. Click the Style Catalog palette menu, and select Embed Style Sheets. Your external style sheet is now part of your internal style sheet.

16. Select File > Open, and change your Files Of Type setting to Adobe LiveCycle Designer Style Sheets (*.xfs).

17. Browse to your myExternalSS.xfs file, and click OK to open it.

18. You can now make additions and updates to the internal styles of this file. After your changes are complete, save it as **myExternalSS.xfs**. You can now use this XFS file in other Designer files as an external style sheet.

Setting a default style sheet

You can set a default style sheet for new forms that will automatically appear in the Style Catalog for each new form you create. Follow these steps to set your new style sheet as a default for new forms:

19. Select Tools > Options to open the Options dialog box (**Figure 1.20**).

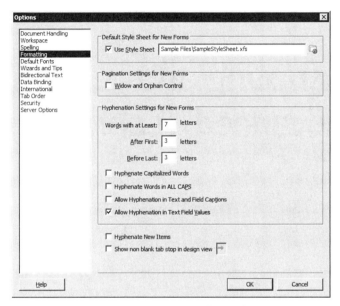

Figure 1.20 You can set a default style sheet for new forms in the Formatting panel of the Options dialog box.

20. Select the Formatting panel.

21. Select Use Style Sheet, and click the browse button to locate your myExternalSS.xfs file.

22. After you select your style sheet, click OK to close the dialog box.

Moving On

Now that you've learned the basics, you're ready to move on to scripting and other advanced techniques in LiveCycle Designer.

2

Scripting and
Advanced Techniques

*There are only 10 kinds of people in this world: those who understand binary
and those who don't.*

—Unknown

Scripting is optional in LiveCycle Designer forms. You can achieve a great deal
of functionality and customization without scripting. You can set most of the
important property values of your form objects at design time by using Designer's
palettes. You learned about this in the last chapter. This chapter will show you
how to set and get these properties at runtime with scripting.

Scripting gives you full control over your form's functionality at runtime. Through
scripting, you have the power to manipulate your form's interactive controls to
provide your users with a richer and more intuitive experience. Designer scripting is similar to HTML scripting in the following ways.

- **Use of JavaScript:** You use JavaScript to write custom scripts that add functionality to your forms like you use JavaScript to add custom functionality
  to a web page. Designer also includes another language, FormCalc, which
  is covered later in this chapter.

- **Use of an object model:** Like web programming, Designer has an object
  model that you can use for your scripting. You can call methods and properties of the object model to provide rich functionality to your forms.

▪ **Range of scripts:** Because JavaScript is a rich, object-oriented scripting language, you can write an incredible range of scripts, from very basic one-line scripts to complex and detailed, object-oriented scripts that can span hundreds and even thousands of lines.

If you're familiar with scripting on the web or another platform, you'll find the scripting concepts in Designer to be very familiar. However, the execution details of scripting in Designer are unique and will be reviewed in this chapter.

The Benefits of Scripting

In many cases, scripting improves the functionality and usability of your forms. You saw an example of this in the last chapter with the Purchase Order form. A number of useful scripts are included in this form. One of these handy scripts is found in the Add Item button's click event. This script creates a new line item in the purchase order (**Figure 2.1**) each time the button is clicked. In the last chapter, you saw how this was made possible by the form's table structure. However, it's the script that calls the subform's instance manager with the directive to create a new instance. This script runs on the button's click event.

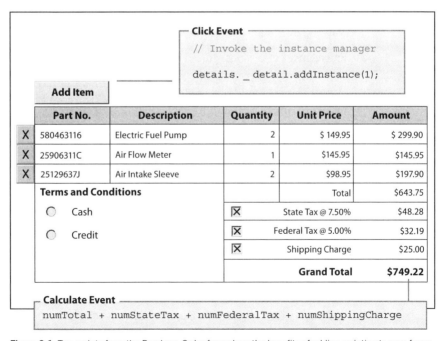

Figure 2.1 Two scripts from the Purchase Order form show the benefits of adding scripting to your forms.

Another practical script is found in the Grand Total text field (numGrandTotal). This script automatically calculates the grand total for the purchase order every time a financial event on the purchase order occurs. When a new item is entered or when a new tax is applied, the grand total is recalculated automatically. This is a useful script for form fillers because they can see how all their changes and additions to the Purchase Order affect the bottom line. Unlike the previous script, which ran on the click event, this script runs on the calculate event of the numeric field.

Although you don't absolutely need scripting in your forms, a small investment in scripting will yield the following benefits to you and your form filler:

- **Automatic calculations at runtime:** As described in the Purchase Order example, the addition of automatic calculations will make your forms much more useful to your form fillers.

- **Ability to control the appearance of form objects at runtime:** In the previous chapter, you set the visual properties of your form objects at design time. With scripting, you can make changes to the visual properties of your form at runtime to provide assistance to your form fillers. For instance, before your user submits a form, you can use a validation script to make sure that all the required fields have been filled in with data. If there are required fields without data, you can call a script to highlight them in yellow. This way, the form filler's attention will be drawn visually to the required task.

- **Enforcement of business rules:** You can use form scripting to enforce the business rules of your company or industry. For instance, the Purchase Order example could have a script that takes an action whenever the grand total goes above a certain threshold. You could create a script that limits users from going above a certain amount, or you could allow them to go above the amount and automatically route the purchase order for a senior manager's approval.

- **Data validation and formatting:** In addition to using patterns and properties to enforce data validation, you can use custom scripting. This approach is valuable because you'll be able to correct many data-entry mistakes before they get to your back-end system.

Using Scripting

Virtually every form object in a Designer form is scriptable at any step in your process. This is a big advantage because scripting will give you full control to respond to events and user actions in your smart forms at runtime.

For the most part, you'll put your scripts into form object events like the click event of a button or the initialize event of a text field. When these events fire, the scripts behind the events are executed. You can see an example of this type of scripting in the SmartDoc Expense Report. The addExpense button on the form has a script in its click event (**Figure 2.2**).

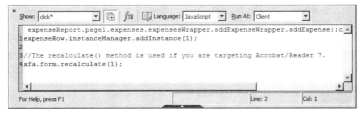

Figure 2.2 The Script Editor showing the click event of the addExpense button.

You can see this script by selecting the addExpense button in Design View. The Designer Script Editor shows you a few important aspects of this script:

- **Show Events:** This drop-down list shows you that the script will run in the click event of the button. The asterisk indicates that the event has scripting associated with it.

- **Language:** The (scripting) Language property is JavaScript, so the script must contain JavaScript with correct structure and syntax.

- **Run At:** The Run At specification is Client so the script will be processed on a user's local machine.

- **Editing window:** The editing window shows the actual script.

FormCalc and JavaScript

Designer supports scripting in two languages: FormCalc and JavaScript. A form can use both languages at the same time, but you can't mix the two languages in one object event. FormCalc is an easy-to-use calculation language that Adobe developed for XFA forms. It's very similar to the calculation language that you use in a spreadsheet program like Microsoft Excel. JavaScript, on the other hand, is a powerful, object-oriented scripting language that many programmers are already familiar with. And with the advent of HTML forms, JavaScript is even more ideal because it runs natively in web browsers.

Surprisingly, FormCalc worked well in many of my HTML form tests, including when I set the scripts to run on the client. However, since JavaScript has so many advantages over FormCalc, I recommend JavaScript for most smart form applications. FormCalc is best suited for PDF-only applications developed by nonprogrammers. Also, Adobe advises against using it for HTML forms in Designer's Help system. This book focuses on JavaScript but includes introductory information about FormCalc in this section.

From the Help System

The following is from Designer's Help System.

Important—If you are developing forms for use with a server-based process (for example, using Forms) with the intent of rendering your forms in HTML, you should develop your calculations and scripts in JavaScript. FormCalc calculations are not valid in HTML browsers, and are removed prior to the form being rendered in HTML.

FormCalc

FormCalc has many built-in functions that cover a range of areas, including finance, logic, dates/times, and mathematics. FormCalc is supported in Designer, Acrobat, and Reader. Like Microsoft Excel, most FormCalc scripts are only one line long. Follow these steps to see some of FormCalc's functions in action:

1. Open formcalc.xdp from the Samples folder.

2. Select TextField1 in the Hierarchy palette, and go to the Script Editor.

3. Select the initialize event in the Show Events drop-down, and make sure Language is set to FormCalc and Run At is set to Client, and then enter this script:

   ```
   TextField1.rawValue = Sum(1,2,3,4)
   ```

4. Select TextField2, and go to the Script Editor.

5. Select the initialize event in the Show Events drop-down, and enter this script:

   ```
   TextField2.rawValue = num2date(date(), DateFmt(3))
   ```

6. Select NumericField1, and go to the Script Editor.

7. Select the initialize event, and enter this script:

   ```
   NumericField1.rawValue = Apr(35000, 269.50, 360)
   ```

If you're working on financial forms, FormCalc has many built-in financial functions that you can add to your form. For instance, it's easy to calculate the APR (annual percentage rate) of a loan with FormCalc. In this example, the principal amount of the loan is $35,000, the monthly payment amount is $269.50, and the number of months is 360. This script will return an annual percentage rate of 0.08515404566 to NumericField1. In the next step, you'll add a display pattern to your field so that this calculation is more relevant to the user.

8. Select NumericField1, select the Field tab of the Object palette, and click Patterns.

9. Enter a display pattern of **num{zzzz9%}** to show the calculation as a percentage. Click OK to close the Patterns dialog box.

10. Select Preview PDF to view your new scripts in action. The form fields should now show 10 (the sum of [1, 2, 3, 4]), today's date, and 9%.

The statement completion feature

These next few steps demonstrate the statement completion feature:

11. While still in the formcalc.xdp file, select Button1, and go to the Script Editor.

12. Select the `click` event, and enter this script. Notice Designer's statement completion feature as you type (**Figure 2.3**).

```
$host.messageBox("Hello, World!")
```

Figure 2.3 The statement completion feature of Designer helps you with your scripting by providing context-sensitive information.

13. Select Preview PDF to view your new scripts in action. When you click Button1, a pop-up message box with the phrase "Hello, World!" will appear. The $host item is a FormCalc shortcut that represents the host object, which is either Adobe Acrobat or Adobe Reader, the host of your PDF form.

14. Select Design View to write a similar script in JavaScript.

15. Select the click event of Button1, switch Language to JavaScript, and replace the FormCalc with this line of JavaScript:

```
xfa.host.messageBox("Hello, World!")
```

16. Select Preview PDF, and click Button1 to see the same pop-up message box. The host object is still either Acrobat or Reader, but the JavaScript syntax for referring to the host object is xfa.host.

 If you're interested in exploring FormCalc further, Adobe has included excellent reference materials in the Help system, including the FormCalc Reference, which you can also find on this book's companion site.

JavaScript

JavaScript is now the default scripting language in Designer. It offers the following advantages:

- **JavaScript is ubiquitous:** It's likely that you'll be able to leverage your organization's existing JavaScript knowledge because JavaScript is a scripting standard that many programmers and designers already know. Designer uses real and complete JavaScript, unlike the earlier versions of Adobe Acroforms, which used a subset of JavaScript.

- **JavaScript is object-oriented:** You can create JavaScript objects and custom functions and use them throughout your form. This feature of JavaScript isn't available in FormCalc, and it enables you to eliminate work by allowing to you reuse your code.

- **50,000 JavaScript fans can't be wrong:** Because JavaScript has been a scripting standard for a long time, you'll be able to find example scripts for almost everything you need to do. You can find these example scripts on the web, in JavaScript books, and in this book.

- **JavaScript works for PDF *and* HTML forms:** JavaScript will work for both PDF and HTML forms, and as you'll see in Part 3, "HTML Forms," you can use JavaScript to create forms that function in a similar fashion when they're rendered as HTML or PDF.

LiveCycle Designer supports JavaScript version 1.6 and earlier.

The Fundamentals

Now that you have seen some scripting examples and learned about the benefits, it's time to explore the fundamentals of scripting in Designer.

The Script Editor in Detail

As you have seen in previous examples, the Script Editor is the tool you'll use to create and edit scripts. It contains a number of features to help you write, test, and organize your scripts (**Figure 2.4**).

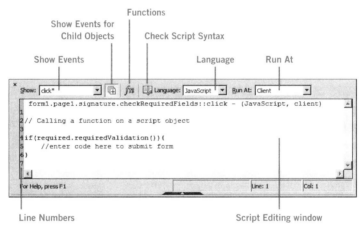

Figure 2.4 Click and drag the Script Editor palette bar to expand the Script Editor.

If you can't see the Script Editor on your screen, select Window > Script Editor. The Script Editor shows the following information:

- **Script Editing window:** This is where you write and edit your scripts.

- **Show Events drop-down:** In this case the event is the button's click event. The asterisk is an indication that there's script in this event. If you select the Show Events drop-down list, you'll see all the events for this object. The events that are grayed out aren't available for this object. Please note that just because an event is available for an object, it doesn't necessarily mean that you should put script behind that event.

- **Show Events for Child Objects:** You can see all the scripts for a subform, a page, or for your entire form at once. This option will show all the scripts for the object that you currently have selected and all its child objects. If you select the top form object in the hierarchy, this option will show you all the scripts associated with a specific event. As an alternative, you can change from a specific event to view all Events With Scripts to see every script in your form.

■   **Functions:** While you're working in the script editing window, you can click this button to view a list of FormCalc or JavaScript functions, depending on your language setting.

■   **Check Script Syntax tool:** This tool provides some basic syntax checking for FormCalc and JavaScript, and it's discussed in the "Debugging Scripts" section later in this chapter.

■   **Language:** In this case, the language is set to JavaScript. If you put proper FormCalc script into this box, it won't work.

■   **Run At:** This option specifies where your script will run. If it is set to Client, the script will be processed by Acrobat, Reader, or a web browser. If the specification is set to Server, the script will be processed by a LiveCycle Server. If your workflow doesn't include a LiveCycle Server, you should always use the Client option. The third option is Client And Server. Use this setting when you aren't sure if your form will be rendered on a client or a server, or for forms that may be rendered on both the client and the server at different times.

Scripting in LiveCycle Designer is simple enough that you can begin today, but it's robust enough that you won't be bored even after years of programming.

Variables

A *variable* is a symbolic representation that refers to a place in computer memory that holds a value. Variables are advantageous because they enable you to define a value in one location but refer to it from many locations on your form. When you need to change the value, you don't need to go back to each variable reference; you only need to go back to the one location where the variable is defined to make your change. All other locations that refer to the variable will be updated. This section focuses on two primary variable types:

■   **Form variables:** These are declared and assigned in the Variables tab of the form's properties dialog box.

■   **Script variables:** These are declared and assigned in your scripts.

NOTE: You can't begin a variable name with a number, but a variable name can contain numbers, letters, and underscores.

Naming Variables

At runtime, naming conflicts occur when the names of variables are identical to those used as XML Form Object Model properties, methods, or form design field names. These conflicts can cause scripts to return unexpected values; therefore, it's important to give each variable a unique name. Here are a couple of examples:

■ Use the variable name `fieldWidth` and `fieldHeight` instead of w and h.

■ Use the form design object name clientName instead of name.

Variable names are case-sensitive and can't contain spaces.

Form variables

A form variable typically acts as a placeholder for a value that you might have to change in the future. For instance, you can create form variables for state tax rates (**Table 2.1**). When you need to calculate the sales tax, you reference the form variable in your script. When you need to change the tax rate, all you have to do is open the Variables panel in the Form Properties dialog box and make the change. Because you referenced the form variable, not a specific numeric value, you don't need to update the tax rate in multiple locations on your form. Form variables are global in nature, which means that you can access them from any part of your form. The values of your form variables will reset each time the form is opened. All form variables are stored as strings; therefore, you may need to convert it to a number before it's used in a calculation.

Table 2.1 State Sales Tax

STATE	VALUE IN 1ST EDITION	VALUE IN 2ND EDITION
Connecticut	5%	6.35%
New Jersey	6%	7%
New York	7%	8.75%

Follow these steps to create a form variable:

1. Open the changeOfBeneficiaryStart.xdp file.

2. Select File > Form Properties > Variables.

3. Click the green plus to enter a new variable.

4. Enter **varUsername** as your variable name, and then enter **Charles Geschke** as your variable value (**Figure 2.5**).

5. Click OK to close the Form Properties dialog box.

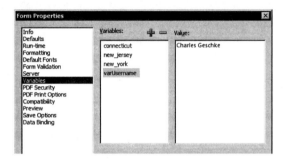

Figure 2.5 Entering a form variable into the Form Properties dialog box. Your form variable values will be reset to their original values each time the form is opened.

6. You can now make a reference to this variable from anywhere on your form. Select the contingentName field on the contingent subform, and expand the Script Editor.

7. Select the initialize event, and add this script:

```
this.rawValue = varUsername.value;
```

This simple script uses two different property values to refer to similar information. When you need to access the value of an XFA field or form object, use the .rawValue property. When you need to access the value of a form variable, use the .value property. If you're working in FormCalc, you can retrieve the value of the variable without explicitly referencing a value property, although adding the value property will also work.

```
order.#subform[0].fromVariable::click: - (FormCalc, client)

$.rawValue = varUsername
```

8. Select Preview PDF, and the value, "Charles Geschke," from your form variable is prefilled in the form.

Even though you were able to create a form variable without scripting, you must use scripting to work with your variables in the following ways:

■ To access the value of your variable

■ To change the value of your variable at runtime

■ To apply the value of your variable to a form object

Script variables

Unlike form variables, script variables are local in nature. A local variable is used only within the scope of the script in which it's declared. If a variable is declared in one script and then referenced in another script, an error will occur. Local variables are used when their stored values aren't needed after the script is completed. Once the script is finished, the memory that was assigned to the local variable is released and is able to be used for other purposes, helping to improve form performance.

You declare a script variable before it's first used in your script. The following example uses the JavaScript var operator to declare a variable named testVar. Once declared, the value of the variable is set to the rawValue of the text field:

```
var testVar;

testVar = textField1.rawValue;
```

Thereafter, you can reference or change the variable at any point throughout the script.

Referencing Objects

You've been writing code to reference objects in all your previous scripting examples. This section covers the various ways that you can reference an object in Designer scripting. Although there are some minor differences, FormCalc and JavaScript follow the same syntax when referencing objects. First we need to create an example object to reference.

1. Open the purchaseOrder.xdp form.

2. Drag and drop a new Button object on the commentsHeader subform next to the addComments button.

3. Name your new button **exampleButton** (**Figure 2.6**). It is very important for the examples in this section that you put this button in the commentsHeader subform.

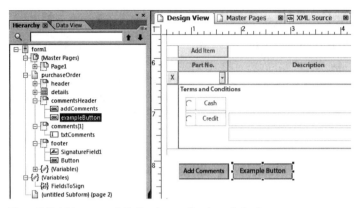

Figure 2.6 Add an exampleButton to your Purchase Order form.

Fully qualified

A *fully qualified* reference uses the complete form hierarchy beginning with the xfa root node. The advantage of a fully qualified statement is that it will work every time regardless of where the script that contains the reference is written. A fully qualified reference for the exampleButton looks like this:

```
xfa.form.form1.purchaseOrder.commentsHeader.exampleButton
```

Notice that form1 is the visible root node of your form in Designer's Hierarchy palette. A fully qualified reference goes two levels above this, all the way to the root node of xfa.

4. While still on the purchaseOrder.xdp form, select your exampleButton, and write the following script in the click event:

```
xfa.form.form1.purchaseOrder.commentsHeader.addComments.presence =
➥ "invisible";
```

5. Select Preview PDF, and click the Example button. Your Add Comments button disappears.

6. Go back to Design View, and put the same script at the end of the click event of the addItem button that appears above the dynamic table on the form.

7. Select Preview PDF, and click the Add Item button. Your Add Comments button disappears even though the script was running from a different place on the form. This works because you're using a fully qualified object reference.

Easy Ways to Create Long References

There are two easy ways to create long references in Designer scripting. The first is to use the statement completion functionality that you've been using. When you're working in the Script Editor, type a period after an object name and Designer will list all the child objects in a pop-up menu. You can repeat this for each level of your hierarchy until your reference is completed.

The second way to easily create a long reference is to use the automatic insert object reference feature. Follow these steps:

1. Place your cursor in the Script Editor where you want your object reference to appear.

2. Go back to the form and select the object while holding down the Ctrl key (your cursor will turn into a V). A new object reference, relative to the selected object, will be created automatically in your Script Editor. You can also select the object while holding down the Ctrl+Shift keys to insert an absolute reference into your script. An absolute reference is similar to a fully qualified reference except it starts with the root node of your form's hierarchy and not with the xfa.form node.

Abbreviated reference

Even though fully qualified references will always work, they usually take longer to write than abbreviated references. The reference syntax for an abbreviated reference is shorter than a fully qualified reference for either or both of the following reasons:

■ **Relative positioning:** You can use an abbreviated reference if two form objects exist in the same container, like a subform or a page. For instance, in the Purchase Order example, the exampleButton and addComments buttons both exist on the commentsHeader subform. You can change your script in the exampleButton's click event to the following abbreviated reference:

```
addComments.presence = "invisible";
```

This works in the exampleButton because of its relative position to the addComments button, but it won't work in the addItem button's click event. In fact, if you put the abbreviated reference at the beginning of the script, not only will this line of script fail but the entire block of script won't execute. The JavaScript interpreter won't step over an improper statement; it will step out of the routine altogether. If you move the improper abbreviated reference to the end of the code block, you'll see that the previous lines will execute but the interpreter will still hang on the abbreviated reference.

You can create a proper abbreviated reference from the addItem button to the addComments button by referring to the first container object that they have in common. For instance, the following script will work from the addItem button:

```
purchaseOrder.commentsHeader.addComments.presence = "invisible";
```

■ **Use of shortcuts:** FormCalc has built-in shortcuts that reduce the effort required to write references. For instance, the $host shortcut makes reference to the host object. You can replace the script of your exampleButton with the following line of code:

```
$host.messageBox("hello world")
```

Remember, you need to change the language to FormCalc. Many more FormCalc shortcuts are documented in the Help system.

Hidden Items in Your Form's Hierarchy

Due to the way the XML Form Object Model is structured, some object properties and methods exist on child objects of the objects on the form. These child objects exist only as part of the XML Form Object Model and don't appear in the Hierarchy and Data View palettes. To access these properties and methods, you must include the child objects in the reference syntax. For example, the following reference syntax sets the tool tip text for the txtCondition field:

```
txtCondition.assist.toolTip.value = "Conditions of purchase.";
```

The current object

Both FormCalc and JavaScript use shortcuts to refer to the current object. You can add the following code to the initialize event of your Example button to customize the tool tip.

JavaScript:

```
exampleButton::initialize: - (JavaScript, client)
this.assist.toolTip.value = "This is the Example Button";
```

FormCalc:

```
exampleButton::initialize: - (FormCalc, client)
$.assist.toolTip.value = "This is the Example Button";
```

Unnamed objects

I recommend providing meaningful names to your form objects. However, occasionally you may come across unnamed objects in Designer. If you need to refer to an unnamed object in a script, you'll need to tweak how you refer to it based on the Language value. Follow these steps to see this in action:

8. Open the referencingObjects.xdp form. Notice that the body page is an unnamed subform.

9. Select the form1 object at the top of the hierarchy, and enter the following script into the `initialize` event. Make sure Language is set to FormCalc.

   ```
   xfa.form.form1.#subform.PrintButton1.presence = "invisible"
   ```

   As you typed the line into the Script Editor, you should've noticed that the unnamed object appeared in the beginning of the statement completion list. All unnamed objects will appear in the beginning of the list and will be preceded by the # symbol.

10. Select Preview PDF, and you'll see that your syntax is correct because the Print button is invisible.

11. Switch back to Design View, and select the form1 object again. This time, switch Language to JavaScript. When you select Preview PDF, this script won't work because JavaScript can't interpret the # symbol correctly. When working with unnamed objects in JavaScript, you must use the `resolveNode` method of the `xfa` object.

12. Enter this script into the `initialize` event:

    ```
    xfa.resolveNode("xfa.form.form1.#subform.PrintButton1").presence =
    ➥ "invisible"
    ```

    Notice that the reference path that's passed to the `resolveNode` method is surrounded by quotes.

Multiple objects with the same name

Designer also supports the creation of multiple objects with the same name. When multiple objects have the same name, each has a different occurrence number represented by a number in brackets directly following the object name.

In the referencingObjects.xdp form, there are three text fields on your form and each has the same name. Designer puts an occurrence number at the end of each name (**Figure 2.7**). The numbers are zero based, so if you have three objects, the highest occurrence number will be 2.

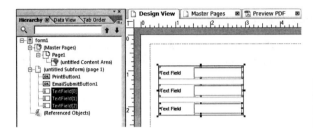

Figure 2.7 You can see the occurrence numbers for your objects in the Hierarchy palette.

13. Select your form1 object, and click the `initialize` event in the Script Editor.

14. Switch back to FormCalc, and enter the following script:

```
xfa.form.form1.#subform.TextField1[0].rawValue = "First"
xfa.form.form1.#subform.TextField1[1].rawValue = "Second"
xfa.form.form1.#subform.TextField1[2].rawValue = "Third"
```

15. Select Preview PDF to see that each of your text fields has a different value.

You'll also need to use the `xfa.resolveNode` method if you're using JavaScript with multiple objects of the same name, because JavaScript can't interpret the occurrence number syntax. The following code will work in JavaScript:

```
xfa.resolveNode("xfa.form.form1.#subform.TextField1[0]").rawValue =
➥ "First";

xfa.resolveNode("xfa.form.form1.#subform.TextField1[1]").rawValue =
➥ "Second";

xfa.resolveNode("xfa.form.form1.#subform.TextField1[2]").rawValue =
➥ "Third";
```

You can find a more advanced example of how occurrence numbers work in the purchase order example. The following script is FormCalc:

```
// Verify at least one instance of the numAmount field exists.
if (exists(detail[0].numAmount) == 1) then
    Sum(detail[*].numAmount)
endif
```

Events

The forms you create in Designer are based on an event-driven programming model. As you've seen in this chapter, the scripts you write are triggered by events. Events are occurrences or actions that change the state of a form.

When these events occur, the scripts behind the events are executed. Because this event-driven model determines how your scripts will perform, you need to consider which events you want to use, when the events will fire, and how often the events will fire.

Types of events

There are three categories of events in Designer forms: process events, interactive events, and application events. Most of your scripts will run in the interactive events, but the process and application events will also be useful to you.

Process events

The following is a list of the process events:

- calculate
- indexChange
- layout:ready
- form:ready
- initialize
- validate

Process events will fire automatically based on an internal process or in response to the firing of an interactive event. As illustrated in **Figure 2.8**, process events are fired following a major form change like the form merging process and the form layout process.

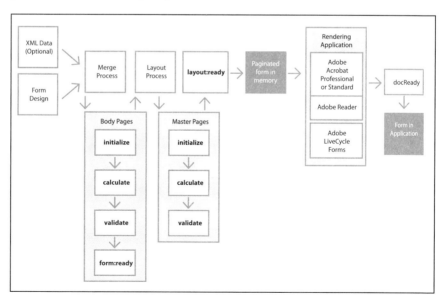

Figure 2.8 This diagram shows the general flow of process events leading up to the PDF form opening in the application. The process events are in bold type. The last event, docReady, is an application event.

Detailed Event Documentation in the Help System

Adobe has done a great job of documenting events in the Help system, providing a list of events and detailed information about each event. However, now that the Help system is online, it's possible that the exact URL will be moved from time to time. Please refer to the book's companion site for a direct link to the Help system support for events. The following details from the Help system describe the `calculate` event:

Description

Initiates in the following situations:

■ When your form design and data merge into your finished form.

■ When a change occurs to any value that the calculation is dependent on, such as the value of a particular field, unless the form filler has manually overridden the calculated value. As a result, the object will display the return value of the event. The properties for manually overridden fields are located in the Value tab of the Object palette.

■ When a field loses focus; for example, when a form filler clicks or uses the Tab key to exit a field.

When using the `calculate` event to perform calculations or scripts, consider the following potential issues:

■ Calculations and scripts on the `calculate` event must not make any changes to the structure of the form, except for the form field and data values.

■ Content inserted by the `calculate` event must conform to the associated validations for the object; otherwise, validation errors will occur.

■ Calculations and scripts must not include an infinite loop because it causes the form to update the value continuously. For example, a script that increments the value of a field as part of a looping expression, such as a `while` or `for` loop, could create an infinite loop.

■ The last expression evaluated in the `calculate` event is used to populate the value of the current form object. For example, if the script on the `calculate` event first sets the value of the current field to 500 and then sets the value of another field to 1000, both fields will display the value 1000 at run time. As a result, you need to limit the scripting that you add to the calculate event to those that deal specifically with setting the value of the current field.

Type

Processing event

Support

■ Acrobat and Adobe Reader

■ HTML browser

Example

Use the `calculate` event for updating numeric values in fields because this event initiates immediately after most other events. For example, on a purchase order form, you can use the `calculate` event for a field to determine the percentage of sales tax due based on the cost of the order. The calculation will initiate every time a change is made to the values in the form fields, ensuring that the value displayed for the sales tax is always correct.

However, because the `calculate` event can initiate many times, you must ensure that the calculation or script you add to the event will not cause data values to increment unnecessarily. For example, if your sales tax calculation adds the value of the sales tax to the total cost each time the calculate event initiates, the resulting total cost value on your form may be too large.

Process events are also fired after interactive events are fired. For instance, a button `click` event will also fire the `layout:ready` event for each object on the form. Process events may fire multiple times based on the situation. For instance, a script in a button's `calculate` event will fire twice when an interactive form is opened.

Interactive events

The following is a list of the interactive events:

- change
- click
- enter
- exit
- mouseDown
- mouseEnter
- mouseUp
- preOpen
- postOpen
- postSign
- preSign
- mouseExit

Interactive events are useful for scripting because they fire as a direct result of a user's action.

Application events

The following is a list of the application events:

- docClose
- docReady
- postPrint
- postSave
- prePrint
- preSave
- preSubmit
- postSubmit

Application events fire as a result of the actions of a client application like Acrobat or a server application like LiveCycle Forms. For example, the post-Print event will fire immediately after Acrobat or Reader has sent the form to a printer or spooler.

Events in action

Follow these steps to see scripts in each of the three types of events:

1. Open the events.xdp form.

2. Select the todaysDate field, and select the `initialize` event in the Show Events drop-down list of the Script Editor. You'll see this script block showing the event and the script. This is an example of a process event.

   ```
   form1.#subform[0].todaysDate::initialize - (JavaScript, client)

   var myDate = new Date();

   var month = myDate.getMonth()+1;
   ```

```
var day = myDate.getDate();

var year = myDate.getFullYear();


this.rawValue = month + "/" + day + "/" + year;
```

3. Select the shirtSize drop-down list, and select the `change` event in the Show Events drop-down list of the Script Editor. You'll see this script block showing the event and the script. This is an example of an interactive event.

```
form1.#subform[0].selectSize::change - (JavaScript, client)

currentSize.rawValue = xfa.event.newText;

previousSize.rawValue = xfa.event.prevText;
```

4. Select the root node of your form (form1), and select the `postPrint` event in the Show Events drop-down list of the Script Editor. You will see this script block showing the event and the script. This is an example of an application event.

```
form1::postPrint - (JavaScript, client)

xfa.host.messageBox("Instruct the user on where to send the printed
➥ form.");
```

5. Select Preview PDF to see these scripts in action. Here is what you will find:

   ■ The form will open with the value of the Today's Date field set to the current date. This is because you used the `initialize` event.

   ■ Select a shirt size in the drop-down list and the Current Selection field will populate with your selection. Select a different size and the Previous Selection field will populate as well. Your script will be executed every time there is a change in the drop-down list.

   ■ Click the Print Form button to see an example of an application event. Acrobat will display the Print dialog box. When you click the Print button in the bottom right, Acrobat will print your file. Immediately after the print action, the XFA `postPrint` event will fire, and your script will run.

Event propagation

You can reduce the number of scripts in your forms with event propagation. This technique will make your scripts global in nature, which will make them easier to maintain. Follow these steps to see an example:

6. Open your changeOfBeneficiaryProp.xdp form from the Samples folder.

7. Select Tools > Options to open the Options dialog box.

8. Select Workspace > Display Event Propagation, and click OK.

9. Select the page1 subform in the Hierarchy palette and expand the Script Editor.

10. Select the exit event from the Show Events drop-down list. You'll see the following script:

```
if(xfa.event.target.rawValue != null)

{

  required.unHighlight(xfa.event.target);

}
```

Notice that the Enable Event Propagation property is checked in the upper right of the Script Editor.

This script will propagate down to all the child nodes of page1 and will execute when an exit event is fired on any of them.

Advanced Scripting

Scripting will improve the functionality and usability of your forms, and Designer uses real and complete JavaScript. This section shows you a few advanced scripting techniques to use in your forms.

Using Script Objects

So far, you've put all your scripts behind form object events like the click event of a button or the initialize event of a text field. This is fine for short scripts that you don't need to reuse from different objects on your form. However, when you start creating longer scripts that you need to reuse from many different objects on your form, you'll want to write them in a Designer script object.

Script objects will reduce your overall scripting efforts and make your forms easier to maintain by putting popular functions into one common location. In many cases, script objects will also improve the performance of your forms based on the following two reasons:

■ **Scripting code rationalization:** You can reduce the overall amount of JavaScript in your form by putting common functions in one location.

This reduction decreases the file size of your PDF forms, which will result in faster download times.

■ **Storage of commonly accessed data:** It's very efficient to retrieve a data value from a script object, so you should use script objects to store commonly accessed data values. This improves the performance of forms that connect to external data resources and web services. Your goal should be to connect to external data resources infrequently and store the important values in script object variables.

The functions that you write in your script objects can be written only in JavaScript. If your script object is written to "Run at Client," the calling script must also be set to "Run at Client." The reverse is also true. You must also write the calling script in JavaScript.

Creating a script object

It's easy to create a script object; the programming challenge comes when you write the functions and methods of your script object.

1. Open the changeOfBeneficiaryStart.xdp file.

   There are already script objects at the bottom of your Hierarchy palette in the (Variables) node (**Figure 2.9**).

2. To create a new script object, right-click the form1 root node object at the top of your form hierarchy. Select Insert Script Object from the pop-up menu. A new script object will appear below the validation script object.

3. Name your script object **required** by clicking it in the Hierarchy palette. You can create a script object at the form level, as you've done here, or at the subform level. To create a subform-level script object, right-click a subform object instead of the form object.

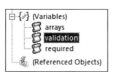

Figure 2.9 The validation script object and the required script object you'll create.

Writing functions in script objects

You can now add functions to your script object. There's no limit to the number of functions you can add to a script object or the number of script objects you can add to a form. You write your functions according to the syntax and rules of JavaScript.

JavaScript Functions

A JavaScript function is a block of code that performs a specific task. This block of code is declared with the keyword `function` and can be called from anyplace on your form. The basic syntax for a JavaScript function is

```
function functionName(argument_0, argument_1,…, argument_N){

   JavaScript statements

}
```

The following is a basic JavaScript function:

```
function helloWorld(){

   app.alert("Hello World");

}
```

All functions must begin with the keyword `function` followed by the function's name. After the name of the function are parentheses that contain zero or more parameters. The next element is an opening curly brace, and the complete JavaScript code for your function will be placed between this opening curly brace and the closing curly brace at the end of your function.

You can write your own JavaScript functions, or you can use one of JavaScript's many built-in functions. As mentioned, you can call a JavaScript function from anyplace on your form; you can even call a function from within another function. This methodology is helpful when you want to simplify a complex function into smaller and more manageable parts.

When you associate a JavaScript function with a script object as you're doing in this chapter, you can refer to your function as a method of the object.

4. Select the required script object in the Hierarchy palette.

5. Select All Events in the Show Events drop-down list, and click in the Script Editor palette.

6. Begin your script by entering two variables—one for the highlight color of yellow and one for the standard color of white.

   ```
   var reqFillColor = "255,255,0";

   var nonReqFillColor = "255,255,255";
   ```

7. Begin the `requiredValidation` function shown and described here. If you have any problems with your script, you can copy and paste it from the changeOfBeneficiaryCompleted.xdp file in the Samples folder. For this example, we're requiring all the fields in the primary beneficiary subform to be completed.

```
function requiredValidation()
{
  var emptyArr = new Array();

  if(page1.primary.primaryItem.primaryName.rawValue == null)
  {
    emptyArr.push(page1.primary.primaryItem.primaryName);
    Highlight(page1.primary.primaryItem.primaryName);
  }
  if(page1.primary.primaryItem.primaryAddress.rawValue == null)
  {
    emptyArr.push(page1.primary.primaryItem.primaryAddress);
    Highlight(page1.primary.primaryItem.primaryAddress);
  }
  if(page1.primary.primaryItem.primaryRelationship.rawValue == null)
  {
    emptyArr.push(page1.primary.primaryItem.primaryRelationship);
    Highlight(page1.primary.primaryItem.primaryRelationship);
  }
  if(page1.primary.primaryItem.primaryCity.rawValue == null)
  {
    emptyArr.push(page1.primary.primaryItem.primaryCity);
    Highlight(page1.primary.primaryItem.primaryCity);
  }
  if(page1.primary.primaryItem.primaryState.rawValue == null)
  {
    emptyArr.push(page1.primary.primaryItem.primaryState);
    Highlight(page1.primary.primaryItem.primaryState);
  }
  if(page1.primary.primaryItem.primaryZipCode.rawValue == null)
  {
```

```
    emptyArr.push(page1.primary.primaryItem.primaryZipCode);

    Highlight(page1.primary.primaryItem.primaryZipCode);

}

if(page1.primary.primaryItem.primaryPercentage.rawValue == null)

{

    emptyArr.push(page1.primary.primaryItem.primaryPercentage);

    Highlight(page1.primary.primaryItem.primaryPercentage);

}
```

The function is defined in the first line, and it doesn't take any parameters. Therefore, when you call it in the next section, you won't pass it any parameters. The body of the function starts after the first opening bracket ({) and closes after the last closing bracket (}).

You'll notice an array variable, which is used to store any field that doesn't meet the validation. The remainder of the function is a series of if statements. Each one evaluates a required field on the form to see whether it has data. If it doesn't, the null condition will evaluate to true and the following two activities will take place:

- The field will be saved to the array variable.

- The field will be passed to the Highlight function.

You will continue and complete this function in step 10.

8. Enter the Highlight function shown and described here:

```
function Highlight(fld)

{

  if(fld.ui.textEdit)
  { // each field has different ui type
    fld.ui.textEdit.border.fill.color.value = reqFillColor;
  }else if(fld.ui.choiceList)
  {
    fld.ui.choiceList.border.fill.color.value = reqFillColor;
  }else if(fld.ui.dateTimeEdit)
  {
    fld.ui.dateTimeEdit.border.fill.color.value = reqFillColor;
  }else if(fld.ui.checkButton)
```

```
  {
     fld.ui.checkButton.border.fill.color.value = reqFillColor;
  }
}
```

The function is defined in the first line, and it takes a parameter of fld. This means that you'll call this function by passing a field object that will be held in the fld variable. The body of the function starts after the first opening bracket ({) and closes after the last closing bracket (}).

The function uses a block of JavaScript if-else statements to determine the type of field being passed in. The fields in Designer have different UI types, and the following types of fields are in this script: textEdit, choiceList, dateTimeEdit, and checkButton.

If one of the if conditions is satisfied, the line within its brackets is executed and the field is highlighted in yellow. The unHighlight function is similar except that it changes the form field's background back to white and doesn't add an item to the array.

9. Enter the unHighlight function as shown here:

```
function unHighlight(fld)
{
  if(fld.ui.textEdit)
  {
     fld.ui.textEdit.border.fill.color.value = nonReqFillColor;
  }else if(fld.ui.choiceList)
  {
     fld.ui.choiceList.border.fill.color.value = nonReqFillColor;
  }else if(fld.ui.dateTimeEdit)
  {
     fld.ui.dateTimeEdit.border.fill.color.value = nonReqFillColor;
  }else if(fld.ui.checkButton)
  {
     fld.ui.checkButton.border.fill.color.value = nonReqFillColor;
  }
}
```

10. Enter the remainder of the `requiredValidation()` function as shown and described here. You should add this script directly after the script you finished in Step 8.

```
var successFlag = true;

   if(emptyArr.length > 0)

   {

      successFlag = false;

      xfa.host.messageBox("Please fill out all required fields that
      ➥ are highlighted in yellow.", "Missing Required Fields", 1,0);

      xfa.host.setFocus(emptyArr[0]); // set focus to first missing
      ➥ item

   }else

   {

      successFlag = true;

      xfa.host.messageBox("Thank you, all Required Fields are
      ➥ completed");

   }

   return successFlag;

}
```

This section starts out with a Boolean variable named successFlag and assigns it a value of true. This is followed by another if-else block that checks to see whether the length of the array is greater than 0.

If the array has a length greater than 0, this is an indication that one or more fields haven't passed the validation and are now stored in the array. Therefore, successFlag is set to false and a message is sent to the user. After the user reads the message, the focus on the form will be set to the first missing item so the user can fill in the missing data.

If the array has a length that isn't greater than 0, this is an indication that all fields have passed the validation and the array is empty. Therefore, successFlag is set to true and a different message is sent to the user. For this example, the return of successFlag isn't relevant. However, if you call this script object from a form submit button, the return value will be very relevant, as you'll see in the next section.

Calling functions in script objects

Now that you have a script object with functions, you just need to call the functions from the appropriate places on your form. This is also referred to as calling the methods of your objects. Follow these steps to call a function in your script object from an interactive form object:

11. Select the checkRequiredFields Button object at the bottom of your form, and go to the Script Editor.

12. Select the `click` event in the Show Events drop-down list, and make sure Language is set to `JavaScript` and the Run At property is set to `Client`.

13. Enter the following script into the `click` event of the button:

```
// Calling a function on a script object


required.requiredValidation();
```

14. Select Preview PDF to see your new script object in action.

If you click Check Required Fields without filling in any data for the Primary beneficiary, the empty fields will highlight in yellow, and you'll receive a JavaScript Warning window with a Missing Required Fields message (**Figure 2.10**).

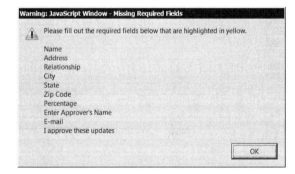

Figure 2.10 The JavaScript Warning window showing the user a message.

In the last section, we showed you that the script object was returning the `successFlag` variable to the calling script. Although this wasn't relevant in the example, it can be relevant if you call this script object from a form submit button. For instance, in the changeOfBeneficiaryCompleted.xdp form we've altered the calling script to act on the returned value:

```
// Calling a function on a script object


if(required.requiredValidation()){
   //enter code here to submit form
}
```

In this example, the script to submit the form data will execute only when the validation is successful and successFlag is set to true.

Using Regular Expressions

Regular expressions are used to validate user-entered data against a pattern. Regular expressions are similar to the wildcard characters you use to search for files in Windows. For instance, if you need to search your computer for all PDF files, you use the "*.pdf" string as a pattern to find all matching filenames. Regular expressions take this concept a step further and can be quite technical in nature.

You don't need to be a regular expression expert to use them in your forms. There are many websites that feature common regular expressions that you can copy and paste into your Designer scripts. Follow these steps to see how regular expressions are used in the Change of Beneficiary form.

1. Open your changeOfBeneficiaryCompleted.xdp form if it's not already open.

2. Select the validation script object in the Hierarchy palette.

3. Expand the Script Editor so you can see the email function.

```
function email(fld){

  if(fld.rawValue != null){

    var r = /^[a-z0-9_\-\.]+\@[a-z0-9_\-\.]+\.[a-z]{2,4}$/


    var result = r.test(fld.rawValue);


    if (result == false){

      app.alert("Please enter a valid email address", 0, 0, "");

      fld.rawValue = null;

      xfa.host.setFocus(fld);

    }

  }

}
```

TIP: If you don't see the line numbering in your Script Editor, you can select Tools > Options > Workspace and select the Show Line Numbers property.

The regular expression is on line 8 in the Script Editor and is assigned to the variable r. Line 10 shows the test method of the regular expression object being called to compare the field's value with the regular expression. The result is assigned to the Boolean variable result. The regular expression pattern is looking for a series of alphanumeric characters and certain symbols followed by an @ symbol, another series of alphanumeric characters and certain symbols followed by a period, and one of the popular domain suffixes used for email addresses (such as com, net, or org).

If the field's value matches this pattern, the script is complete and the user can move on with the form. If the value doesn't match, the user is alerted with a message box, the entry is cleared, and the focus is set back to the field so the user can try again to enter a valid email address.

The USZipCode function uses regular expressions in a similar way, but there are now three distinct regular expressions to support three different validation patterns:

- The first expression accepts entries of 99999, 999999999, or 99999-9999.

- The second expression only accepts entries of 99999.

- The third expression only accepts entries of 999999999 or 99999-9999.

Using Arrays to Store Data

Arrays are useful in programming, and JavaScript arrays use a syntax similar to arrays that you create in Java. An array will hold a group of items and each item will occupy a specific index of the array, much like a parking lot holds a group of cars, with each car in a specific parking spot. JavaScript uses an Array class, and you can call methods of this class as you work with your array. You create an array like this:

```
var aValues = new Array();
```

If you know the size of your array, you can pass it a size parameter. The following line creates an array of 20 items:

```
var aValues = new Array(20);
```

Like Java, JavaScript arrays are zero-based, so the first item in this array will occupy the index 0 and the last item will occupy the index 19. You can retrieve the length of an array by calling its length property:

```
var arrayLength = aValues.length // will return 20
```

If you know the values for your array, you can pass them when you create the array. The following will create an array with a length of 4:

```
var aBeatles = new Array("John", "Paul", "George", "Ringo");
```

Storing form data in arrays

You can store form data in arrays and add these arrays to your script objects. This enables you to store common form data in one location for easy edits and updates. For instance, the state drop-down lists on your forms can retrieve their data from an array in a script object. Follow these steps to learn how to add arrays to script objects and retrieve data from the arrays for use in your forms:

1. Select the arrays script object in your Hierarchy palette. You can see the existing state array that holds the abbreviations for all 50 U.S. states.

2. Create a new array below your state array with this script:

```
var relationship = new Array("Wife", "Husband", "Daughter", "Son",
➡ "Grandson", "Granddaughter");
```

3. Select the primaryRelationship Drop-down List in the primaryItem subform.

4. Expand the Script Editor, and add this script to the initialize event:

```
this.clearItems();

var arrayList = arrays.relationship;

for(var i=0; i<arrayList.length; i++)

{

  this.addItem(arrayList[i]);

}
```

The first line will clear any existing items from this Drop-down List. The second line creates an arrayList variable that's local to this script. The second line also fills the arrayList variable with the contents of the array from the script object.

The remainder of this script is a for loop that iterates through the array and adds each item to the Drop-down List. The i variable represents the index of the array, so the for loop starts at index 0 (the first item in the array) and continues to iterate through the array as long as the counter is less than the length value of the array (the total number of items in the array).

5. Select the contingentRelationship Drop-down List in the contingentItem subform.

6. Expand the Script Editor and add the same script to the `initialize` event.

7. Select Preview PDF to see your scripts in action. When you select either drop-down, your array values will be in the list (**Figure 2.11**).

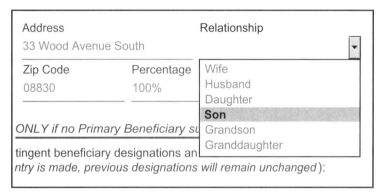

Figure 2.11 Your array values in your drop-down list.

Handling Exceptions

Your smart forms can call web services at runtime to retrieve data. This is a useful technique to retrieve real-time, customized, or personalized information for your user. Unfortunately, there may be problems connecting to the service and a JavaScript exception may be generated. A JavaScript *exception* is an event that disrupts the normal flow and execution of your script. You need to handle possible exceptions by adding exception handling to your script. Follow these steps to learn how:

1. Open your changeOfBeneficiaryCompleted.xdp form if it's not already open.

2. Select the prefillInformation Button object in the header, and go to the Script Editor.

3. Select the `click` event in the Show Events drop-down list, and make sure Language is set to `JavaScript` and the Run At property is set to `Client`.

4. The script is currently commented out. Remove the beginning of the comment block on line 3 (the /* line) and the end of the comment block on line 41 (the */ line).

5. Select Preview PDF to see your new script object in action.

6. Click the Prefill Information button in the top right of the form, and you may see your form prefilling with data from the web service (**Figure 2.12**).

Change of Beneficiary

SmartDoc Technologies
New York, New Jersey, and Beijing, China

SmartDoc
TECHNOLOGIES™

You can use this form to update your beneficiary information on our contract records.

Prefill Information

| Policy Number | Name of Insured | Policyowner's Name |
| 0001-00002-00003 | John Smith | John Patrick Smith |

Figure 2.12 The data from the web service prefilled in your form.

You may not see the results illustrated here. Since we're calling a web service and our script is using a `try-catch` block to catch an exception, you may see either of the following results as well:

■ **The Adobe Acrobat Security Warning:** Adobe Acrobat may prompt you with a security warning about connecting to an external web service (**Figure 2.13**).

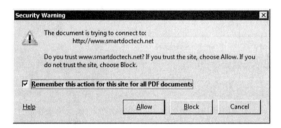

Figure 2.13 Adobe Acrobat Security Warning.

■ **The message box from our JavaScript:** You may see a message box advising you that the web service is down. This message box is the result of using exception handling in our JavaScript. Whenever a runtime exception is possible, it's a best practice to add a `try-catch` block to your JavaScript.

The try block

The connection to the web service and the retrieval of data is all executed within the `try` block. The other parts of the script can be tested at design time, but it's always possible that either the server is down or you have some other network problem that prohibits you from getting data at runtime. You want to make sure to add script to the `try` block at design time so these exceptions will be caught at runtime.

```
try {
    var oGetIdandNameRequest = {
        GetPolicyInfoById:{
            id:selId
```

```
      }
   };


   var cSOAPAction = "http://tempuri.org/GetPolicyInfoById";

   var myNamespace = "http://tempuri.org/";


   var oResults = SOAP.request ({

      cURL: cURL,

      oRequest: oGetIdandNameRequest,

      cAction: cSOAPAction,

      bEncoded: false,   // If false then document/literal encoding will
      ➥ be used.

      cNamespace: myNamespace,

      cResponseStyle: SOAPMessageStyle.Message

   });

}
```

The exception is caught in the catch block

If an exception occurs, it's caught in the catch block that starts on line 43 of
the Script Editor:

```
catch(e)

{

xfa.host.messageBox("There is a problem connecting to the web
➥ service:\n\n" + e);

}
```

The catch block alerts the user with a message box (**Figure 2.14**). Without this
exception handling, users would be left wondering what was happening with
their form and they wouldn't know how to proceed with completing the form.

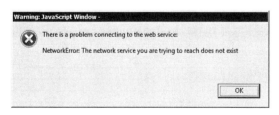

Figure 2.14 You can add a message box to the `catch` block of your JavaScripts to alert the user to the exception that occurred.

The data is displayed in the form

The last section of the script populates the form fields with the data from the web service:

```
var concatStr = oResults[0].soapValue[0].soapValue;


var stringArr = new Array();
stringArr = concatStr.split("~$~");


policyNumber.rawValue = stringArr[0];
insuredName.rawValue = stringArr[1];
policyOwnerName.rawValue = stringArr[2];
```

Using the Date Class

JavaScript also includes the Date class, which is useful in interactive forms. Follow these steps to review an example of the JavaScript Date class:

1. Open the dateClass.xdp file.

2. Select Preview PDF to see how the form functions. After you enter dates in both date fields, the script will determine which date comes first, or whether both fields have the same date.

This script creates two Date objects in the calculate event of the Text Field object and compares them to determine which came first. Notice that the first line tests the text fields for null values.

```
if(DateTimeField1.rawValue != null && DateTimeField2.rawValue != null){
    var date1 = DateTimeField1.rawValue; //create Date variable with
    ➥ the date
    var date1Year = date1.substr(0,4); //extract the year
    var date1Month = date1.substr(5,2); //extract the Month
    var date1Day = date1.substr(8,2); //extract the Day of the month
    var newDate1Date = new Date(date1Year, date1Month-1, date1Day);


    var date2 = DateTimeField2.rawValue;
    var date2Year = date2.substr(0,4);
```

```
var date2Month = date2.substr(5,2);

var date2Day = date2.substr(8,2);

var newDate2Date = new Date(date2Year, date2Month-1, date2Day);


if(newDate1Date > newDate2Date ){

   this.rawValue = "Date 1 is AFTER Date 2";

}else if(newDate1Date < newDate2Date ){

   this.rawValue = "Date 1 is BEFORE Date 2";

}else{

   this.rawValue = "Date 1 is EQUAL TO Date 2";

}

}else{

   this.rawValue = "Please enter a value in Date 1 and Date 2 above";

}
```

The script starts by testing for null values because there's no reason for us to attempt a comparison if only one date is entered. Once Date 1 and Date 2 contain dates, we'll use the substr function to extract the month, day, and year from each value and store them in appropriate variables. A new variable is then created using the Date constructor with the appropriate month, day, and year variables. Using the Date constructor will create a variable with the value of an actual date instead of a string. The two new date variables can then be compared. After the comparison, the text field is updated with the results.

Your Personal JavaScript Assistant

If you need the benefits of scripting but don't have the time to master JavaScript, Designer's Action Builder may be the tool you're looking for. Action Builder is a script-creating assistant that you can access by selecting Tools > Action Builder. You select form objects, conditions, and results and Action Builder generates the script for you. For instance, you can select a Button object and indicate that you want an action performed when the button is clicked. You can define the result of the action as a message box. Action Builder will generate the script and add it to your Button object's click event in the Script Editor. When a user clicks the button at runtime, the pop-up message box will appear.

For a complete Action Builder exercise, visit the book's companion site.

Debugging Scripts

The debugging tools in Designer keep improving with each version. If you come from a programming background, you'll find that these tools don't have all the debugging features found in modern integrated development environments (IDEs) like Microsoft's Visual Studio and Eclipse. However, Designer does provide the following features and tools to help you track down problems with your forms and scripts.

The Report Palette

The Report palette should be the first place you go to examine the behavior of your form. It has a Warnings tab, a Binding tab, and a Log tab.

The Warnings tab

Designer logs useful information about your form to the Warnings tab when you save your file or when you select Preview PDF. The important information includes script syntax errors and picture clause errors (**Figure 2.15**).

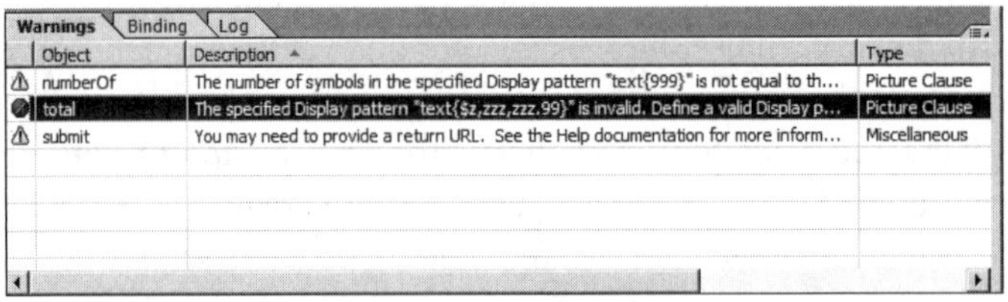

Figure 2.15 The Warnings tab of the Report palette.

Follow these steps to see the Report palette in action:

1. Open the expenseReportWithErrors.xdp file.

2. Expand the Report palette. If you don't see the Report palette, select Window > Report.

3. Select the Warnings tab to see the warnings displayed in Figure 2.15. There are a number of warnings. The highlighted one is a picture clause warning because the specified display pattern on the total field is invalid. Let's fix this.

4. Select the total field in the expenseRow subform.

5. Select the Field tab of the Object palette, and click the Patterns button.

6. Change the word "text" to **num** in the display pattern.

7. Click Apply, and then OK. You'll notice that the warning is no longer in the Warnings tab.

The Binding tab

If you include fields on your form that are bound to a data source, the Binding tab can assist you by displaying lists of fields based on how you defined their data binding. For example, you can list only fields with global data binding or only those with no data binding defined. This feature is especially useful on forms that have a large number of data bound fields.

8. While still in the expenseReportWithErrors.xdp file, select the Binding tab on the Report palette.

9. Click the arrow icon in the top right of the Binding tab, and select Fields Using Data Binding By Reference in the pop-up menu to see the bindings displayed in **Figure 2.16**.

Figure 2.16 The Binding tab of the Report palette.

The warning icons (the red exclamation point in the triangle) indicate the binding problems on your form. You can correct these issues.

10. Select firstName in the Binding tab, and Designer will tell you that your data reference isn't defined by any data connection.

11. Select the firstName field in the Employee section at the top of your form.

12. Select the Binding tab of the Object palette to change the data binding for this form object.

13. Remove the *s* character from the end of your data binding so you now have the following data binding:

```
$.UserInfo.txtEmployeeFirstName
```

Notice that the warning icon next to the firstName item in the Report palette has now disappeared. You can repeat this technique to correct other binding issues.

14. Select the notes field in the Employee section at the top of your form.

15. Select the Binding tab of the Object palette to change the data binding for this form object.

16. Add an **s** character to the end of your data binding so you now have the following data binding:

```
$.UserInfo.txtNotes
```

The warning icon next to the notes item in the Report palette has disappeared.

The Log tab

Designer also sends messages about your form to the Log tab (**Figure 2.17**) when you save your file or when you select Preview PDF. These messages can be benign status messages like "PDF generated successfully" or messages about problematic issues in your form.

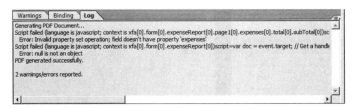

Figure 2.17 The Log tab of the Report palette.

Follow these steps to see the Log tab in action:

17. While still in the expenseReportWithErrors.xdp file, select Preview PDF to generate a current log message.

18. Select Design View and then the Log tab to review and correct issues. The log shows a "Script failed" message in the following field:

```
xfa.form.expenseReport.page1.expenses.total.subTotal
```

The log also tells us "Invalid property set operation; field doesn't have property 'expenses'."

19. Select the subTotal field, and select Events With Scripts in the Show Events drop-down list of the Script Editor. The issue is that this script declares a variable with the same name as a subform in your form. You can correct this by changing the name of the variable from expenses to myExpenses in all three instances where it occurs in the script. Your corrected script will look like this:

```
var myExpenses = expenseReport.page1.expenses.expensesWrapper.
➥ resolveNodes("expenseRow[*]");

var sum = 0.0;

for (var i = 0; i < myExpenses.length; i++){

  sum += myExpenses.item(i).total.rawValue;

}

this.rawValue = sum;
```

20. Select Preview PDF to generate a new log message.

21. Select Design View to review your Log tab message. You will now see "0 warnings/errors reported."

The Check Script Syntax Tool

Designer includes the Check Script Syntax tool (**Figure 2.18**) as part of the Script Editor.

Figure 2.18 The Check Script Syntax tool can be accessed in the toolbar of the Script Editor.

In this example, line 7 contains an additional and unnecessary closing bracket. Designer will highlight this in the Check Script Syntax window and list this error in the Warnings tab of the Report palette.

```
Error: Too many closing braces, Line 7.
```

Follow these steps to see the Check Script Syntax tool in action:

1. Open the changeOfBeneficiaryCompleted.xdp form.

2. Select the checkRequiredFields Button object in the signature subform, and go to the Script Editor.

3. Select the click event in the Show Events drop-down list, and add an extra close bracket on line 7 (Figure 2.18).

4. Click the Check Script Syntax tool, and you'll see line 7 highlighted and the error message appear in the Warnings tab of your Report palette.

5. Remove the extra close bracket on line 7.

6. Click the Check Script Syntax tool again, and you'll see the error message removed from the Warnings tab of your Report palette.

Stepping Through Your Scripts

A practical and useful method of debugging your scripts is to step through them at design time. You can do this with the messageBox method of the host object. The trick is to position your messageBox script at the appropriate point in your script to retrieve the information that you need. Follow these steps to see this technique in action:

1. Open the changeOfBeneficiaryCompleted.xdp form.

2. Select the required script object, and expand your Script Editor. There are two message box scripts in the requiredValidation function. Each of these is commented out.

3. Remove the comment characters at the beginning of each line so your scripts look like these:

```
// You will remove the comment characters from the next line in the
// exercise.
xfa.host.messageBox("Begin populating required field array.");
...
// You will remove the comment characters from the next line in the
// exercise.
xfa.host.messageBox("Required field array has successfully
➥ populated.");
```

After these comment marks have been removed, preview your form to see when the message boxes appear at runtime.

4. Select Preview PDF.

5. Click the Check Required Fields button. As long as some of the required fields are empty, your requiredValidation function will execute. However, before you see the Missing Required Fields message box, you'll see the Begin Populating Array info message (**Figure 2.19**).

6. Click OK to close this message box. You'll now see the Finish Populating Array info message (**Figure 2.20**).

7. Click OK to close this message box. You'll now see the Missing Required Fields message box that you saw in previous examples.

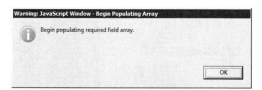

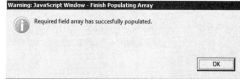

Figure 2.19 The Begin Populating Array info message shows you that your runtime execution has successfully reached this point in your script.

Figure 2.20 The Finish Populating Array info message occurs at a different point in your script.

If you saw all three of the message boxes, you know that your script has successfully executed. If you saw only the first message box and not the other two, you probably have a script error within the requiredValidation function of your script object. Since you know the first message box script executed, all of your script up to that point including this line is OK:

```
var emptyArr = new Array();
```

You have now narrowed down your problematic scripting and can focus on the other areas.

The JavaScript Debugger

Another useful tool for debugging your scripts is the JavaScript Debugger, which is included with Adobe Acrobat Professional. To enable the JavaScript Debugger for Designer, you must first enable JavaScript and the JavaScript Debugger in Acrobat Professional:

1. Launch Acrobat Professional, and select Edit > Preferences.

2. Select JavaScript from the list on the left.

3. Select Enable Acrobat JavaScript if it's not already selected.

4. In the JavaScript Debugger panel, select "Enable JavaScript debugger after Acrobat is restarted."

5. Select Enable Interactive Console.

6. Select Show Console On Errors And Messages.

7. Click OK to close the Preferences dialog box.

8. Select File > Exit to close Acrobat Professional.

9. Restart Acrobat, and open expenseReportWithErrors.pdf. You'll now see the Acrobat JavaScript Debugger (**Figure 2.21**). If you don't see this dialog box, press Ctrl+J (Windows) or Command+J (Mac).

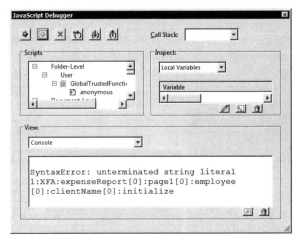

Figure 2.21 The JavaScript Debugger launches when there's a problematic script.

The debugger will display information about what went wrong, including the full path of the field containing the erroneous script, the event where the script is located, the line number of the script, and a basic explanation of the error.

TIP: You can clear the messages in the JavaScript Debugger's window by clicking the trash can icon in the bottom right of the window.

Tabbing

The tabbing order of your form is important because many of your form users will navigate your form by tabbing through the fields. Tabbing order is also critical if your forms need to be accessible to users who rely on keyboard commands because of vision or mobility impairments.

We recommend setting the tabbing order last because it can often be affected by other form changes that occur during development. After completion of all form changes, you'll have to apply the tabbing order only once. Otherwise, you may duplicate your efforts by re-creating the tab order after a new set of form changes.

How Tabbing Order Works

Designer's default tabbing order works from left to right and top to bottom, starting from the upper-left corner of the page. The default order is based on the precise X and Y coordinates of each object. A difference of 0.0001 inches in the Y coordinate may not be seen by the naked eye, but it will affect the tabbing order.

The tabbing order takes into account complex container objects like subforms and content areas. For instance, if you have two vertical subforms side by side on a form and each is filled with text fields, the tabbing order will work through each text field in the subform on the left before it moves to the sub-form on the right.

The following form objects aren't tabbed to when a form filler is navigating the form with the Tab key:

■ Circle, Line, or Rectangle objects.

■ Objects with a Presence property of Invisible or Hidden.

■ Objects with an Access property of Protected. This property can be set with the following JavaScript:

```
TextField1.access = "protected";
```

Designer treats a RadioButtonList object as a single stop in the tabbing order. A form filler must use the Up Arrow and Down Arrow keys on the keyboard to navigate through the radio buttons in a radio button list.

The Tab Order Palette

You can use the Tab Order palette to override the default tabbing order for your form. If you're working on a long and complicated form, you can edit the tabbing order one page at a time and save your changes intermittently. You rearrange the order of the accessible fields within the Tab Order palette by dragging and dropping the object names or by selecting an item and using the up and down arrows at the top of the palette. Designer will highlight each field in the tab order with a numbered icon in the Design View (**Figure 2.22**).

Some objects that aren't tabbed to are still part of the tabbing order because the tabbing order is also used to determine the reading order in accessible forms. If your objects are set to Invisible, Hidden, or Protected, the form filler won't tab to them when tabbing through the form, but the objects will still be part of the form's tabbing order.

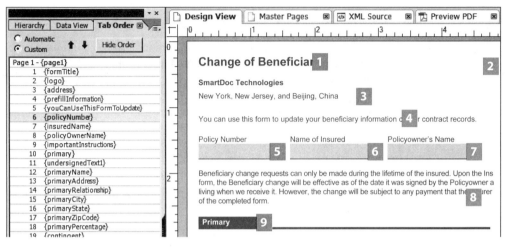

Figure 2.22 The Tab Order palette showing custom tabbing.

Options for Tab Order

Designer provides some tab order options in the Options dialog box, which you can access by selecting Tools > Options (**Figure 2.23**).

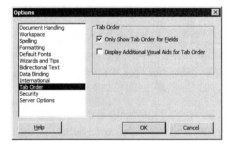

Figure 2.23 The Tab Order panel of the Options dialog box.

▪ **Only Show Tab Order For Fields:** By default, the tab order includes all the fields and objects on the form. However, if you're creating a custom tab order for your form's interactive fields, it's more cumbersome if all the form's objects are in the tab order. You can select this option to hide static Text objects and Image objects in the tab order view.

▪ **Display Additional Visual Aids For Tab Order:** Selecting this option will provide you with additional visual aids for your tab order. Designer will show blue arrows (**Figure 2.24**) displayed on your form when you hover over a field. The arrows show the two previous fields and the two subsequent fields in your tab order relative to the field you're hovering over.

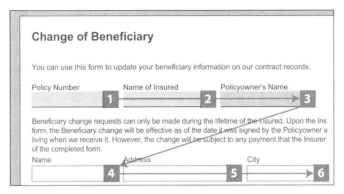

Figure 2.24 Designer's Display Additional Visual Aids For Tab Order option enables you to view the flow of your tab order.

Barcodes

Even when you supply an interactive form to your users, it's possible that they'll send back a printed form to complete the workflow. In these cases, you can encode some or all of the form data into barcodes, making it easier to bring the encoded data into your database via a barcode scanner.

Designer supports two software barcode types: the one-dimensional, or linear, type and the two-dimensional type (**Figure 2.25**). You can find Designer's barcode objects in the Barcodes tab of the Library palette. One-dimensional barcodes enable you to encode a single value into a barcode object. If you need to encode more than one value into a single barcode, use the two-dimensional Paper Forms Barcode. This barcode object encodes data that a user types into a form and works with a LiveCycle Server module called Adobe LiveCycle Barcoded Forms.

Figure 2.25 Designer supports one-dimensional barcodes (A) and two-dimensional barcodes (B).

One-Dimensional Barcodes

You can encode a single value into a one-dimensional barcode at design time or at runtime. At design time, you can enter a value into the Default field of the Value tab. If you need to encode a single value at runtime, you can use the rawValue property of your barcode:

```
PostUS5ZipBarCode1.rawValue = "90210";
```

Two-Dimensional Barcodes

The Paper Forms Barcode is an example of a two-dimensional barcode. This barcode object implements the industry standard PDF417 format. You can add this barcode object to a form to encode the user's data at runtime. To see this functionality, the form must be opened in Acrobat Professional or Reader Extended for use in Adobe Reader. You will learn how to Reader extend a form in Chapter 4. Follow these steps to see an example.

1. Create a new form in Designer by selecting File > New to launch the New Form Assistant.

2. Select Use A Blank Form, click Next, and click Finish.

3. Drag and drop a Text Field object from the Standard Object Library to the form.

4. Drag and drop a Paper Forms Barcode object from the Barcodes Object Library to the form. Click OK if you receive a Tips and Hints message box.

5. With the barcode selected, highlight the Value tab of the Object palette.

6. Select <<New/Manage Collection>> in the Collection drop-down list at the bottom of the palette.

7. In the Collection List dialog box, click New, and enter a new collection named **myCollection**.

8. Select myCollection in the list and click Modify. The Collection Editor dialog box appears (**Figure 2.26**).

Figure 2.26 The Collection Editor dialog box.

9. Select the TextField1 node in the Collection Editor dialog box.

10. Click OK and close the Collection List dialog box.

11. Select Preview PDF, and you'll see that the Paper Forms Barcode object is automatically updated when you exit the text field after updating its value.

PDF417 Barcodes

In this case, PDF stands for Portable Data File, which is not the same as Adobe's PDF (Portable Document Format). Barcodes of this type are typically used in identification cards and inventory management. PDF417 is an industry-standard two-dimensional barcode format with the following features:

- **More storage:** PDF417 barcodes can store up to 2710 characters of data, which is more than one-dimensional barcodes can store.

- **Fast reading:** PDF417 barcodes can be read nearly as fast as one-dimensional barcodes.

- **Redundancy:** Even if part of the barcode becomes damaged through faxing or some other activity, the data that the barcode represents can be reconstructed.

Designer includes two PDF417 barcodes: the Paper Forms Barcode and the PDF417 barcode object. Unlike the Paper Forms Barcode, the PDF417 barcode accepts only one value. However, unlike the other one-dimensional barcodes, the PDF417 barcode includes the redundancy of the PDF417 standard.

Web Services

Web services are similar in some ways to web pages, but they're also different and unique. Like a web page, a web service has a specific URL and can be called by making a reference to its URL. Web services also work with a request/response mechanism similar to web pages. However, unlike web pages, web services aren't designed to be viewed by humans. They're designed to serve data and functionality across the web to other computer programs.

You can call a web service from your form at runtime, and your form fillers will benefit because your web service call will retrieve real-time data to assist your form filler with completing your form. For instance, your form can call a web service to retrieve current home mortgage interest rates to make a mortgage form more relevant and accurate. In a similar way, a brokerage form or a bank account form can retrieve current financial information on mutual funds and money market accounts. Many third-party companies provide stable and accurate web services for free or for a small monthly charge.

Web services are described by WSDL (pronounced wiz-dull) files. WSDL (Web Services Description Language) is based on XML. The WSDL file specifies how to communicate with a particular web service. Earlier in this chapter, you saw an example of connecting to a web service with JavaScript. You can also use Designer's interface tools to connect to a WSDL file at design time. To see this functionality, you must open the form in Acrobat Professional or Reader Extended (for use in Adobe Reader).

Connecting to a WSDL File

When you connect to a WSDL file at design time, Designer reads the file to determine which operations are available to call. It then creates data objects that are bound to the request and response objects of the web service. Once your form is connected, you can call the web service at runtime (**Figure 2.27**).

Follow these steps to create a data connection to a WSDL file:

1. Create a new form in Designer by selecting File > New to launch the New Form Assistant.

2. Select Use A Blank Form, click Next, and click Finish.

3. Select the Data View palette on the left side of your workspace. If you don't see the Data View tab, select Window > Data View.

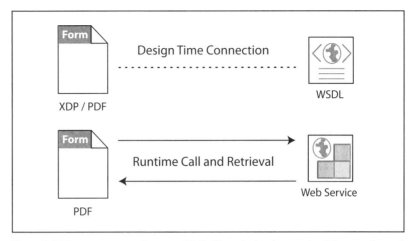

Figure 2.27 You connect your form to a WSDL file at design time, and call the operations of the web service at runtime.

4. Right-click the empty Data View palette and select New Data Connection from the pop-up menu.

5. Select the WSDL File option and name your data connection **myWebService** (**Figure 2.28**). Click Next to continue.

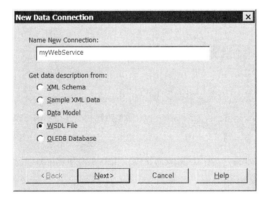

Figure 2.28 The name you enter here will be the name that you use when calling the web service at runtime.

6. Enter the following URL into the WSDL File text field and click Next to continue:

http://www.webservicex.net/stockquote.asmx?WSDL

A web service URL is similar to a web page URL, but the service's URL ends with the .asmx suffix. In this case, the ?WSDL string has been appended to request the WSDL file.

NOTE: The URL provided points to a WSDL file for a free web service that's available as of this writing. However, I have no control over this web service. So, if you're unable to connect to it, I recommend trying another web service. You can find others at www.webservicex.net. If you want to connect to a different WSDL file, use the appropriate URL for that WSDL file.

7. The next screen (**Figure 2.29**) lists all the operations available from the web service. For this particular web service, select the topmost GetQuote option. Click Next to continue.

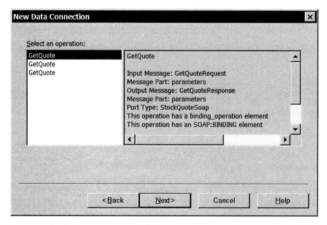

Figure 2.29 If you select an operation in the left panel, the right panel displays details about the operation.

Each Designer data connection is mapped to one specific operation of the web service. If you need more than one operation of the web service, you'll need to create multiple data connections.

8. Click Finish to create your connection to the WSDL file. Designer will automatically generate some data objects in your Data View palette.

9. Expand the nodes in your Data View palette so you can see the entire hierarchy of objects.

10. Drag the symbol object to your form.

11. Drag the GetQuoteBtn object to your form.

12. Drag the GetQuoteResult object to your form.

13. With the GetQuoteResult object selected, click the Field tab of the Object palette.

14. Select Allow Multiple Lines.

15. Make the GetQuoteResult object larger (**Figure 2.30**). The web service will return a block of XML, so you need to enlarge this text field to view the entire block.

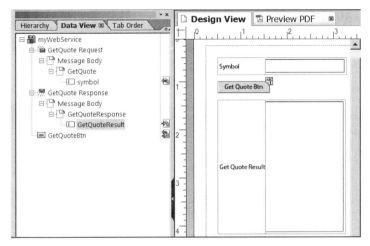

Figure 2.30 The Design View of your WSDL connection.

Your data objects in the Data View palette are in a series of wrappers culminating in one of the following top-level wrappers:

■ GetQuote Request

■ GetQuote Response

Each of these top-level wrappers corresponds to the request/response nature of a web service. However, your form hierarchy doesn't need to match this data hierarchy.

Calling the Web Service

This web service is called at runtime when the user clicks the GetQuoteBtn button. This button has some important property settings that you can see at design time. Select the GetQuoteBtn button and select the Execute tab of the Object palette to view these important property settings:

■ The Connection property is set to myWebService.

■ The Web Service URL is set to http://www.webservicex.net/stockquote.asmx.

■ The Operation is set to GetQuote.

■ The Run At property is set to Client.

Follow these steps to see how your form performs at runtime:

1. Select Preview PDF to launch your form into the runtime environment.

2. Enter **adbe** into the Symbol text field. This is the stock symbol for Adobe.

3. Click the GetQuoteBtn button. Depending on your Acrobat settings, you may see the Adobe Acrobat Security Warning message box. You'll need to allow connection to this web service for your form to populate with the return data.

Your form will load with the return data from the web service (**Figure 2.31**).

Figure 2.31 Your PDF forms can be filled with real-time data by calling web services at runtime.

Moving On

Now that you've significantly added to your LiveCycle Designer knowledge, you're ready to create your first form.

3

Creating the SmartDoc Expense Report

Creativity is just connecting things. When you ask creative people how they did something, they feel a little guilty because they didn't really do it, they just saw something. It seemed obvious to them after a while.

—Steve Jobs

LiveCycle Designer is the ideal authoring tool for smart forms, but it can be challenging to learn. If this is your first experience with Designer, you may find this exercise to be demanding and exacting. However, this thorough walkthrough will give you a chance to practice what you learned in the first two chapters.

To help you along, I have included seven master XDP files in the Samples folder that represent the completed results of each part of the exercise (**Figure 3.1**). If you find parts of this exercise to be formidable, compare your results to the step-by-step sample files. If you struggle with a step in the process, begin the next step with one of the completed files so you can continue through the exercise.

Figure 3.1 The SmartDoc Expense Report exercise is saved as a series of steps and separate XDP files in your Samples folder.

My goal is to give you a thorough Designer exercise to introduce you to the key parts of the program and the important concepts of smart forms. You'll create master pages, body pages, and dynamic subforms in this exercise. You'll also add scripting to form object events and to script objects. At the end, you'll preview your form with sample data.

Creating a Custom Object Library

Designer supports the creation of custom objects and custom object libraries. That means you can create the perfect interface object using just the right font you want and functionality you need, and then save it for reuse on any LiveCycle form. Follow these steps to create a custom object library and add the SmartDoc objects to your library:

1. Click the Object Library palette menu and choose Add Group (**Figure 3.2**, left). Designer launches the Add Library Group dialog box.

2. Enter **SmartDoc** as the name for your new library. Click OK to close the window.

3. Click the SmartDoc category menu and choose Group Properties. The Library Group Properties dialog box appears (Figure 3.2, right).

4. Click the icon to the right of the Location field and locate the SmartDoc Objects folder in the Samples folder. Click OK to close the dialog boxes.

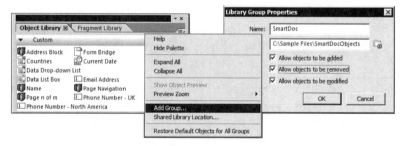

Figure 3.2 Adding a group to your Object Library palette (left) and associating this group with a folder on your computer (right).

Now you'll be able to drag and drop form objects from the SmartDoc Object Library to your form. All the form objects in the SmartDoc Object Library were created in Designer based on the standard Designer objects that you can find in the other tabs of the Object Library. You will learn how to create your own custom objects in Chapter 5, "Best Practices for PDFs."

Creating the Pages and Subforms

Follow these steps to create the high-level structure of your form. When you've completed these steps, you'll have two master pages and some body page elements.

1. Create a new blank form by choosing File > New. Designer opens the New Form Assistant.

2. Select Use A Blank Form and click Next to continue.

3. Keep the defaults on all subsequent screens and keep clicking Next until you get to the Finish button. Click Finish to create your new form.

4. Right-click the Page1 master page in the Hierarchy palette, choose Rename Object, and change its name to **masterPage1**.

5. Right-click the (Master Pages) node in the Hierarchy palette, and choose New Master Page. Name this master page **masterPage2**.

6. Right-click the body page (untitled Subform) (page 1) in the Hierarchy palette, choose Rename Object, and change its name to **page1**.

7. With page1 selected, select the Subform tab of the Object palette and set the Content property to Flowed and Flow Direction to Top To Bottom. This will flow all the child subforms from the top of your page to the bottom.

8. Right-click the page1 node in the hierarchy and choose Insert Subform. Name this subform **employee**. Create another subform the same way and name it **expenses**.

9. Save your file as **myExpenseReport_1.xdp**. Your file type should be Adobe XML Form (*.xdp).

TIP: If you had difficulty with the exercises in this section, you can compare your form to the expenseReport_1.xdp file in your Samples folder. This file contains all the form elements in their proper structure. You can correct your file based on this sample or simply use this sample as a base for the next exercise.

Creating the Master Pages

Now that your form has some structure, you can begin to construct your pages using master pages.

1. Right-click the Content Area object on masterPage1, and choose Rename Object to change its name to **contentArea**. You can use the Layout palette to change the dimensions of the content area to the following: Width = **7.5** inches, Height = **9** inches, X = **0.5** inches, Y = **1.5** inches. You now have room at the top of the page for some header elements.

2. Drag and drop an Image object from your Standard Object Library to the header section of masterPage1 and rename it **smartDocLogo**. With this object selected, enter these values into the Layout palette: X = **0.5**, Y = **0.4375**.

3. Drag and drop a header object and a dateRequested object from your SmartDoc Object Library to the header section of masterPage1.

4. Select the dateRequested object and enter these values into the Layout palette: X = **6.3**, Y = **0.7625**.

5. Select the header object and change its name to **expensesTitle**. With this object selected, enter these values into the Layout palette: X = **6**, Y = **0.4375**

6. Select smartDocLogo on masterPage1, and select Use Original Size on the Object palette. Click the icon to the right of the URL text field, and locate and select the smartDocLogo.jpg file in the Samples folder.

7. Double-click the expensesTitle object and enter **Expense Report** as the header copy on your form.

8. Drag and drop a Text object from your Standard Object Library to the footer section of masterPage1. Double-click this object and enter **Copyright 2014 - SmartDoc Technologies** or type some other suitable footer. Rename this object **copyrightFooter** in the hierarchy. With this object selected, enter these values into the Layout palette: X = **3**, Y = **10.5**.

9. Right-click the Content Area object on masterPage2, and choose Rename Object to change its name to **contentArea**. You can also use the Layout palette to change the dimensions of the content area to the following: Width = **7.5** inches, Height = **10** inches, X = **0.5** inches, Y = **0.5** inches.

10. Copy the Copyright statement Text object from masterPage1, and paste it at the bottom of masterPage2. Enter the same X and Y coordinates for this object in the Layout palette that you used on masterPage1: X = **3**, Y = **10.5**.

11. Drag and drop the "*Page n of m*" object from the Custom Object Library to the bottom right of masterPage2. Notice that this action adds three objects to your form hierarchy.

12. Select masterPage1 in the hierarchy and select the Master Page tab on the Object palette. Select the Restrict Page Occurrence option, and then set the Min Count and Max Count properties to **1**.

13. Save your file as **myExpenseReport_2.xdp**.

You've just created the master pages for the SmartDoc Expense Report. To finalize your work, you can take some additional steps. For instance, you can properly name each object in the form hierarchy. You can also style your text according to the graphic styles used in the sample file. However, even without completing these additional steps you have the basics that you need to continue.

TIP: If you had difficulty with the exercises in this section, you can compare your form to the expenseReport_2.xdp file in your Samples folder. This file contains all the form elements in their proper structure. You can correct your file based on this sample or simply use this sample as a base for the next exercise.

Creating the Body Page and Subforms

The creation of a body page and subforms requires more work than the master pages did. To simplify this task, set up your Layout Editor in the following way:

■ Select View > Grids & Guidelines > Snap To Grid.

■ Select Window > Drawing Aids and set your grid to a suitable measurement for form design. I use inches as a measurement unit, and I set my grid interval to be 16/in on the X axis and 16/in on the Y axis. I use these settings because they give me the consistency and the flexibility I need for my form design work. If another measurement system works better for you, that's fine. The goal is to produce a professional-looking graphic layout by keeping the size of your form fields consistent and standard.

With these settings in place, follow these steps to create the employee subform:

1. Select the employee subform in the Hierarchy palette.

2. Select the Subform tab of the Object palette and ensure that the Content property is set to Positioned to enable you to move form objects around to create your layout.

3. Select the Layout palette and enter the following: Width = **7.5** inches, Height = **2** inches.

4. Drag and drop a Line object from your Standard Object Library to the upper-left corner of the employee subform.

5. Stretch the line to be the full width of the subform, and set the line weight to **0.02** inches in the field to the right of Line Style in the Object palette. Your finished line should have the following dimensions in the Layout palette: X: 0.5in, Y: 1.5in, Width: 7.5 in, Height: 0in.

6. Drag and drop the following form objects from your SmartDoc Object Library to the employee subform: a subHead, three captionFields, a captionDropDown, and a notesField.

7. Double-click the subHead object and enter **Employee** as the subhead copy on your form. You can style this text with the Font and Paragraph palettes.

8. Enter the names and captions shown in **Table 3.1** for these form objects. You can change the caption properties in the Field tab of the Object palette.

Table 3.1 Form Object Names and Captions (Employee Subform)

FORM OBJECT	NAME IN HIERARCHY	CAPTION
Line1	line	none
subHead	subHead	none
captionField	firstName	First Name
captionField	lastName	Last Name
captionDropDown	clientName	Client Name
captionField	otherClientName	Other Client Name
notesField	notes	Notes

9. Arrange the form objects on your subform according to **Figure 3.3**. Stretch the captionFields so the row extends the entire width of the subform. As you work, you should notice the form objects snapping to the grid. You can see this table illustrated in the blue form in Figure 3.3.

10. Select the otherClientName object and select the Field tab of the Object palette. Change the Presence property from Visible to Invisible.

11. Save your file as **myExpenseReport_3.xdp**.

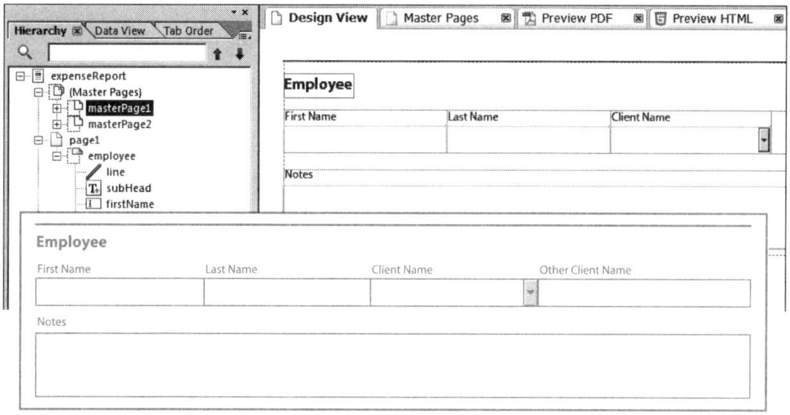

Figure 3.3 The Employee subform showing the form objects with their proper names in the hierarchy (left) and their proper positions in the layout (right). The blue form illustrates how the subform will look at runtime.

TIP: If you had difficulty with the exercises in this section, you can compare your form to the expenseReport_3.xdp file in your Samples folder. This file contains all the form elements in their proper structure. You can correct your file based on this sample or simply use this sample as a base for the next exercise.

Creating a Data Connection

Although you copied custom objects from the SmartDoc library, you could've also created these objects from Designer's standard objects. You can compare the SmartDoc objects to standard Designer objects by selecting form objects and viewing their properties in the Object, Border, Font, and Paragraph palettes.

After you've finished styling your subform, you can bind the employee form fields to the schema by following these steps:

1. Choose File > New Data Connection to launch the New Data Connection wizard.

2. Enter **expenseReport** for the name of your connection, select the XML Schema option, and click Next.

3. Locate expenseReport.xsd in the Samples folder, ensure that expenseReport is the root element, and then select the Embed XML Schema option. Click Finish to create your connection. Click Yes in the pop-up asking if you want to clear the Use Name settings.

4. Bind the clientName drop-down list to the schema by selecting the field and selecting the Binding tab of the Object palette.

5. Click the icon to the right of the Data Binding field and choose Use expenseReport > UserInfo > ddSmartDocClientName (**Figure 3.4**). Designer prompts you with the Binding Properties dialog box. Select Update The Following Properties Only, select Default Value and List Items, and click OK. The list of SmartDoc clients will be imported from the XML schema to your form in the same way that the shirt sizes were imported in the previous binding example in Chapter 2, "Scripting and Advanced Techniques." Select the Field tab of the Object palette and you'll see that Designer has updated the list of items. If you're using Designer 9 or later, you can also copy and paste a list of values from another application like Microsoft Word or Excel directly into the List Items property.

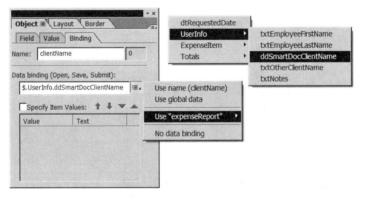

Figure 3.4 Binding a form field to an XML schema.

6. Bind the First Name field to the schema by selecting the firstName form field and selecting the Binding tab of the Object palette. Click the icon to the right of the Data Binding field and select Use expenseReport > UserInfo > txtEmployeeFirstName. This time when Designer prompts you with the Binding Properties dialog box, select Don't Update Any Related Properties.

7. Repeat the previous step and bind these fields to their corresponding schema nodes:

   ▪ **lastName:** $.UserInfo.txtEmployeeLastName

   ▪ **otherClientName:** $.UserInfo.txtOtherClientName

   ▪ **notes:** $.UserInfo.txtNotes

8. Select the employee subform and select the Binding tab of the Object palette. Set Data Binding to No Data Binding. This is a good practice to follow when a subform isn't bound to data.

9. Save your file as **myExpenseReport_4.xdp**.

TIP: If you had difficulty with the exercises in this section, you can compare your form to the expenseReport_4.xdp file in your Samples folder. This file contains all the form elements in their proper structure. You can correct your file based on this sample or simply use this sample as a base for the next exercise.

Previewing a Dynamic Subform

You've completed a simple subform. The next subform is more complex, so before you start, let's see how it works by previewing the completed SmartDoc Expense Report. Open the expenseReportCompleted.xdp file if it isn't already open. Follow these steps to see the dynamic expenses subform in action:

1. Select Preview PDF to view the form.

2. Click the Add Expense button to add a new expense item. The form dynamically creates a new row and moves the Add Expense button down.

3. Create five expense items and enter some information for each. If you enter data into the Cost column, the Sub Total and Total fields will update automatically.

4. Select the **X** to the left of your third entry to delete it. The expense item is deleted and your Sub Total and Total fields are updated. Your form should look something like **Figure 3.5**.

5. Select the Design View tab to complete the preview.

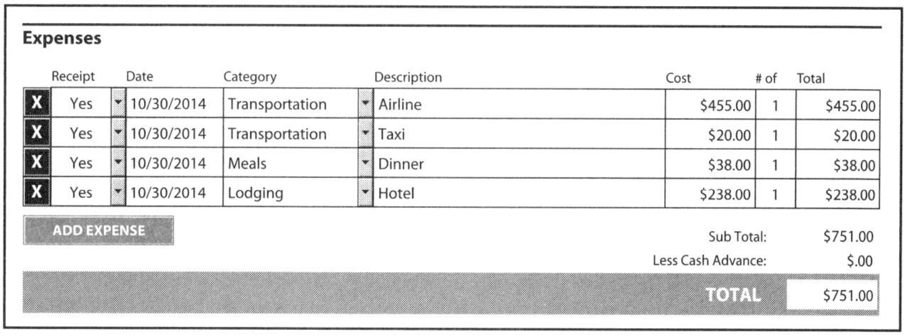

	Receipt	Date	Category	Description	Cost	# of	Total
Expenses							
X	Yes	10/30/2014	Transportation	Airline	$455.00	1	$455.00
X	Yes	10/30/2014	Transportation	Taxi	$20.00	1	$20.00
X	Yes	10/30/2014	Meals	Dinner	$38.00	1	$38.00
X	Yes	10/30/2014	Lodging	Hotel	$238.00	1	$238.00

ADD EXPENSE

Sub Total: $751.00
Less Cash Advance: $.00

TOTAL $751.00

Figure 3.5 The Expenses subform in action. Notice that the Add Expense button changes to blue when you hover over it.

Creating a Dynamic Subform

Now that you know how the completed form works, go back to your working form (myExpenseReport_4.xdp) and follow these steps to make the dynamic expenses subform. In this exercise, you will create an expenseRow subform. This subform will repeat for every expense item and will be the core of your dynamic form.

1. Right-click the expenses subform and choose Insert Subform. Create three subforms and name them **header**, **expensesWrapper**, and **total** from top to bottom in the hierarchy.

2. Select the expenses subform in the Hierarchy palette and set the Content property to Flowed in the Subform tab of the Object palette. This will enable the Auto-fit Height property, resulting in the subform being able to expand as needed.

3. Set the Width property for the header, expensesWrapper, and total subforms to **7.5** inches in the Layout palette.

4. Set the Width property of the expenses parent subform to **7.5** inches in the Layout palette.

5. Select the header subform and ensure the Content property is set to Positioned.

6. Set the Height property for the header subform to **.4375** inches in the Layout palette.

7. Drag and drop a subHead and a line from your SmartDoc Object Library to the upper-left corner of the header subform.

8. Double-click the subHead object and enter **Expenses** as the subhead copy on your form.

9. Right-click the expensesWrapper subform and choose Insert Subform. Create three subforms and name them **columnHeaders**, **expenseRow**, and **addExpenseWrapper** from top to bottom in the hierarchy.

10. Set the Width property for each of these subforms to **7.5** inches in the Layout palette.

11. Review the Content properties on the other subforms in the Subform tab of the Object palette and make sure they match the following:

    ■ **expensesWrapper:** Flowed

    ■ **columnHeaders:** Positioned

- **expenseRow:** Positioned

- **addExpenseWrapper:** Positioned

- **total:** Positioned

12. Select the page1 body page subform and make sure the Allow Page Breaks Within Content property in the Subform tab of the Object palette is selected. Also ensure that this property is selected for the expenses and the expensesWrapper subforms to enable your expense report to flow over to page 2 when a user has numerous entries.

13. Select the expenseRow subform and select the Binding tab of the Object palette. Select Repeat Subform For Each Data Item and set your Min Count to **1**. Be sure not to set a maximum count so your form filler can enter as many expense items as desired.

14. Drag and drop a columnHeaders object from your SmartDoc Object Library to the top of the columnHeaders subform.

15. Select the columnHeaders subform and set the Height property to Auto-fit in the Layout palette.

16. Drag and drop the following form objects from your SmartDoc Object Library to the expenseRow subform: a delete button, two dropDown objects, and five decimalField objects.

17. Enter the names shown in **Table 3.2** for these form objects and place them below the column headers listed in the column on the right.

Table 3.2 Form Object Names (Expenses Subform)

FORM OBJECT	NAME IN HIERARCHY	COLUMN HEADER
delete	delete	none
dropDown	receipt	Receipt
decimalField	date	Date
dropDown	category	Category
decimalField	description	Description
decimalField	cost	Cost
decimalField	numberOf	# of
decimalField	total	Total

18. Select the Date object and change the Type property in the Field tab of the Object palette to Date/Time Field.

19. Select the description object and change the Type property in the Field tab of the Object palette to Text Field.

20. Arrange the form objects on your expenses subform according to **Figure 3.6**. Adjust the text fields so they all fit on one row that runs the width of the expensesRow subform. Although this subform appears as only one row at design time, it will repeat at runtime to form a table of expense items. It's good practice to order your form fields on the Hierarchy palette in the same way they're ordered on the form.

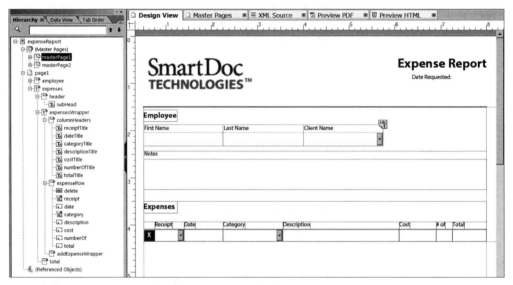

Figure 3.6 The expenses subform showing the form objects with their proper names in the hierarchy (left) and their proper positions in the layout (right).

21. After you arrange the form objects into one row, as shown in Figure 3.6, select the expenseRow subform and set the Height property to Auto-fit in the Layout palette.

22. Bind the following fields on the expenseRow subform to their corresponding nodes in the XML schema. Choose Don't Update Any Related Properties when Designer prompts you with the Binding Properties dialog box.

■ **receipt:** $.ExpenseItem[*].ddReceipt

■ **date:** $.ExpenseItem[*].dtDate

- **category:** $.ExpenseItem[*].ddCategory

- **description:** $.ExpenseItem[*].txtDescription

- **cost:** $.ExpenseItem[*].numCost

- **numberOf:** $.ExpenseItem[*].numNumberOf

- **total:** $.ExpenseItem[*].numLineTotal

The [*] in this list of bindings indicates that these form elements will be bound to a repeating part of the schema.

23. Select the receipt object and select the Field tab on the Object palette. Click the green plus sign and type **Yes** as a list item. Press Enter on your keyboard and type **No** as a second list item.

24. Repeat the previous step with the Category Drop-down List object. Add a few expense-related categories like Lodging and Transportation.

25. Drag and drop the addExpense object from your SmartDoc Object Library to the addExpenseWrapper subform.

26. Drag and drop the following form objects from your SmartDoc Object Library to the total subform: a subTotal object, a lessCash object, a rectangle object, and a grandTotal object.

27. Arrange the form objects on your subform according to **Figure 3.7**. The grandTotal object needs to be on top of the background object. You can use the options at the bottom of the Layout menu to move objects forward or backward in the layout.

Figure 3.7 The total subform showing the form objects with their proper names in the hierarchy (left) and their proper positions in the layout (right).

28. Select the addExpenseWrapper subform and the total subform, and set their Height properties to Auto-fit in the Layout palette.

29. Save your file as **myExpenseReport_5.xdp**.

*NOTE: As you can see in the SmartDoc Expense Report sample (**Figure 3.8**), I like to use the Adobe Myriad Pro font in my form design for two reasons. Design wise, Myriad Pro is an easily read, comprehensive sans serif font. It offers excellent font contrast between its light and heavy versions, and Adobe offers over 40 different styles of Myriad Pro. In addition, the common versions (Regular, Italic, Bold, and Bold Italic) of Myriad Pro ship with Reader and Acrobat, so you don't need to embed the font with your files.*

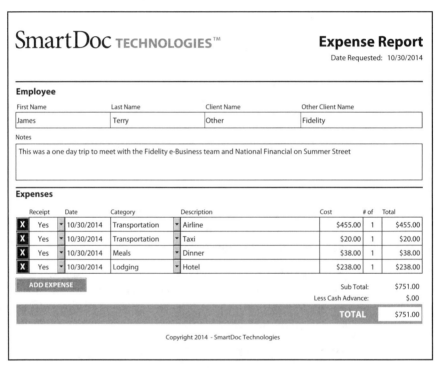

Figure 3.8 The SmartDoc dynamic expense report with four expense items.

When your form elements are complete, you can move on to scripting.

TIP: If you had difficulty with the exercises in this section, you can compare your form to the expenseReport_5.xdp file in your Samples folder. This file contains all the form elements in their proper structure. You can correct your file based on this sample or simply use this sample as a base for the next exercise.

Creating the Scripts and the Script Object

As you learned in the last chapter, you can add script to form object events and to functions in script objects. You'll do both in this section.

Changing the Button Color

Using script in a form object event is ideal for short scripts that are specific to a particular form object event. In this exercise, you'll add short scripts to the following form objects: the addExpense button, the clientName drop-down list, and the total and subTotal decimal fields. Follow these steps to add scripts to your form:

1. Select the addExpense Button object in the Design View.

2. Go to the Script Editor and select mouseEnter from the event list.

3. Select JavaScript as the Language and Client as the Run At property.

4. Enter this script in the Script Editor:

    ```
    this.border.fill.color.value = "0,102,174";
    ```

5. Switch the event to mouseExit, set Language to JavaScript, and enter this script into the editor:

    ```
    this.border.fill.color.value = "0,0,0";
    ```

6. Save your file as **myExpenseReport_6.xdp** and click Preview PDF to see your script in action.

This is a simple example of how you can add cosmetic enhancements to your forms. When your mouse pointer enters the Add Expense button area in preview mode, the button will change from black to blue. When your mouse pointer exits this area, the button color will change back to black.

NOTE: This cosmetic enhancement will work with only PDF forms. Currently, the mouseEnter and mouseExit events are not supported in HTML forms.

Progressive Disclosure

You'll now use script to change the functionality of your form. This is an example of *progressive disclosure*, which is a dynamic form technique to reduce complexity and make your form filler's job easier. In this case, the user will never see the Other Client Name text field unless they select Other in the Client drop-down list.

1. Select the clientName Drop-down List object.

2. Go to the Script Editor and select change from the event list.

3. Select JavaScript as Language and Client as the Run At property.

4. Enter this script in the Script Editor:

```
if(xfa.event.newText == "Other"){
  otherClientName.presence = "visible";
}else{
  otherClientName.presence = "invisible";
}
```

5. Save your file as **myExpenseReport_6.xdp** and click Preview PDF to see your script in action. If this doesn't work, check your script and check your default preview settings by choosing File > Form Properties > Preview. Your defaults should be:

   ■ Preview Type: Interactive Form

   ■ Preview Adobe XML Form As: Dynamic XML Form

In this script, you used a different XFA event, the change event. When there's a change made to the clientName Drop-down List object at runtime, this script will execute. The script performs a simple test to see if the user chose Other in the drop-down list. If so, the Other Client Name text field becomes visible; if not, the Presence property of this text field is set to Invisible.

TIP: If you had difficulty with the exercises in this section, you can compare your form to the expenseReport_6.xdp file in your Samples folder. This file contains all the form elements in their proper structure. You can correct your file based on this sample or simply use this sample as a base for the next exercise.

Calculating Totals

You'll now use the calculate event in the total Decimal Field. The calculate event fires often in Designer forms, so this is an ideal event for the total calculation. Whenever a change is made to the numberOf or cost fields, this script executes to update the total of the row.

1. Select the total Decimal Field object.

2. Go to the Script Editor and select calculate from the Show Events drop-down.

3. Select JavaScript as Language and Client as the Run At property.

4. Enter this script in the Script Editor:

```
if(cost.rawValue != null && numberOf.rawValue != null){

  this.rawValue = cost.rawValue * numberOf.rawValue;

}else{

  this.rawValue = null;

}
```

5. Select Preview PDF to see your script in action.

Calculating Totals for Repeating Objects

You'll now use the calculate event in the subTotal field. This script demonstrates how you can calculate the sum of a series of numbers even when the amount of numbers is determined by the form filler at runtime.

Because the expense report is dynamic, a user can't determine the total amount of expense line items. Each expense item is represented by an instance of the expenseRow subform. You can add a script to the calculate event of the subTotal field that calculates the sum of the repeating subforms.

The total field in each expenseRow item holds the total of that line item. The script first resolves all of the expenseRow instances and assigns them to the myExpenses variable. It then defines a sum variable with an initial value of 0.0 to hold the running total. The heart of the script is a for loop that iterates through all the instances of the expenseRow held in the myExpenses variable. Within the loop, the sum is calculated by adding the values held in all the total fields. The last line assigns the sum variable to the rawValue property of the subTotal field.

1. Select the subTotal Decimal Field object.

2. Go to the Script Editor and select calculate from the Show Events drop-down.

3. Select JavaScript as Language and Client as the Run At property.

4. Enter this script in the Script Editor:

```
var myExpenses = expenseReport.page1.expenses.expensesWrapper.
➥ resolveNodes("expenseRow[*]");
```

```
var sum = 0.0;

for (var i = 0; i < myExpenses.length; i++){

  sum += myExpenses.item(i).total.rawValue;

}

this.rawValue = sum;
```

5. Save your file as **myExpenseReport_7.xdp** and click Preview PDF to see your script in action.

As mentioned, the calculate event in this field fires often as changes are made to the form. As you can see, adding form object scripts to your forms is beneficial. If you need to create a longer script or a function that can be reused by many different objects on your form, it's usually best to create a script object.

Creating and Referencing Script Objects

A good example of a script object is the validation script object in the SmartDoc Expense Report. Open the expenseReportCompleted.xdp file from the Samples folder along with your working file, and follow these steps to create a script object on your working file:

1. Select the topmost node (expenseReport) of your form in the Hierarchy palette.

2. Right-click this node and choose Insert Script Object. Designer inserts a script object at the bottom of your form hierarchy.

3. Right-click this new script object (untitled Script Object) and choose Rename Object. Enter **validation** as the new name.

4. Enter the following comment block into the Script Editor:

```
/*  Author: < enter your name here >

  dateValidation function - Last Updated < enter date >

  Use case: Check that the value entered is a valid date.

  Input Parameters: The field that will be checked.

  if type = 0 then any date can be entered as long as it is real

  if type = 1 then no future dates can be entered, only real dates
  ➥ allowed

  if type = 2 then no past dates can be entered, only real dates
  ➥ allowed

*/
```

5. Copy and paste the JavaScript functions from the script object in the expenseReportCompleted.xdp file to the script objects in your working file. You can copy one function at a time or copy the entire block of code from the SmartDoc script object to your script object.

6. Save your file as **myExpenseReport_7.xdp**.

There's no limit to the number of functions that you can add to a script object or the number of script objects that you can add to a form. But you must write your functions according to the syntax and rules of JavaScript.

The `validation` script object on the form provides common date validations that test any date entry on your form in a variety of ways, including:

■ **Testing for real dates:** A variety of tests are available to ascertain that a date entry is for a date that actually exists. These tests include logic that accounts for different month lengths and for leap years.

■ **Testing for future dates:** These tests are valuable for birth date entries. You usually want to screen out future dates in a birth date field.

■ **Testing for past dates:** These tests are valuable for shipping date entries; you don't want to accept a ship date that has already passed (the warehouse team would find this request rather challenging).

This `validation` script object contains approximately 300 lines of JavaScript, so you wouldn't want to replicate it in each Date Field object on your form. The script object is organized into five functions that work together. The main function, dateValidation(), calls each of the other functions. The following code shows the snippet of the dateValidation() function that references the other functions.

```
function dateValidation(field, type){

[..]

flagYear = checkYear(nYear, currYear, field, type);

flagMonth = checkMonth(nMonth, currMonth, flagYear, field, type);

flagDay = checkDay(flagYear, flagMonth, nDay, nMonth, leapYear, field,
➥ type);

compareDay(flagDay, flagMonth, flagYear, nDay, currDay, field, type);

[..]

}
```

You can find the complete script (with comments) in the expenseReport Completed.xdp file.

Referencing Functions in Script Objects

Now that you have a dateValidation() function within your validation script object, you just need to call it from the Date objects on your form. Follow these steps to add the calling script:

1. Select the date object in your expenseRow subform.

2. Go to the Script Editor and select exit from the Event List drop-down.

3. Select JavaScript as Language and Client as the Run At property.

4. Enter this script in the Script Editor:

```
validation.dateValidation(this,0);
```

This script is added to the exit event and not to the validate event of the field because scripts in the validate event should return a value of true or false. Since the dateValidation() function of the script object doesn't return a value, it shouldn't be placed in the validate event.

You reference script objects just like you reference other Designer objects: by using a dot to indicate different levels of hierarchy. The first item is the script object (validation) and the second item is the function (dateValidation). The function takes two parameters, which are in the parentheses (this,0). The first parameter is the object that you're testing. The this keyword indicates that you'll test this Date object. The second parameter indicates the "type," which is represented by an integer value between 0 and 2. The type descriptions are found at the top of the script object:

```
if type = 0 then any date can be entered as long as it is real

if type = 1 then no future dates can be entered, only real dates
➥ allowed

if type = 2 then no past dates can be entered, only real dates allowed
```

Testing Your Form

After you finish developing your form, it's a good idea to test it with some data files so you can see how it will perform with different data scenarios (**Figure 3.9**). You'll find the following two test files in your Samples folder:

- expenseDataShort.xml

- expenseDataLong.xml

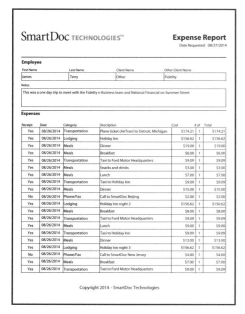
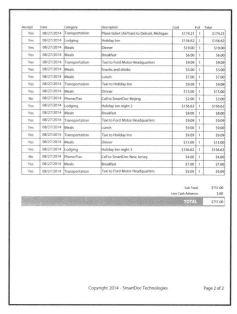

Figure 3.9 Designer will create two pages when you preview the expenseReportCompleted.xdp file with the expenseDataLong.xml data file.

Testing Your Form with Data Files

Because Designer forms are dynamic, it's best to test them using data files that show every possible runtime data scenario.

1. Open the expenseReportCompleted.xdp form or your completed form and follow these steps to test it with the data files.

2. Choose File > Form Properties. Designer opens the Form Properties dialog box.

3. Select the Preview tab and click the icon to the right of the Data File field. The Open XML File dialog box appears.

4. Locate and select the expenseDataShort.xml file in the Samples folder and click Open.

5. Click OK to close the Form Properties dialog box.

6. Select Preview PDF to see the expense report fill with data. This test illustrates how the form will render when there's less than a page of expenses.

7. Return to Design View and repeat steps 2 through 5, but this time select the expenseDataLong.xml file.

8. Select Preview PDF to see the expense report fill with two pages of data. This test illustrates how the pagination and other layout controls will work when the user enters numerous expense items.

Moving On

Now that you've learned about the Designer tool, it's time to learn more about PDFs and Acrobat. Part 2 covers different types of PDFs, Adobe's tools for working with PDFs, and best practices for using PDFs to automate your business.

PDF Forms

You learned how to create dynamic forms with LiveCycle Designer in Part 1, "The Designer Tool." Part 2 shows you how to render and deploy these forms as PDFs. You will also learn about the different PDF viewers your end users will use to work with your dynamic forms and files.

4

PDF and Acrobat

There is no such thing as fun for the whole family.

— Jerry Seinfeld

Portable Document Format (PDF) is actually a family of file formats, and this chapter focuses on the ones that are relevant to LiveCycle Designer. You'll learn how to create these various types of PDFs and understand how and why to use each one. All these types work best in the premier client tool for viewing and working with PDFs—Adobe Acrobat.

Like PDF, Adobe Acrobat is a family with many members. It's important to understand the features of the various Acrobat programs because their features affect how your PDF forms function. Acrobat has the agility to run as a stand-alone application or as a plug-in to your web browser, and it gracefully balances these two modes. It can also handle the requirements of different types of users working with different types of PDFs. And it works on virtually every computer system and renders PDF files faithfully and efficiently regardless of the system's fonts and software.

Although Acrobat is the ideal tool, there are also many non-Adobe PDF viewers on the market. If you're deploying PDFs to a heterogeneous user base, you need to know how your PDFs will perform in these third-party tools.

The PDF Family

The term *PDF* refers to a family of file formats and an evolving set of technical specifications. Many of these formats and specifications are International Organization for Standardization (ISO) standards, and some are specific intellectual property owned by Adobe.

XFA PDF (PDF Form)

Adobe uses the term *PDF form* to refer to the interactive and dynamic forms you create with Designer. It's important to note that there's another type of PDF form, called an *Acroform*, that's different from the PDF forms you create in Designer. The forms and files you create with Designer are based on Adobe's XML Forms Architecture (XFA). In many ways, the XFA PDF file format is closer to an HTML file than it is to a traditional PDF file. For instance, the following code shows you what a simple text object looks like in an XFA PDF file:

```
<draw name="StaticText1" y="15.875mm" x="28.575mm" w="29.2864mm"
➡ h="5.2331mm">

  <ui>

    <textEdit/>

  </ui>

  <value>

    <text>Text</text>

  </value>

  <font typeface="Myriad Pro"/>

  <margin topInset="0.5mm" bottomInset="0.5mm" leftInset="0.5mm"
➡ rightInset="0.5mm"/>

</draw>
```

As you can see, XFA forms are XML based. This well-structured and flexible format enables a LiveCycle Server to transform your Designer files into many different formats, including traditional PDF and HTML. You can see the complete XML structure of your forms in Designer by selecting the XML Source tab of the Layout Editor. As you learned in Part 1, "The Designer Tool," all the objects and events in these XFA PDFs are scriptable at runtime, so this PDF type offers you a great deal of flexibility and power. You can create both static and dynamic XFA forms in Designer.

NOTE: The step-by-step instructions in this chapter were created with Acrobat Professional 11 for Windows. If you have a different version, the exact steps and screenshots may differ.

Static forms

Static XFA PDF forms won't change their layout at runtime, but they can be interactive for the user. The following are a few advantages of static XFA PDF forms:

- Static forms support Acrobat's Comment and Markup tools.

- Static forms enable you to import and export Acrobat comments.

- Static forms support font subsetting, which you will learn about in the next chapter.

- Static forms work in early versions of Acrobat like 6 and 7, but dynamic forms are recommended only for version 8.1 and above.

You can create a static XFA PDF in Designer with the SmartDoc Expense Report form that you developed in Chapter 3, "Creating the SmartDoc Expense Report." Follow these steps to create and view a static PDF form:

1. Launch your Designer program, and open the expenseReportCompleted. xdp file from the Samples folder.

2. Select File > Save As to open the Save As dialog box.

3. Enter **expenseReportStatic.pdf** as your filename, select Adobe Static PDF Form (*.pdf) as your file type, and click Save.

4. Launch Adobe Acrobat from the Windows Start menu. Please note that if you're using the free Adobe Reader program, you won't yet be able to use the commenting tools because this file has not been Reader extended. You'll learn how to do this in an upcoming exercise.

5. Select File > Open and browse to the static PDF you just created.

6. Click the Add Expense button on the form. Notice that a new row is not created because this isn't a dynamic PDF.

7. Open your Comment tools and notice that you can add comments to this type of PDF because it's a static form.

Dynamic forms

Dynamic XFA PDFs can change their layout at runtime, so the commenting and markup features aren't supported. However, dynamic XFA PDFs do offer the following advantages:

- Dynamic forms support client-side scripts that change the layout and pagination of the form. For instance, your SmartDoc Expense Report will expand and paginate to accommodate an endless amount of data if you save it as a dynamic form.

- Dynamic forms support all the properties of your form at runtime, whereas static forms support only a subset (**Figure 4.1**).

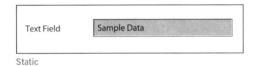

Static

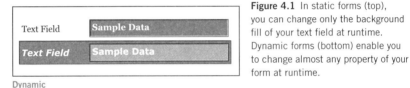

Dynamic

Figure 4.1 In static forms (top), you can change only the background fill of your text field at runtime. Dynamic forms (bottom) enable you to change almost any property of your form at runtime.

Follow these steps to create and view a dynamic PDF form:

8. Go back to your expenseReportCompleted.xdp file in Designer.

9. Select File > Save As to open the Save As dialog box.

10. Enter **expenseReportDynamic.pdf** as your filename, select Adobe Dynamic XML Form (*.pdf) as your file type, and click Save.

11. Launch your Adobe Acrobat or Adobe Reader program from the Windows Start menu.

12. Select File > Open and browse to the dynamic PDF you just created.

13. Click the Add Expense button on the form. Notice that a new row is added because this is a dynamic PDF.

14. Open your Comment tools and try to add a comment. Notice that you can't add comments to this type of PDF form (**Figure 4.2**).

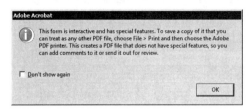

Figure 4.2 Acrobat's commenting features don't work on dynamic PDF forms.

If your Designer form works equally well as either a static or dynamic XFA PDF form, Adobe recommends creating dynamic XFA PDFs for performance benefits.

NOTE: Dynamic PDF forms support all the XFA script constructs. However, HTML forms currently don't support all the XFA scripting constructs. You'll learn more about this in Part 3, "HTML Forms."

PDF File (Traditional PDF)

The most popular and pervasive PDF format is the traditional PDF file. There are many ways of creating a traditional PDF file, including using Acrobat and many third-party tools. Acrobat provides all the following ways to create traditional PDF files. If you don't have Acrobat installed, you may not see these options on your computer.

- **By capturing the print stream of a desktop application:** Choose the Print command of an authoring application and select the Adobe PDF printer icon. Instead of a printed copy of your document, you'll have created a PDF file of your document.

- **By using the Acrobat PDFMaker plug-in with Microsoft Office applications:** When you install Acrobat, it adds an Adobe PDF menu to Microsoft Office applications and an icon to the Office ribbon. You can use these added features to create PDF files directly in Microsoft Office.

- **By using Acrobat Distiller to convert PostScript and Encapsulated PostScript (EPS) files into PDFs:** Distiller is typically used in print publishing and other workflows that require a conversion from the PostScript format to the PDF format.

Static documents

Under the hood, a traditional PDF is very different than an XFA PDF. It doesn't have the same XML structure, and since it's created by capturing the print stream of a file, a traditional PDF is a static and read-only file. You can create a traditional PDF file from a dynamic Designer file by following these steps:

1. Launch your Designer program, and open the dunningNotice.xdp file from the Samples folder.

2. Select File > Form Properties > Preview.

3. Select Print Form (One-sided) as your preview type.

4. Locate a data file by clicking the Browse button to the right of the Data Field entry field.

5. Select dunningNoticeData.xml from the Samples folder and click Open.

6. Select Dynamic XML Form as your preview type.

7. Click OK to save these preview settings.

8. Select Preview PDF to see your dynamic form merged with your data file. At this stage, your PDF is still an XFA PDF.

9. Press F8 on your keyboard to display the Acrobat toolbar (**Figure 4.3**).

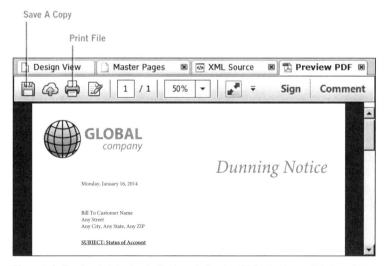

Figure 4.3 The Acrobat toolbar in Designer's Preview PDF tab. If you click Save A Copy, you'll create an XFA PDF. If you click Print File, you'll create a traditional PDF.

10. Click the Print File button. Select Adobe PDF as your printer, and click the Print button on the bottom right.

11. Enter **dunningNoticeTraditional.pdf** as your filename, and click Save. You have now created a traditional PDF file by capturing the print stream of your XFA PDF file. This new PDF file is static and read-only.

Dynamic documents

Since the source file for the Dunning Notice is a dynamic Designer file, the rendered files will grow or shrink based on the length of your data (**Figure 4.4**). There are additional data files in the Samples folder, and each has a different amount of data. You can repeat the steps in this exercise with these data files to see how different PDFs will be created each time. This is an example of dynamic document generation.

1 page's worth of data   2 pages' worth of data

Figure 4.4 The Dunning Notice is a dynamic Designer file that will grow or shrink to accommodate the data that's merged with it.

PDF Is an ISO Standard

In 2008, PDF became an official ISO standard document format. ISO is a worldwide federation of national standards organizations, and its goal is to work with member countries to develop and promote international standards. The American National Standards Institute (ANSI) represents the United States of America in ISO. There are approximately 100 other countries represented in ISO.

Acroforms

Acroforms are Adobe's older interactive form technology; they date back to Acrobat version 3. Adobe provides the Acrobat Forms API Reference, dated May 2003, to provide the technical details for this technology. You can find a link to this on the book's companion site. Acroforms are a combination of the following items:

- A traditional PDF that defines the static layout and graphics of the form.

- Interactive form fields that are bolted on top with the form tools of the Adobe Acrobat program. Please note that these form tools are a small subset of what's available in Designer.

Acroforms can be enhanced and expanded with Designer. However, even when you enhance an Acroform in Designer, it's still a traditional PDF under the hood, and there are limits to how interactive and dynamic you can make these forms. For instance, only some of the form fields in Designer's Object Library are supported in Acroforms, and even the ones that work are only partially supported.

To move beyond the limits of Acroform technology, Adobe has invested in XFA to provide an XML form structure that's both interactive and dynamic. If you're moving from Acroforms to XFA PDFs, you need to know a couple of important facts about these two technologies:

- Designer can edit a PDF form created in Acrobat, but Acrobat *cannot* edit a PDF form created in Designer.

- JavaScript works differently in these two technologies. Some of the JavaScript routines that work in Acroforms won't work in XFA forms. Adobe has documented these differences in a 43-page online PDF called "Converting Acrobat JavaScript for Use in LiveCycle Designer Forms." You can find a link to this on the book's companion site. As mentioned previously, Designer is a much more robust tool for using JavaScript in your forms, so I recommend that you learn how to script in Designer with the XFA object model.

PDF/A

PDF/A (PDF for Archives) builds on the document storage benefits of traditional PDFs with many specific details that enhance long-term archiving. The traditional PDF file format offers many benefits for long-term document storage. The compact nature of PDF facilitates easy transfer and conserves space, and its well-structured nature enables powerful indexing and search capabilities. Traditional PDF has extensive support for metadata, and PDF has a long history of supporting many different computer environments.

Like PDF, PDF/A is an ISO standard specification. It was developed by a task force that included AIIM (Association for Information and Image Management), NPES (National Printing Equipment Association), and the Administrative Office of the U.S. Courts. Since the goal of the PDF/A specification is to provide a long-term archive format, many PDF features are omitted so the files can be self-contained. The following are some key points about the specification that enhance the long-term reproducibility of the PDF/A file:

- All content must be contained in the file, and there can be no dependencies on external sources like hyperlinks, fonts, or software programs.

- All fonts must be embedded, and they need to be fonts that have an unlimited-use license for electronic documents.

- JavaScript isn't allowed.

- Transparency isn't allowed.

- Encryption isn't allowed.

- Audio and video content aren't allowed.

- Color spaces must be defined in a device-independent way.

- All metadata must follow certain standards.

Different PDF/A versions

Although the original standard was based on Adobe's PDF Reference Version 1.4, the ISO technical committee maintains the specification and has created the following versions:

- **PDF/A—1b:** This level is based on PDF version 1.4, and it ensures that the file can be accurately reproduced visually on a computer system in the future.

- **PDF/A—1a:** This level is also based on PDF version 1.4, and it includes all the requirements of 1b plus some additional requirements to ensure the long-term reproducibility of the document's text stream in other devices besides a traditional computer.

- **PDF/A—2:** This is a newer specification (released 2011), and it addresses some of the new features in PDF versions 1.5, 1.6, and 1.7.

- **PDF/A—3:** This is the newest specification (released 2012), and it allows embedding of compliant archived objects, including XML, word processing, and spreadsheet documents.

Viewing a PDF/A file

Two files in the Samples folder were created from the same Microsoft Word file. One was created as a traditional PDF and the other as a PDF/A file. Open these two files in Acrobat Professional:

- simpleWordFile.pdf

- simpleWordFilePDFA.pdf

Although the documents look the same, the PDF/A file opens with a blue bar across the top, indicating that you're viewing this document in PDF/A mode. This blue bar is Acrobat's document message bar (**Figure 4.5**), which you'll see when you open certain types of PDF files.

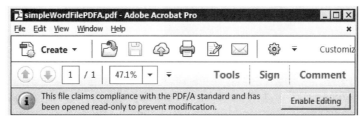

Figure 4.5 Acrobat's document message bar highlighted in blue.

The document message bar includes instructions, and possibly buttons, to help you complete a task. It's color coded, and you'll see the blue color when you open special types of PDFs (like this PDF/A file) as well as certified and digitally signed PDFs. The bar changes to purple for PDF forms and to yellow when you're participating in a PDF review.

NOTE: It's possible that your document message bar is hidden. You can change this Acrobat setting by going to Edit > Preferences > Forms > and deselecting Always Hide Forms Document Message Bar.

This message bar indicates that your file conforms to the PDF/A specification. Another compliance indicator is found in the Results pane of Acrobat Professional's Preflight tool. Follow these steps to see how it works:

1. Open the simpleWordFilePDFA.pdf file in Acrobat Professional if it isn't already open.

2. Choose Tools > Print Production > Preflight to open the Preflight dialog box (**Figure 4.6**). If you don't see this option, select the Show Or Hide Panels option in the Tools drop-down in the upper-right corner of the Tools panel.

3. Scroll down to the PDF/A compliance section and select Verify Compliance With PDF/A-1b.

4. Click the Analyze button at the bottom of the dialog box. Acrobat will compare your file to the PDF/A-1b profile and issue a report (**Figure 4.7**).

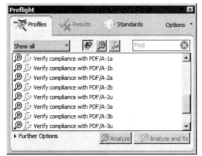 

Figure 4.6 The Acrobat Preflight tool shows you various PDF/A profiles that you can test your file against.

Figure 4.7 The Acrobat Preflight tool shows you the results of the analysis.

If you go back to the Profiles tab and compare your file against other PDF/A profiles, you'll find that it doesn't meet all requirements. You can also open simpleWordFile.pdf and see the issues that this file has. Experiment with the features of this tool. In many cases, you can use the Convert To PDF/A options to make your PDFs compliant with the various specifications. In some cases, you'll need to go back to the source files of your PDFs and make changes in order to reach compliance. LiveCycle Server can automatically convert your Designer files into PDF/A documents.

The Acrobat Family

Now that we've reviewed the PDF family of file formats, let's take a look at the Acrobat family of software tools. The Acrobat family includes various commercial versions of the software used to create and view PDFs, and the free Adobe Reader program used to view PDFs. You can launch Acrobat/Reader as a standalone application and work with it in the same way that you use traditional desktop software. Acrobat/Reader is also launched automatically when you navigate to a PDF file with your web browser if your web browser's default PDF Viewer is set to Acrobat/Reader (**Figure 4.8**).

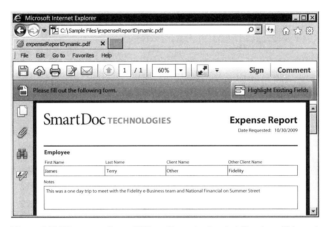

Figure 4.8 When you view a PDF on the web, Acrobat/Reader will launch as a browser plug-in.

All versions of Acrobat and Reader work in this dual way, and all can be used to view PDF forms and files. However, because each is unique, you should be aware of your users' versions so you know their capabilities.

Adobe Reader

You can download the free Reader program for various languages and operating systems, including Windows, Macintosh, and Linux. It's the only free PDF file viewer that works with the entire PDF family of file types. Adobe updates Reader when it updates the commercial versions of Acrobat, so the XFA support is synchronized between the two products. Reader has the same look and feel as the rest of the family but only a subset of the functionality.

As its name implies, Reader is primarily used to read or view PDF files. However, the functionality of Reader can be extended through Reader Extensions. You apply Reader Extensions at the file level. When these extensions have been applied to a file, a user's Reader application automatically unlocks the Acrobat features that have been lying dormant in the program. There are multiple ways and reasons to apply Reader Extensions. For instance, if your user base only has Reader but you need your users to participate in a document review process, you can Reader extend the file. Once the file is extended, your Reader users can access the Acrobat commenting tools, including sticky notes, highlighting, and stamps. Another valuable use of Reader Extensions is to give Reader users the ability to save their data with their form.

Acrobat Standard

Acrobat Standard is available for the Windows platform. This version contains most of the Acrobat features and includes the ability to do the following:

- Reader extend a file so users of Reader 8 or later can save form data
- Create a PDF document from any application that can print a file
- Scan paper documents and convert the text to digital text with Acrobat's OCR (optical character recognition) functionality
- Apply restrictions on copying, printing, and changing PDF files
- Encrypt and digitally sign PDFs
- Save PDFs in the PDF/A (PDF for Archives) format

Acrobat Professional

Acrobat Professional is available for the Windows and Macintosh platforms. Acrobat Professional includes the following tools in addition to those found in Acrobat Standard:

- Redaction tools, used to permanently delete specific text and illustrations (Redaction tools are used by legal professionals to completely remove sections of a document.)
- High-end print production and digital publishing tools, used to preflight and correct PDF files
- Optimization tools, used to enhance PDF reading experiences for mobile users

Acrobat Professional also enables you to

- Validate PDF documents against ISO standards, including PDF/A, PDF/X (high-end graphics), PDF/E (engineering), and PDF/VT (variable-data printing)

- Combine a wide range of file types into a PDF Portfolio with custom layouts, themes, and colors

- Compare two different PDFs and highlight the differences between them

- Create and validate accessible PDF files to meet WCAG (Web Content Accessibility Guidelines) 2.0 and PDF/UA (Universal Accessibility) standards

- Insert Flash video (FLV format) and H.264 video into PDF files

- Automate PDF creation tasks

Understanding Reader Extensions

As mentioned, some of the interactive and dynamic features in your forms won't work in Reader until the form has been Reader extended. In this section, you'll learn about the limitations of Reader and how to transcend these confines with Reader Extensions.

Understanding Adobe Reader Limitations

Although Reader is primarily used to read or view PDF files, you'll often need your Reader users to do more to effectively participate in your smart form workflow. Fortunately, you can extend the features of Reader by applying Reader Extensions to your PDF forms. In this section, you'll explore the following two files to understand and transcend Reader's limitations.

- **notReaderExtended.pdf:** This file was created in Designer and saved as a dynamic XFA PDF.

- **readerExtended.pdf:** This is the same file created in Designer, but it was also Reader extended with LiveCycle Reader Extensions.

Saving data with the form

Believe it or not, Reader users won't be able to save a copy of your PDF form with their data until the form has been extended. When a nonextended PDF is opened, Reader displays a message in the document message bar. If you open the notReaderExtended.pdf file in Reader 9 or above, you'll see a purple document message bar with the following message: *Please fill out the following form. You cannot save data typed into this form. Please print your completed form if you would like a copy for your records.*

Although it's helpful to know this before filling in a complex form, it's hardly in keeping with a smart form workflow to print out the form to retain the data. It's usually best to store the information digitally; your Reader users will be able to do this after the form is extended. Look at the readerExtended.pdf file, and you'll see a purple document message bar with the following message: *Please fill out the following form. You can save data typed into this form.* You'll also need to Reader extend a form if you want to use Reader to import or export XML data into PDF forms at runtime.

Using digital signatures

Digital signatures play an important role in secure smart form workflows. Just think about the many times you have had to sign paper documents. Digital signatures will replace the tasks in your workflow that previously required a handwritten signature on paper. In many ways, digital signatures are more trustworthy than traditional signatures, and there are various ways that you can use them in your Designer forms.

When you open the notReaderExtended.pdf file in Reader 9 or later, the digital signature field is unresponsive. However, when you open the readerExtended. pdf file, you're able to sign the document by clicking the digital signature field.

Connecting to data in real time

The two sample files you've been working with also contain a connection to a web service. However, you'll notice that this web service call works only in the Reader extended file. Follow these steps to call a web service from that sample file:

1. Open the readerExtended.pdf sample file in Adobe Reader 9 or later.

2. Enter **1001** in the Enter ID field.

3. Click the Call Web Service button. This will call a web service at the SmartDoc data center to retrieve a record from a Microsoft SQL Server database. Depending on your security settings, you may see Acrobat Security Warning messages like the one in **Figure 4.9**. You'll need to *trust this document* as explained in step 5 to bypass these messages.

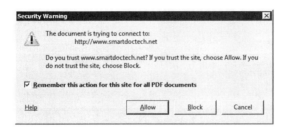

Figure 4.9 The Acrobat Security Warning message.

4. Deselect the "Remember this action for this site for all PDF documents" option, and click Allow.

5. Click the Options drop-down list in the Acrobat document message bar, and select "Trust this document one time only."

6. Click No if you're prompted to save changes.

7. Now that the security questions are answered, you can enter **1001** in the Enter ID field, and click the Call Web Service button.

   The data will automatically flow into the form fields of the PDF. This happens because the form has been Reader extended and the fields are bound to the data connection.

If you try to repeat the preceding steps in Adobe Reader with the notReaderExtended.pdf file, nothing will happen when you click the Call Web Service button.

NOTE: Acrobat has sophisticated security features, and Adobe provides features and techniques for tuning your PDF applications to meet both your security and functionality requirements. For instance, you can create trusted JavaScript functions that will be handled differently by Acrobat than your standard JavaScript functions.

Submitting electronic forms

Some types of electronic form submission won't work in Reader until the file has been extended. Reader enables you to submit XML data from a nonextended form, but if you want to submit the form and the data, the form must be Reader extended. Follow these steps with your sample files to see how this works:

8. Open the readerExtended.pdf sample file in Adobe Reader 9 or later.

9. Click the Submit Form button. The Send Email dialog box appears (**Figure 4.10**).

10. If you have Microsoft Outlook, select Default Email Application, and click Continue. Acrobat passes this form to your Outlook program. Note that this functionality doesn't work with all email programs.

The Outlook screen shows your email message with your attached PDF form (**Figure 4.11**).

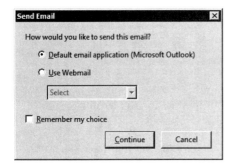

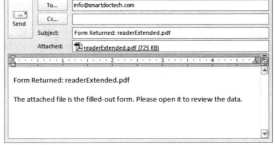

Figure 4.10 The Send Email dialog box.

Figure 4.11 An Outlook email message with an attached PDF form.

If you're using Reader and you try to click Submit Form in the notReader Extended.pdf file, nothing will happen. Form submission isn't supported in Reader until the form has been Reader extended. However, you can submit the XML data. Click the Submit Data button and you'll be able to complete the process.

The Submit Data button will work with both files. This button will submit your form data as an XML email attachment. Reader supports XML data submission for both extended and nonextended forms.

Using barcodes

You may sometimes need to integrate paper-based tasks in a digital workflow. Barcodes can help you do this. For instance, if you send an interactive PDF form to users and they fill it out with Reader, they may not necessarily submit the form to you electronically. For various reasons, your users may decide to print out the form and submit it via fax or traditional mail.

In these cases, barcodes can encode the users' form data as they enter it into Reader. You saw an example of this at the end of Chapter 2, "Scripting and Advanced Techniques." These barcodes on the paper forms can be scanned, and the data they contain will be automatically read into your back-end system. If you open the readerExtended.pdf file in Reader 9 or later, you'll see the barcode in action. The code is wired to encode the data only in the Name field. As you make changes to this data, the visual appearance of the barcode changes. This barcode is an instance of Adobe's Paper Forms barcode, which you can add to your forms with Designer. This two-dimensional barcode is read by a barcode scanner, which retrieves the data you entered in the Name field. You can encode most types of form data into a barcode.

Attaching files

Acrobat enables users to attach other files to a PDF. This capability is useful in cases when a user wants to include supporting documents with a form. These files appear in the Attachments panel, which is always available in Acrobat and active in Reader when a PDF has been extended. Follow these steps to see how to add attachments to PDF forms and files:

11. To open the Attachments panel in Acrobat, select View > Show/Hide > Navigation Panes > Attachments. Alternatively, you can click the paperclip icon in the Navigation pane on the left of the main window.

12. Click the drop-down list and select Add Attachment (**Figure 4.12**, left). The Add Files dialog box will open.

13. Select the file you need to attach to your PDF form and click Open. Your attached file now displays in the Attachments panel.

You won't see this option in Reader when you open the notReaderExtended.pdf file. However, when you open the readerExtended.pdf file, this feature is enabled. You can also open the Attachments panel in Reader by clicking the icon in the Extended Features panel that displays in Reader when a Reader Extended file is active (Figure 4.12, right).

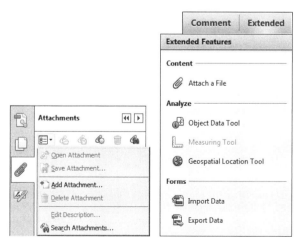

Figure 4.12 The Attachments panel (left) and the Extended Features panel in Reader (right).

Using the Comment and Markup tools

The Acrobat Comment and Markup tools aren't normally a feature of Adobe Reader. However, these tools lie dormant in the program and can be activated when a Reader extended PDF form is opened. Remember, it must be a static XFA PDF in order for you to use these tools. You'll Reader extend a static form in the next exercise.

Extending a PDF Form with Acrobat

Now that you've learned the benefits of Reader extending your form, it's time to learn how to do so with a hands-on exercise. There are two tools you can use to extend a form:

- Adobe Acrobat will do a partial Reader extension of your PDF form.

- LiveCycle Reader Extensions will do a complete extension of your XFA PDF. LiveCycle Reader Extensions is a LiveCycle Server module that needs to be licensed from Adobe separately from Acrobat.

Partial Reader extension with Acrobat Professional

These steps allow you to Reader extend a form using Acrobat Professional:

1. Open the changeOfBeneficiaryStatic.pdf form in Adobe Reader. Notice that the commenting tools in the upper right are grayed-out and inactive.

2. Close the changeOfBeneficiaryStatic.pdf form in Adobe Reader.

3. Open the changeOfBeneficiaryStatic.pdf form in Acrobat Professional.

4. Select File > Save As Other > Reader Extended PDF > Enable More Tools (includes form fill-in and save).

   Acrobat displays a message box describing the features that will be available for this file when it's opened in Reader (**Figure 4.13**).

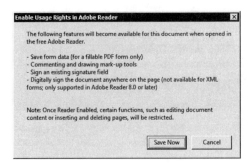

Figure 4.13 Enabling Adobe Reader usage rights.

5. Click Save Now to open the Save As dialog box.

6. Change the filename to **changeOfBeneficiaryStatic_RE.pdf** and click Save.

   Your file is now Reader extended, and it supports the following features:

   ■ Saving data with the form

   ■ Using the Comment and Markup tools

   ■ Submitting electronic forms

   ■ Using digital signatures

7. Open your new changeOfBeneficiaryStatic_RE.pdf in Adobe Reader. Notice that the commenting tools in the upper right are now active.

NOTE: The Adobe Acrobat EULA (End User License Agreement) includes a limit of 500 unique data responses for a Reader extended document. If you work for a government agency or a corporation with needs that extend beyond this limit, you must buy LiveCycle Reader Extensions. You can read the complete Adobe Acrobat EULA at www.adobe.com/products/eulas.

Although Reader extending with Acrobat Professional is good for many cases, you'll have to extend your forms with LiveCycle Reader Extensions if you need Reader users to access any of the following functionality in your XFA PDFs:

■ Connecting to data in real time

■ Using barcodes

■ Attaching files

Complete Reader extension with LiveCycle Reader Extensions

To completely Reader extend your PDF forms, you need to use LiveCycle Reader Extensions. Unlike the previous Acrobat method, Reader Extensions can extend files at design time and at runtime. If you have a license for this LiveCycle Server module, you can extend a file at design time by launching your browser and navigating to the Reader Extensions URL of your LiveCycle Server. The path will follow this format.

http://[*Server Address*]:[Port *Number*]/ReaderExtensions

After you log in with your username and password, the main screen appears (**Figure 4.14**). You can select your PDF file and your usage rights on this screen. After making your choices, click Apply to Reader extend your file.

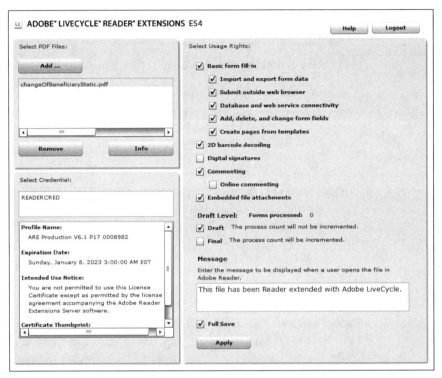

Figure 4.14 The web interface for LiveCycle Reader Extensions. You need this software to enable Reader users to work with barcodes and embed file attachments.

Since this module runs as a LiveCycle service, you can call it at runtime from your LiveCycle, Java, or .NET programs. This is an ideal module to use at runtime to make sure all users of your form will realize its full functionality regardless of whether they are using Acrobat or the free Reader program. As you can see in Figure 4.14, you can even add a custom message that users will see when they open your Reader extended files.

NOTE: Adobe LiveCycle Reader Extensions is one of Adobe's LiveCycle Server modules for automating enterprise forms and documents. Other important modules include Forms Standard and Pro, Forms Portal, Output, PDF Generator, Rights Management, Digital Signatures, Process Management, and Correspondence Management.

Third-Party Viewers

There are over 20 commercially available PDF viewing/reading applications for Windows and many others available for tablet devices. Bear in mind that these programs were designed to open, view, and sometimes annotate traditional PDF files. They weren't designed to work with your interactive and dynamic XFA PDF forms.

Because they were designed to read traditional PDF files, these third-party PDF viewers are typically lightweight applications that don't include a JavaScript engine or support for Adobe's XFA object model. If your user base includes third-party PDF readers and you're using XFA PDF forms, it's best to advise your end users to open your forms with the free Adobe Reader. This will enable them to realize all the features and functionality in your forms.

Viewing PDFs on Tablet Devices

Your XFA PDFs also won't work in the third-party PDF viewers that are available for the Apple iPad and Android tablets. Even Adobe's own Reader application for tablet devices doesn't support XFA PDFs. If you're targeting mobile devices with your Designer forms, you should render them as HTML mobile forms; you'll see how to do this in Part 3, "HTML Forms."

Web Browsers with Default Viewers

But perhaps the biggest challenge with non-Adobe PDF readers is the new web browsers that include their own default PDF viewers. The following is a short list of web browsers that have a non-Adobe PDF viewer as their default helper application for PDF files:

- Apple Safari defaults to Apple's own Preview application.

- Google Chrome includes a default viewer that opens PDFs directly in the browser window.

- Mozilla Firefox has its own default PDF viewer.

Changing the default for Google Chrome

Fortunately, you can change your browser's default PDF viewers. Follow these steps to change the default PDF helper application in the Google Chrome browser:

1. Launch your Google Chrome browser.

2. Enter **chrome://plugins** in the navigation bar, and press Enter. You'll see the Chrome Plug-ins panel (**Figure 4.15**).

3. Click Disable in the Chrome PDF Viewer section (Figure 4.15).

   If you have Adobe Acrobat or Adobe Reader on this machine, you can enable it as your default PDF viewer for Chrome. If you don't have it, you must download it first before proceeding with these next steps.

4. Scroll down in your Plug-ins panel until you see the entry for Adobe Acrobat or Reader. Click the Enable link. You will see the grayed-out version become active (**Figure 4.16**).

5. Press Ctrl+O on your keyboard to launch Google's Open File dialog box.

6. Browse to the dynamic XFA PDF expenseReportDynamic.pdf, which you created earlier in this chapter.

7. Click Open, and you'll see your Acrobat/Reader plug-in working inside the Google Chrome window. You now have the full functionality of your dynamic form.

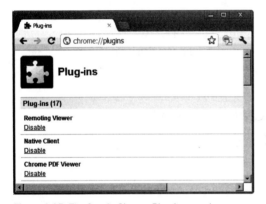

Figure 4.15 The Google Chrome Plug-ins panel.

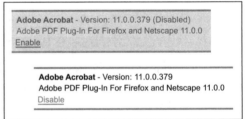

Figure 4.16 Enabling Adobe Acrobat in Google Chrome.

 For current information on this topic and to learn how to change the default PDF viewer in other browsers, please refer to the book's companion site.

Moving On

Now that you know more about PDF file types and PDF viewers, let's move on to review the best practices for creating PDFs with Adobe LiveCycle Designer.

5

Best Practices for PDFs

When all else fails, read the manual.

—Unknown

This chapter covers specific LiveCycle Designer techniques that consistently show superior results in the real world. These strategies and tools will help you achieve quality results in an efficient and effective way. It's quite possible that you'll choose not to follow one or more of these practices. That's OK; you need to balance your organization's needs with these best practices.

Target Versioning

Each version of Adobe Acrobat and Designer includes a specific version of
Adobe's XML Forms Architecture (XFA). As you saw in Chapter 4, "PDF and
Acrobat," it's a good idea to know the Acrobat version your form fillers are
using. It's also a good idea to know the version of XFA that's supported in your
version of Designer and your user's version of Acrobat. **Table 5.1** shows the XFA
specification for different versions of Acrobat and Designer.

Table 5.1 XFA Versions for Acrobat and Designer

ACROBAT VERSION	DESIGNER VERSION	XFA VERSION
Acrobat 6	Designer 6	2.1
Acrobat 7	Designer 7.0 Designer 7.1	2.2 2.4
Acrobat 8	Designer 8	2.5
Acrobat 8.1	Designer ES (8.1) Designer ES (8.1.2)	2.6 2.7
Acrobat 9	Designer ES (8.2)	2.8
Acrobat 9.1	Designer ES (8.2.1) Designer ES2 (9) Designer ES2 (9.0.1)	3.0 3.1 3.2
Acrobat 10	Designer ES3(10) Designer ES3(10)	3.3 3.5
Acrobat 11	Designer ES4(11)	3.6

Fortunately, Designer enables you to set a specific target version for each form
in the Form Properties dialog box (**Figure 5.1**).

If you use a form object that isn't supported in your Target Version setting,
Designer will provide the following information in the Warnings tab of the
Report palette:

■ The problematic form object

■ A description of the problem

■ The remedy for the problem, with a recommendation of the newer version
that will support the form object

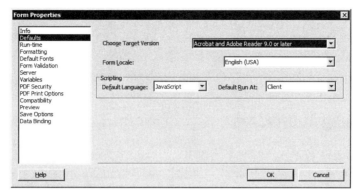

Figure 5.1 The Target Version feature showing an Acrobat and Adobe Reader target of version 9.0 or later.

If you don't see the Report palette, choose Window > Report; it appears at the bottom of your workspace. Follow these steps to see this feature in action:

1. Open the basicSubform.xdp file from the Samples folder.

2. Select File > Form Properties > Defaults.

3. Select Acrobat And Adobe Reader 9.0 Or Later in the Choose Target Version drop-down list. Designer will prompt you with the message *This form may behave differently in the selected target version*. This is your first indication that something is awry. Click the **X** to close the message.

4. Click OK to close the Form Properties dialog box.

5. Select the Warnings tab of your Report palette. You'll notice that you have a Target Version warning message.

   As you learned in Chapter 1, "The Basics," Designer supports a Right to Left flow direction for subforms. However, this is a relatively new feature that was added to XFA Specification version 3.3. This version also supports a Right to Left flow direction for tables. Using Table 5.1 or the description of the problem detailed in the Warnings tab, you can determine that Reader version 10 will support this new feature.

6. Select File > Form Properties > Defaults.

7. Select Acrobat And Adobe Reader 10.0 Or Later in the Choose Target Version drop-down list.

8. Click OK to close the Form Properties dialog box.

   You'll notice that the Warning message is now gone from your Report palette.

Templates and Custom Objects

In addition to the style sheets that you learned about previously, Designer enables you to maintain consistent form standards with templates and custom objects.

Using Templates

Templates enable you to control layout properties across many forms or documents. Adobe includes many standard templates with the Designer program. As a best practice, you can use a template for the common form objects and properties that create the foundation of many forms. Templates can be used for all the following aspects of your forms:

- Layout properties, including page size, margins, headers, and footers
- Graphic design properties, including font, color, and style
- Common script objects and form variables

You can see templates in action by following these steps:

1. Select File > New to launch the New Form Assistant.

2. Select Based On A Template, and click Next. Review the many categories and templates included in the Designer program.

3. Select Forms – Blue from the Select A Category drop-down list, and choose the Check Request template. Click Next.

4. Enter your company name, and click Next.

5. Browse to locate globalLogo.png in your Samples folder, and click Next.

6. Use the default address or enter your own, and click Next.

7. Use the default contact information or enter your own, and click Finish.

   As you can see, your new form is created and a great deal of work on the form is already completed.

Creating Templates

In addition to using Designer's standard templates, you can create a template by saving your XDP as a TDS file.

1. Open the expenseReportTemplate.xdp file from the Samples folder.

2. Select File > Save As, and choose the Adobe LiveCycle Designer Template (.tds) option in the Save As Type drop-down list.

   After you create your template, you can add it to Designer with the Template Manager.

3. Select Tools > Template Manager to open the dialog box shown in **Figure 5.2**.

4. Open the menu on the top right of the Template Manager, and select Add Category.

5. Enter **SmartDoc** as the template category name, and click OK. Your new SmartDoc category is added as a new tab in the Template Manager.

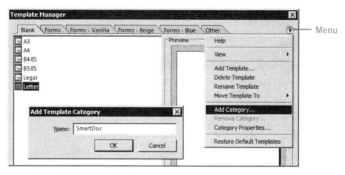

Figure 5.2 Adding a category to the Template Manager.

6. Make sure you are in the SmartDoc tab, open the menu on the top right, and select Add Template.

7. Browse to the Samples folder, select the expenseReportTemplate.tds file, and click Open.

8. Click OK to close the Template Imported pop-up. You'll see the expenseReportTemplate in the SmartDoc tab. If you select expenseReportTemplate and click Set Selected As Default, this will be your default template when you create a new blank form in the New Form Assistant. I do not recommend doing this because Designer's standard default template is better for blank forms.

Your new template is now active in Designer. You can use it to create new forms by launching the New Form Assistant (File > New).

NOTE: Some of the best practices discussed in this chapter, including templates, custom objects, and form fragments, will also benefit your work with HTML forms.

Creating Custom Objects

In the same way that templates enable you to maintain consistent forms, custom objects enable you to maintain consistent form objects. You learned how this works in Chapter 3, "Creating the SmartDoc Expense Report." In this section, you'll learn how to create your own custom object and add it to the SmartDoc Object Library. The following are some advantages of creating your own custom objects:

■ Your custom objects can be made to match your company's graphic standards and data pattern requirements.

■ You can group multiple form objects into one custom object. You'll see an example of this in the following exercise.

■ Senior developers can add JavaScript to custom objects and share them with junior developers in your organization. Custom objects are saved as XFO files and can be shared on a network.

Follow these steps to create a custom object:

1. Create a blank form if you don't already have one open.

2. Drag and drop an Email Address field from the Custom Object Library. Change the graphic style by selecting Solid Box as the Appearance property on the Field tab of your Object palette.

3. Drag and drop a Check Box field from the Standard Object Library. Change the graphic style by selecting Solid Square as the Appearance property on the Field tab of your Object palette. Change the Caption property to **Notify me by email**. Select the Layout palette and change the width to **2** inches.

4. Expand the Script Editor, and select the change event.

5. Enter this if statement into the change event.

```
if (this.rawValue == "1")
  {
  email.presence = "visible";
  }
else
  {
  email.presence = "invisible";
  }
```

6. Select the Email Address field, and select the `validate` event.

7. Change the regular expression on line 3 from the old to the new code below. Be sure to change only the regular expression within the parentheses.

   Old: `"^[a-z0-9_\\-\\.]+\\@[a-z0-9_\\-\\.]+\\.[a-z]{2,3}$"`

   New: `"^[A-Z0-9._%-]+@[A-Z0-9.-]+\.(com|org|net)$","i"`

8. You can put scripts on multiple events of a form object. Select the `initialize` event of your Email Address field, and enter the following script:

   `this.presence = "invisible";`

9. Expand the SmartDoc Object Library. This was created in Chapter 3, Creating the SmartDoc Expense Report.

10. Select the Email Address field and the Check Box field together (by holding down your Shift key), and drag them both to your SmartDoc Object Library.

11. Enter **Email Notification** as the name of your new custom object.

12. Click OK to create your new custom object.

    You can now drag and drop this object to any form. Follow these steps to use your new custom object in a form.

13. Drag and drop your Email Notification object from your SmartDoc Object Library to your form.

14. Select Preview PDF to see your object in action. Notice that the Email Address field is hidden when the form opens. This was accomplished by the script you added to the `initialize` event.

15. Click the Notify Me By Email check box. Each time a click causes the `change` event to fire, your script will either show or hide the Email Address field.

Your new object has all the same formatting and functionality of your custom object. However, your new object is a unique and independent object that isn't linked to your custom object. You can make changes to your new object that won't affect your custom object. Likewise, you can update your custom object, but any objects that were previously created from this object won't be updated.

Form Fragments

You can take the concepts of templates and custom objects one step further by using form fragments. Fragments enable you to create a section of a form and reuse it across many different forms. The following points are true about form fragments:

■ All instances of a form fragment are exactly the same because each maintains a link to one master form fragment (which is saved as a separate XDP file).

■ When the form fragment is updated, all forms that use the fragment are updated automatically.

■ Form fragments enable you to manage and maintain a library of forms more efficiently and effectively. You'll no longer need to execute and test the same change across many forms.

■ If you do need to edit and change an instance of a form fragment, you can embed it in your form. However, this breaks the link to the master so automatic updating is no longer possible.

You can use Designer's form fragment technology at design time and at runtime.

Fragments at Design Time

Designer doesn't include any standard fragments out-of-the-box, but it does include the Fragment Library panel, to which you can add your own custom fragments and that you can access by selecting Window > Fragment Library. Follow these steps to add fragments to your library:

1. Select the Fragment Library tab, which is next to the Object Library tab.

2. Select Open Fragment Library from the menu in the top right of the Fragment Library tab (**Figure 5.3**).

3. Browse to the SmartDoc Fragments folder in the Samples folder, and click OK. The header and signatureSection fragments are added to your library.

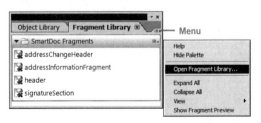

Figure 5.3 Opening a Fragment Library.

Using fragments

Fragments make it easier to create a series of forms that all share a similar object. In this example, you will create three forms that all use the same signature section.

4. Create a blank form in Designer.

5. Drag and drop the signatureSection fragment from the SmartDoc Fragments library onto your form. Notice that the fragment has a purple color in Design View and the objects are grayed-out in the Hierarchy palette.

6. Save this file three times with the following names: **fragmentTest1.xdp**, **fragmentTest2.xdp**, and **fragmentTest3.xdp**.

7. Save and close all files.

8. Right-click the signatureSection fragment (this will be your master fragment) in the Fragment Library, and select Edit Fragment. This will open the fragment's source XDP file.

9. Select the Instructions text object, and enter **Thank you.** at the end of the instructions.

10. Save and close the file.

11. Open any of the three files you created previously. You'll see that each one of the signature sections has been automatically updated because each was a link to the master fragment.

This technique has its advantages, but you can't edit an individual instance of a fragment.

Embedding fragments

If you want to edit a fragment instance, you need to embed it in your form, which will break the link to the master fragment.

12. Open fragmentTest3.xdp in Designer.

13. Right-click the signature subform in the hierarchy, and select Fragments > Convert To Embedded Object.

14. Click Yes on the Warning message, letting you know that embedding the fragment into the form removes all references to the external fragment file. Your objects are now local to your form, and you're able to edit them without affecting the fragment.

15. Save and close fragmentTest3.xdp.

16. Right-click the signatureSection fragment in the Fragment Library, and select Edit Fragment. This will open the fragment's source XDP file.

17. Select the dateSigned field, click the Patterns button on the Field tab of the Object palette, and select Sunday, April 1, 2007 in the Type list. This changes the display pattern to date(EEEE, MMMM D, YYYY).

18. Click Apply, and then click OK to close the dialog box.

19. Save and close the file.

20. Open any of the three files you created previously. The signature sections of the first two files have been updated, but the signature in fragment-Test3.xdp hasn't been updated because the link to the master fragment was broken when you embedded the fragment.

Creating fragments

Fragment references retain the graphic style and functionality of the source (or master) fragment. Creating a fragment is as easy as creating a custom object. Follow these steps to add a fragment to your SmartDoc library:

21. Open the expenseReportCompleted.xdp file from the Samples folder.

22. Right-click the employee subform on page1.

23. Select Fragments > Create Fragment, and the Create Fragment dialog box will open (**Figure 5.4**).

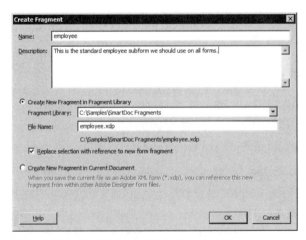

Figure 5.4 The Create Fragment dialog box.

24. Enter a description, leave all the defaults, and click OK. This will add a new fragment to your library and create a reference to the fragment in your current form. This new fragment will have all the graphic styles and functionality of the employee subform.

Bringing it all home

You can balance these important strategies and techniques to meet your form creation and management goals. The following steps will show you one example.

25. Select File > New in Designer.

26. Select Based On A Template, and click Next.

27. Select the SmartDoc category from the Select A Category drop-down list.

28. Select expenseReportTemplate, and click Finish to open the template. Notice that the filename starts with *Untitled*, because you've opened a template and not a form.

29. Select the SmartDoc panel in the Object Library palette.

30. Drag and drop the Expenses Section custom object to the bottom of your form.

31. Select the SmartDoc Fragments panel in the Fragment Library palette.

32. Drag and drop the signatureSection fragment to the bottom of your form.

33. Select Preview PDF to see your new dynamic form in action.

This example demonstrated how easy and quick form creation can be when you have a properly designed library of templates, custom components, and fragments.

Fragments at Runtime

As valuable as fragments can be at design time, they're even more valuable at runtime. You'll need an Adobe LiveCycle Server to use fragments at runtime. The combination of a LiveCycle Server and a properly designed fragment library will enable you to manage your forms effectively and efficiently. **Figure 5.5** on the next page shows an example of how this works at runtime.

As you can see in the illustration, using form fragments at runtime will enable you to meet all the following goals to improve your enterprise form management:

■ Common sections like headers and signature subforms can be reused by multiple forms and managed in one source file.

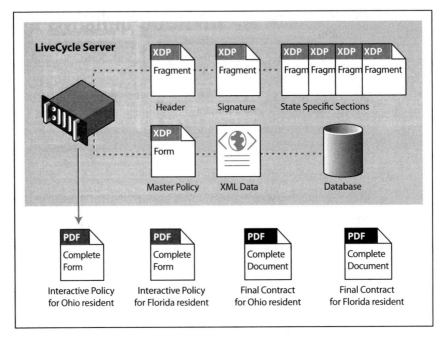

Figure 5.5 An optimal architecture for enterprise form management.

- Unique sections like state-specific subforms and business rules can be created and updated independently from the master policy form.

- The LiveCycle Server combines the master policy forms with the common and unique fragments to generate complete interactive forms and read-only documents for each unique user.

LiveCycle Enterprise Suite includes the LiveCycle Forms Manager, which simplifies the management of your forms and fragments. You will learn about this in Chapter 9, "LiveCycle Enterprise Suite."

Fonts

The fonts you choose and the technical approaches you take will greatly affect the readability and usability of your forms. There are two basic types of fonts: serif and sans serif. Serif fonts feature fine lines that finish off the main strokes of the letterform. And, as you might have guessed, sans serif fonts do not have serifs. Sans serif fonts also have very little variation in the thickness of the stroke, a taller x-height, and a more modern appearance. You can see the main differences between serif and sans serif fonts in **Figure 5.6**.

Figure 5.6 Adobe Garamond Pro (left) is a serif font, and Adobe Myriad Pro (right) is a sans serif font. Sans serif fonts have a taller x-height, which is the height of a lowercase x.

Because quality design will improve the success of your forms, they should be designed by a professional graphic designer who's experienced with typography and typographic layout. This section focuses on the best technical approaches for controlling typographic quality in Acrobat, Designer, and LiveCycle Server.

Fonts in Acrobat

The most important consideration is to make sure your end users experience your fonts and typographic layouts as you intended them. Just because you see a font in Designer and it looks good on your machine, that doesn't mean your end users have the same font on their machine. If the user doesn't have the same font you're using, the missing fonts are substituted, causing unintended changes to your layout. If you can't control the fonts on your end users' machines, there are a number of best practices you can follow to improve the typographic quality of your user's forms.

Use the standard fonts

The following fonts are installed by Adobe with every installation of Acrobat and Reader, so they're always available:

- Courier Standard, Courier Standard Bold, Courier Standard Bold Oblique, Courier Standard Oblique
- Minion Pro Bold, Minion Pro Bold Italic, Minion Pro Italic, Minion Pro Regular
- Myriad Pro Bold, Myriad Pro Bold Italic, Myriad Pro Italic, Myriad Pro Regular
- Symbol (Type 1)

If you choose one of these fonts, you'll have the best of both worlds: typographic and layout fidelity and a small PDF file size.

Trust Acrobat's font substitution

If you can't use one of the standard fonts, you can always trust Acrobat's font substitution feature. Adobe Acrobat was designed to open PDF files and render them properly even when the file's fonts don't exist on the viewer's computer. Acrobat uses an Adobe Multiple Master typeface as a substitute for the missing font. Two Adobe Multiple Master font families are included in Acrobat—AdobeSerifMM for serif fonts, and AdobeSansMM for sans serif fonts. Acrobat's font substitution works best if your form is using a font that's stylistically similar to one of these fonts.

However, you may have a font that isn't similar. In these cases, the layout can be changed and captions can be truncated. This is a problem for complex layouts with many fields that are packed into a small space. Once part of the layout changes, it will have a ripple effect and graphic imperfections will cascade down your form. In these cases, you may want to embed your font into your form.

Embed your fonts

This option includes specific font information in your PDF file. On one hand this is beneficial because you can be assured that your fonts will render properly on a form-filler's machine. On the other hand, selecting this option makes your file much larger, which results in longer download times for your user. Consider the Purchase Order form. The poFontsEmbedded.pdf file has embedded fonts, and its file size is 188 KB. However, if you resave this same form without embedding fonts, the file size decreases to 56 KB. The performance advantage of smaller PDF forms is so substantial that you should think twice before choosing to embed fonts.

However, if you must embed fonts, try to minimize the number of different fonts you use in your form. Embedding fonts is an all or nothing proposition; there's no option to select the specific fonts or characters that you'd want to embed.

1. Open the expenseReportCompleted.xdp file in Designer.

2. Select File > Save As.

3. Select Adobe Dynamic XML Form (*.pdf) in the Save As Type drop-down list.

4. Save your file as **expenseReportFontsEmbedded.pdf**.

5. Select File > Form Properties > Save Options.

6. Deselect the Embed Fonts option. The ability to choose to embed or not embed fonts is available only to a PDF file.

7. Click OK.

8. Save your file as **expenseReportFontsNotEmbedded.pdf**.

   Here are some important points about these two files.

   ▪ expenseReportFontsNotEmbedded.pdf is only 70 KB in size, so it will download and render much quicker for the user. In this case, this is all you need because the SmartDoc Expense Report uses MyriadPro-Bold and MyriadPro-Regular, which are both included with Adobe Acrobat.

   ▪ expenseReportFontsEmbedded.pdf is 346 KB in size because it includes the fonts. When this form is opened, Acrobat will use the embedded fonts even though there's already a valid version of these fonts available on the system.

   Let's view these forms in Acrobat.

9. Open expenseReportFontsEmbedded.pdf in Acrobat.

10. Select File > Properties to view the Document Properties dialog box.

11. Select the Fonts tab to view the fonts used in this document.

12. Open expenseReportFontsNotEmbedded.pdf.

13. Select File > Properties to view the Document Properties dialog box.

14. Select the Fonts tab to view the fonts used in this document.

    The Fonts tab shows you slightly different information for each form, but in both cases the fonts will be MyriadPro-Bold and MyriadPro-Regular.

Fonts in Designer

You can also control the font substitution within your Designer program. This is beneficial if you want all your form creators to map fonts on input PDFs to certain corporate standard fonts available on their systems. Designer controls this font-mapping with a table stored in your Designer.xci file that maps available system fonts to the fonts in your files. You can programmatically modify this file according to this syntax:

```
<equate from='input_font_*_*' to='Designer_font_*_*' force="0"/>
```

The following line will substitute the Courier New system font for a Courier font in the input PDF when the Courier font isn't available on the system:

```
<equate from='Courier_*_*' to='Courier New_*_*' force="0"/>
```

TIP: For more details on programmatically modifying the Designer.xci file, see the Designer.xci link on the book's companion site.

Modifying the font map

You can modify this font-mapping table interactively in Designer:

1. Select Tools > Options to open the Options dialog box.

2. Select Document Handling, and click the Modify Font Substitutions button. The Change Font Substitutions dialog box will appear (**Figure 5.7**).

3. Select the mapping that you want to change, and click Change Substitute Font.

4. Select the substitute font and style that you want, and click OK.

5. Click OK to close the Change Font Substitutions dialog box.

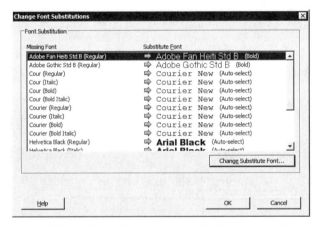

Figure 5.7 This table enables you to control the font mappings that Designer uses to map your system fonts to the fonts in your input PDFs.

Replacing a form's font

You can permanently replace a form's fonts with the substitute fonts on your system. You can do this with the Missing Fonts dialog box (**Figure 5.8**), which you can access at either of the following times:

■   When you open a form with missing fonts, you will be prompted with this dialog box. Select the option Permanently Replace Unavailable Fonts. After you save the file, the fonts will be changed, and you'll no longer see this dialog box when you open the file.

■   You can also access this dialog box at any time by selecting Tools > Missing Fonts. If this option is grayed out for your form, that means your form doesn't have any missing fonts.

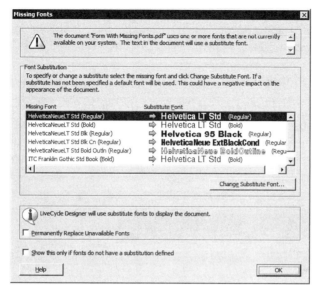

Figure 5.8 The Missing Fonts dialog box showing substitute font mappings for the missing fonts in the form.

Fonts on the Server

If you have a LiveCycle Server, there are two more important font strategies to follow.

Font subsetting

As an alternative to font embedding, you can use Font Subsetting for static PDF forms. As you've seen, embedding a font will greatly increase the file size of your PDF. This is because modern Unicode fonts often contain thousands of characters. Font Subsetting enables you to embed only the characters that you need for your form to render properly. The font you select should be set to the Print & Preview Embedding Allowed level. Also consider these points:

■ Fonts can be subset only in static PDF forms and won't work with dynamic PDF forms.

■ Font Subsetting can be used for static text on a document, such as boiler-plate text and captions for interactive fields.

■ If you need to support interactive fields where the user can enter any character from the font, you should embed your fonts.

■ You can have the best of both worlds by subsetting your corporate font for captions and static text and using an Acrobat standard font for the interactive user input fields.

If you can meet all these requirements, a form with Font Subsetting enabled will have full graphic fidelity at a much smaller file size than a similar form with font embedding.

Server rendering of PDFs

Oftentimes, Designer forms are created with Windows fonts but rendered in LiveCycle on a Linux server. In these cases, you must have a compatible Linux version of the font resident on the LiveCycle Server. You also must stipulate the path to your server fonts in the LiveCycle Administrator console (AdminUI) (**Figure 5.9**).

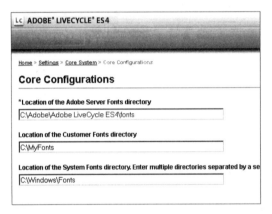

Figure 5.9 The LiveCycle AdminUI showing the paths to the fonts directories.

You can edit the font paths on your LiveCycle Server by selecting Settings > Core System > Core Configurations in the LiveCycle AdminUI. If you make any changes to the core configurations, be sure to restart the application server where LiveCycle resides.

Localization

In addition to making sure your forms have the proper fonts, it's also important to make sure they are displaying the proper currency symbols and date formatting. If you're developing forms for an international audience, consider the expectations and requirements that different cultures have. For instance, Americans see a date formatted as 10/12 and think it's October 12th. However, Europeans will see the same date format and think it's December 10th.

Designer enables you to address these differences with the locale property. You can set this property at the field or form level. **Table 5.2** shows the patterns and symbols that different locales will use by default. Setting a specific display pattern on these fields will override the default locale setting.

Table 5.2 Locale Settings Defaults

	DEFAULT LOCALE (ENGLISH USA)	ENGLISH UK	SPANISH (SPAIN)	CHINESE (CHINA)
Dates	MMM DD, YYYY	DD MM YYYY	DD/MM/YYYY	YYYY-MM-DD
Currency	$9,999.99	£9,999.99	9.999,99	¥9,999.99
Numbers	9,999.99	9,999.99	9.999,99	9,999.99
Time	hh:MM:SS A	HH:MM:SS	HH:MM:SS	Ahh:MM:SS

You can see how different locale settings affect your form by changing the locale property in the SmartDoc Expense Report:

1. Open the expenseReportCompleted.xdp file in Designer.

2. Select the date field in the expensesRow subform.

3. In the Field tab of the Object palette, select Spanish (Spain) in the Locale drop-down list. Locales are listed by language first and then by country or region.

4. Click the Patterns button, and remove the prefilled Display, Edit, and Data patterns.

5. Click Apply, and then click OK.

6. Select the cost field in the expensesRow subform.

7. In the Field tab of the Object palette, select Spanish (Spain) in the Locale drop-down list.

8. Click the Patterns button, and change the prefilled Display and Edit patterns to the `num.currency{}` option. Please note that you must first delete the existing pattern, which is `num{$z,zzz,zzz.99}`. The new currency pattern will put the Euro symbol after the amount.

9. Click Apply, and then click OK.

10. Select the total field in the expensesRow subform, and follow steps 7 through 9. Please note that the Type drop-down list in the Value tab of the Object palette is set to Calculated – Read Only, so there's no Edit pattern to update.

11. Select Preview PDF.

12. Select December 23, 2013 from the calendar drop-down list of the Date field of the Expenses row. Note how the date is now formatted as 23/12/2013, which is the proper formatting for Spain.

13. Enter **1234** in the Cost field of the Expenses row. Note how the value is now formatted as 1.234,00€. The calculated Total field at the end of the row is also displayed as 1.234,00€. However, the Sub Total and Total fields at the bottom of the form are all still formatted as $1,234.00 because the form's default locale is English (USA).

    These steps show how to set the locale on individual fields. This is a valid approach, but it's more common for the entire form to use the same locale.

14. Select Design View.

15. Select File > Form Properties, and click Defaults.

16. Select English (United Kingdom) in the Form Locale drop-down list.

17. Click OK to close the Form Properties dialog box.

18. Select the date field in the expensesRow subform.

19. In the Field tab of the Object palette, change your Locale from Spanish (Spain) to Default locale.

20. Repeat step 19 for the cost field and total field in the expensesRow subform. You previously gave each one of these fields a unique locale that will override your form's locale. You are now setting them to use the form's default locale.

21. Select Preview PDF. Your form is now consistently using the English (United Kingdom) locale.

TIP: *There's another option to set the locale to your viewer's system locale. This isn't a recommended practice because it doesn't deliver reliable and predictable results.*

Accessibility

Accessibility features improve the accuracy and usability of your form for the following users:

- People who navigate your form with an audible screen reader
- People who navigate your form by tabbing through it
- People who are color blind

You can add accessibility features to XFA PDFs with the Accessibility palette (**Figure 5.10**).

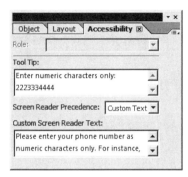

Figure 5.10 Designer's Accessibility palette.

Viewing Features in an Accessible Form

Let's view some accessible form features in action:

1. Open accessibleForm.pdf in Designer.

2. Select the header subform, and click the Accessibility palette to see its properties. If you don't see this palette, select Window > Accessibility. The Role option of this subform is set to (None), which means that it won't be read by the screen reader.

3. Select the information subform, and click the Accessibility palette to see its properties. The Role option of this subform is set to List, which means the screen reader will check the nested child subforms that make up the list to determine how many items are in the list, how the list is structured, and where the list ends. This information will then be read by the screen reader.

4. Select the phoneNumber field, and click the Accessibility palette to see its properties. Notice that the Tool Tip and the Custom Screen Reader Text have different messages. The Tool Tip text will be shown when interactive users place their mouse over the phone number field at runtime (**Figure 5.11**).

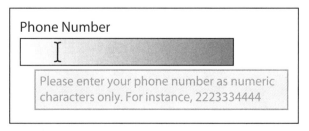

Figure 5.11 Tool tips are valuable for interactive users of your form.

The tool tips will also be read by screen readers if your Screen Reader Precedence option is set to Tool Tip. In our example, the precedence is set to Custom Text (Figure 5.10) because we need to provide a more extended message for the users of our audible form. The Screen Reader Precedence drop-down list determines which of the following text will be read to the user when this field becomes active:

■ **Custom Text:** The message that you enter in the Custom Screen Reader Textfield.

■ **Tool Tip:** The message that you enter in the Tool Tip field.

■ **Caption:** The caption that appears in the Field tab of the Object palette.

■ **Name:** The name of the field displayed in the Hierarchy palette.

■ **None:** No message is read.

Setting Custom Reader Text

You should also set custom screen reader text for the images on your form. Follow these steps to add this to your form and save it with accessibility tags for Acrobat:

1. Select the imageField object and click the Accessibility palette.

2. Enter **This is a table showing data from 2012** as your Custom Screen Reader Text.

3. Make sure your Screen Reader Precedence property for the image field object is set to Custom Text.

4. Select File > Form Properties > Save Options.

5. Make sure the Generate Accessibility Information (Tags) for Acrobat check box is selected (**Figure 5.12**). You must have this property selected when saving your PDF form for screen readers to navigate your form.

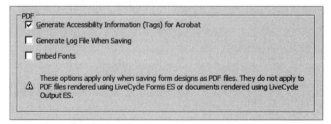

Figure 5.12 The Generate Accessibility Information (Tags) for Acrobat setting is selected in the Save Options panel for PDF files.

6. Click OK to close the Form Properties dialog box.

7. Select File > Save As, and name your file **myAccessibleForm.pdf**. You can now test this form in Acrobat with screen readers.

In addition to optimizing your forms for screen readers, you should optimize your forms for tabbing and color. The tabbing techniques you learned in Chapter 2, "Scripting and Advanced Techniques," will help you create an accessible form for users who don't use a mouse. These users will likely tab through the form to navigate the form-filling process.

You should also consider the needs of a color-blind user. These users will benefit from designs that offer a strong contrast between the background and foreground object. If you're using a color to represent something in your design, make sure there's an alternate method for users who can't distinguish the color. For instance, the form validation you did in Part 1, "The Designer Tool," relies on yellow to highlight required fields that are missing data. This yellow highlight may be difficult for some people to differentiate from the white background of the non-required fields. To make this form more accessible, we also listed these fields in the message box on the changeOfBeneficiaryCompleted.xdp form.

Optimizing Performance

Complex PDF forms can be sluggish. You should balance the features and functionality of your forms with their responsiveness. You can do so by optimizing the performance of your forms and system.

Form Strategies

You can increase the performance of your forms by decreasing their file size and rendering time. This section provides tips to help meet both goals.

Form graphics

Here are some performance tips for your form graphics:

■ As you saw in the font section, embedding fonts will greatly increase the file size of your forms. If you must embed fonts, try to use as few fonts as possible in your form. In addition to improving rendering speed, a small file size will decrease download times across slow network connections.

■ Don't use more form objects than you need. For instance, use the caption property of a Text Field instead of a separate Text object; use the border property of a subform instead of creating a separate rectangle box; and use a Rectangle object instead of four lines.

■ Combine smaller Text objects into a single Text object. This is often required after converting a form from another program into Designer.

■ Use the Background Fill property of an object instead of creating an additional rectangle box.

■ Use compressed and optimized image graphics to decrease file size.

■ Size your images in Photoshop to the precise size you need so you can set the Sizing property in Designer to Use Original Size and avoid dynamic resizing.

■ Make sure your straight lines are straight and not sloped to optimize rendering speed. Horizontal lines that are completely straight will have a Height property of 0 (**Figure 5.13**). Vertical lines that are completely straight will have a Width property of 0. Using Designer's Snap To Grid feature will help keep your objects straight. You can set this property by selecting View > Grids & Guidelines > Snap To Grid.

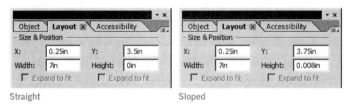

Straight   Sloped

Figure 5.13 Lines that are exactly horizontal and exactly vertical will render faster.

NOTE: If you're creating HTML forms with Designer, you'll create your layout graphics differently. For instance, certain browsers won't render the border property of your objects correctly. In these cases, it's better to use Designer objects like rectangles and lines in your XDPs. This topic will be discussed further in Part 3, "HTML Forms."

Scripting

As with form graphics, you can improve performance by keeping your form scripting as limited and as simple as possible. Because scripts increase the processing time for form rendering, consider if you can meet your requirements without a script. The following steps show techniques for meeting functional requirements without scripting:

1. Open propertiesAndScripting.xdp from the Samples folder.

2. Select Preview PDF.

3. Enter **Hello World** into each of the Limit Length fields. Notice that they don't allow you to finish entering the text because each field is limited to 10 characters.

4. Select Design View to examine these two fields.

5. Select the limitLengthProperty field in the hierarchy.

6. Select the Field tab of the Object Palette. Notice that the Limit Length Property is selected and that the Max Chars field is populated with 10. This is an example of using an XFA property to meet your requirement.

7. Select the limitLengthJavaScript field in the hierarchy.

8. Select the Field tab of the Object palette. Notice that the Limit Length Property isn't selected and that the Max Chars field is blank.

9. Expand the Script Editor and select the change event. In this case, we're using JavaScript to enforce the limit of 10 characters:

```
if(xfa.event.newText.length > 10){
  xfa.event.change = "";
}
```

10. Select Preview PDF.

11. Enter **Hello World** into the JavaScript Mask field and into the Field Property Mask field. Notice that they both mask your entry.

12. Select Design View to examine these two fields.

13. Select the fieldPropertyMask field in the hierarchy. This is another example of using a Designer property instead of JavaScript to meet a functional requirement. In this case, the Password Display Character property is set to *, which will mask the user's entry at runtime.

14. Select the javaScriptMask field in the hierarchy. Expand the Script Editor, and select the change event. In this case, we're using JavaScript to mask the user's entry:

```
var pwdStr = maskValue.rawValue;

if(xfa.event.change != "")

{

  if(pwdStr != null && pwdStr.length > 0){

    pwdStr += xfa.event.change;

  }else{

    pwdStr = xfa.event.change;

  }

  xfa.event.change = "*";

}

else

{

  var newStr = xfa.event.newText;

  if(newStr == null || newStr.length == 0){

    pwdStr = "";

  }else{

    pwdStr = pwdStr.substr(0,newStr.length);

  }

}

maskValue.rawValue = pwdStr;
```

In both cases, we were able to use native Designer properties to meet the requirements instead of JavaScript. This approach may or may not work with HTML forms. In some cases, custom JavaScript will enable you to define functionality in your Designer forms that will produce results for both PDF and HTML forms. Part 3 will cover this in more detail.

Here are a few more ideas to help improve the performance of your forms when using scripting:

■ Use the exit event for your validation scripts instead of the validate event.

■ Limit the number of times you call the `.resolveNode()` and `.resolveNodes()` methods in your scripts. Call these methods as few times as possible, and store the values you retrieve in a form or local variable. It's more efficient to retrieve a value from a variable than it is to call the methods to reevaluate the expressions again.

■ Avoid using using the `..` token (double periods) within the `.resolveNode()` and `.resolveNodes()` methods. When you're trying to access descendant nodes, it's better to write out as much of the path that's known before using this token. For instance, the expression `xfa.resolveNode("expenses.` `.subTotal").rawValue` on the page1 node of the SmartDoc Expense Report will iterate through most of form's objects before locating the `subTotal` field. This expression is more efficient: `expenses.total.subTotal.rawValue`.

Data binding

Here are some techniques for improving the performance of your PDF forms that are bound to data sources:

■ Simplify the structure of the data source. If the structure is too complex and/or too deep, the performance of your forms will suffer.

■ Set the binding of all fields that aren't explicitly bound to No Data Binding. This will improve performance because the fields will be ignored when data is merged with the form. To make things easier when developing forms, you can create and use custom objects that already have their bindings set to No Data Binding. You can also set the Default Binding For New Subforms option in Tools > Options > Data Binding.

■ Use absolute binding to bind repeating data groups to repeating subforms. Then use relative bindings to bind the individual data elements to the form fields (**Figure 5.14**).

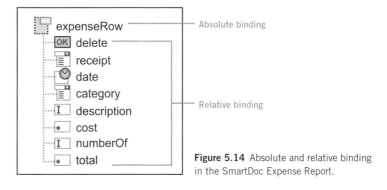

Figure 5.14 Absolute and relative binding in the SmartDoc Expense Report.

Follow these steps to see how absolute and relative binding is used in the SmartDoc Expense Report:

15. Open expenseReportCompleted.xdp in Designer.

16. Select the expenseRow subform in the hierarchy. You'll find it in this path: page1 > expenses > expensesWrapper > expenseRow.

17. Select the Binding tab of the Object palette. Notice that the binding is set to $.ExpenseItem[*]. The asterisk is there to show that there may be multiple ExpenseItem nodes.

18. Select the receipt drop-down list in the expenseRow subform.

19. Select the Binding tab of the Object palette. Notice that the binding is set to $.ddReceipt. This is because the binding of the field is set relative to the binding of the parent subform. In this case, the parent subform is already bound to ExpenseItem, so the field needs to bind only to the relative ddReceipt node. This is the structure of the relevant section of the XML schema:

```
<xs:complexType name="ExpenseItemType">

<xs:sequence>

   <xs:element name="ddReceipt" type="xs:string" minOccurs="0"/>

   <xs:element name="dtDate" type="xs:date" minOccurs="0"/>

   <xs:element name="ddCategory" type="xs:string" minOccurs="0"/>

   <xs:element name="txtDescription" type="xs:string" minOccurs="0"/>

   <xs:element name="numCost" type="xs:float" minOccurs="0"/>

   <xs:element name="numNumberOf" type="xs:int" minOccurs="0"/>

   <xs:element name="numLineTotal" type="xs:float" minOccurs="0"/>

</xs:sequence>

</xs:complexType>
```

20. Select the other fields in the expenseRow subform, and select the Binding tab of the Object palette to view their relative bindings.

Log messages

Designer sends messages about your form to the Log tab of the Report palette when you save your file or when you select Preview PDF. Generating these messages reduces the rendering performance of your form, so you should resolve as many of them as possible.

Balancing performance and functionality

You might choose not to follow some performance tips. That's OK. As mentioned earlier, you need to balance your goals with the ideas covered in this chapter; you may be decreasing form functionality to increase form performance. The following suggestions will improve performance at the expense of graphics or functionality:

- Fixed form objects will render faster than dynamic objects that grow in size.

- Plain text in Text Fields will render faster than rich text. Rich text is an option in Designer's Text Field objects that enables your users to add graphic styling to their text entry, including bold and italic fonts, bullets and numbering, and color.

- Check boxes will render faster than radio buttons.

- Adding accessibility tags to your form will decrease performance.

- Selecting the Allow Page Breaks Within Content property on a subform will cause additional processing time.

System Strategies

If you have a LiveCycle Server, you can optimize the performance of your PDF form system in a variety of ways. Here are a few ideas to explore.

Submit XML

When your users complete a form, they can submit the whole form or just the data to a LiveCycle process on your server. You'll learn more about how to create a LiveCycle process later in this book. A LiveCycle Server process can receive and process a PDF, an XDP, an HTTP Post, and an XML data file. As long as you're maintaining a copy of the template on the server, it will greatly increase the performance of your system to just send the XML and not the template each time (**Figure 5.15** on the next page).

The XML data file is a much smaller and safer file to send across the Internet. Once your server receives it, the LiveCycle process can transfer it to a database or merge it with an XDP template to render the final PDF document of record. Follow these steps to learn how to configure your form to submit XML data by setting properties on a Button object:

1. Open the changeOfBeneficiaryCompleted.xdp file.

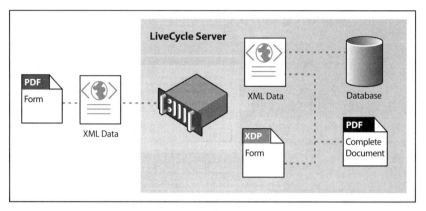

Figure 5.15 A LiveCycle Server process can combine your user's data with the template on the server to render the PDF document.

2. Select File > Save As, name your new file **changeOfBeneficiarySubmit.pdf**, and select the Adobe Dynamic XML Form (*.pdf) file type.

3. Drag and drop two Button objects from the Standard Object Library to the signature subform, next to the checkRequiredFields button object.

4. Right-click Button1 in the Hierarchy palette and select Rename Object. Name this button **submitXML**.

5. Right-click Button2 in the Hierarchy palette and select Rename Object. Name this button **submitPDF**. You'll use this button later in the exercise.

6. Select the submitXML button and highlight the Field tab of the Object palette.

7. Set Control Type to Submit. The Submit tab will appear.

8. Select the Submit tab and enter the URL for your LiveCycle Server process in the Submit To URL field (**Figure 5.16**). This URL can be retrieved with the LiveCycle Workbench application, which is part of LiveCycle Enterprise Suite. There is more information on LiveCycle Enterprise Suite in Chapter 7, "Best Practices for HTML Forms," and Chapter 9, "LiveCycle Enterprise Suite."

Figure 5.16 You can use a standard Button object as a submit button by setting its Control Type to Submit.

9. Click the Submit drop-down list and select XML Data (XML). This will result in your form data being submitted as XML when the button is clicked.

10. Select the Field tab of the Object palette.

11. Set the Presence property to Hidden (Exclude From Layout). Your user won't see this button, but you'll call it from script.

    It's a best practice to validate your form data before you execute a form submission. Since you already have a checkRequiredFields button, you can update in the following way to check and submit your XML data.

12. Right-click the checkRequiredFields button in the Hierarchy palette and select Rename Object.

13. Enter **submitButton** as the new name.

14. Expand the Script Editor and select the click event in the Show Events drop-down list. Add this line of script to execute the click event on your submitXML button. Add the script directly below the comment line that reads //Enter code here to submit form:

    ```
    submitXML.execEvent("click");
    ```

Submit PDF

Although it's faster to send the XML data, there may be times when your users need to submit the whole PDF document to your LiveCycle Server process. Here are a couple of use cases that require PDF document submission:

■ Your user needs to submit a digitally signed PDF.

■ Your user needs to submit document attachments.

Follow these steps to configure the submitPDF button you created earlier in the exercise:

15. Select the submitPDF button and highlight the Field tab of the Object palette.

16. Set Control Type to Submit. The Submit tab will appear.

17. Select the Submit tab and enter the URL for your LiveCycle Service process in the Submit To URL field (**Figure 5.17**).

18. Click the Submit drop-down and select PDF. This will result in your PDF with data being submitted when the button is clicked.

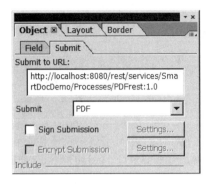

Figure 5.17 You can use a standard Button object to submit a PDF to a LiveCycle Server process.

19. Select the Field tab of the Object palette.

20. Set the Presence property to Hidden (Exclude From Layout). Your user won't see this button, but you'll call it from script.

21. Select submitButton in the Hierarchy palette and expand the Script Editor.

22. Select the click event in the Show Events drop-down. If you want to make this change to your form, you simply update the script to call the submit-PDF button.

```
submitPDF.execEvent("click");
```

NOTE: As you learned in Chapter 4, Adobe Reader enables you to submit XML data from a nonextended form, but if you want to submit the form and the data, the form must be Reader extended. Adobe Acrobat supports both types of submission.

23. Save your updated file.

Optimize caching

LiveCycle Server enables you to cache commonly used resource files, including all of the following:

- XDP form templates
- XDP form fragments
- Images
- Rendered PDF forms

You can optimize your resource caching for LiveCycle Forms and LiveCycle Output in these locations of your LiveCycle Administration Console:

- **LiveCycle Forms:** Home > Services > LiveCycle Forms
- **LiveCycle Output:** Home > Services > LiveCycle Output

All rendered PDF forms are stored without data in the rendered cache unless your Form Rendering Cache option is disabled. This improves performance because the template isn't required to be parsed every time and the bytes are available without having to read from an HTTP or repository resource. PDF forms are cached the first time they're called. This cache is available in the Form Service but not the Output Service. You can configure this cache with the In Memory Form Rendering Cache panel of the AdminUI (**Figure 5.18**).

In Memory Form Rendering Cache

Specify the cache size. A change in this setting requires Service restart to take effect.

Cache Size: 100

Specify whether in memory cache should be enabled. A change in this setting requires Service restart to take effect.

☑ Enabled

Figure 5.18 The In Memory Form Rendering Cache panel in the LiveCycle AdminUI.

The Cache Size field displays the number of rendered PDFs the server will cache. When the maximum number is reached, the oldest template in the cache makes way for the newest one. Your rendered PDFs are being cached on your server's hard disk. By selecting Enabled, as you see in Figure 5.18, you ensure that your files will also be cached in your server's RAM, which improves performance.

Other resources can also be cached. You can use the Template Resource Cache Settings panel (**Figure 5.19**) to configure your cache settings for XDP templates, fragments, and images. You can set the resource level to any of these options:

- **Enabled for Fragments and Images:** This option will cache fragments, images, and XDP templates together in the Template Pre-Render Cache.

- **Enabled for Fragments:** This option will cache just the fragments and XDP templates together in the Template Pre-Render Cache.

- **Disabled:** This option will cache only the XDP templates in the Template Cache.

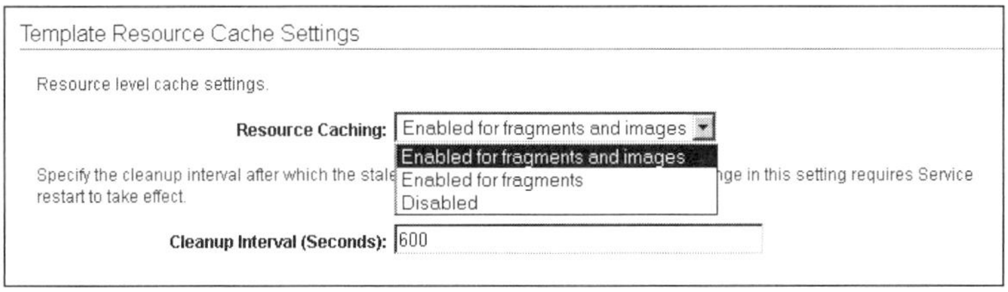

Template Resource Cache Settings

Resource level cache settings.

Resource Caching: Enabled for fragments and images ▾
Enabled for fragments and images
Enabled for fragments
Disabled

Specify the cleanup interval after which the stale [...]ge in this setting requires Service restart to take effect.

Cleanup Interval (Seconds): 600

Figure 5.19 The Template Resource Cache Settings panel in the LiveCycle AdminUI.

The files that LiveCycle caches are stored in the following two places:

■ **In memory:** This is the quickest cache because it resides in your server's RAM. However, it's also more limited in size and will be cleared whenever you restart the server.

■ **On disk:** This is a slower cache, but it holds more data because the assets are cached in your server's file system. This cache is retained when the server is rebooted.

Configuring your form for caching

There's a property in Designer that you can set on your forms to allow them to be cached by Adobe Form Server.

24. Open expenseReportCompleted.xdp from the Samples folder.

25. Select Files > Form Properties > Server.

26. Select Allow Form Rendering To Be Cached On Server (**Figure 5.20**).

27. Select Dynamic XML Form as your Default PDF Render Format.

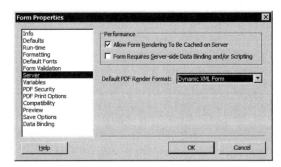

Figure 5.20 The Server properties of your form in Designer.

Maintaining a unique UUID

For caching to work, your LiveCycle Server must be able to identify your unique form. One of the properties that LiveCycle Server uses to find a specific form is your form's UUID (universally unique identifier). Designer will create this automatically every time you save your file. You can see this ID at the top of your form's XML source:

```
<xdp:xdp xmlns:xdp="http://ns.adobe.com/xdp/" timeStamp=
➥ "2013-08-27T21:39:17Z" uuid="285932ef-2b3d-4096-b270-01223a7f677d">
```

Be sure to avoid creating new forms by copying and pasting XDP files in your computer's file system. When you use this method to create a new file, both files will have the same UUID. This will cause unwanted results for your form caching.

Managing multiple instances of an image

LiveCycle Forms enables you to optimize forms that contain multiple instances of an image. Since a PDF is a fully contained and "portable" format, it shouldn't contain links to external images. When you're working with Designer, you should embed your images as you did with the SmartDoc Expense Report.

28. Open expenseReportCompleted.xdp from the Samples folder.

29. Select the smartDocHeader image on masterPage1.

30. Select the Draw tab of the Object palette. You'll see that the Embed Image Data property is selected.

This image is stored in the form as a Base64-encoded value. When Acrobat renders this image, it reads the value and renders the image to the screen. If the form contains multiple copies of the image, the Base64-encoded value will be embedded multiple times in the form. However, LiveCycle Forms will render an alternate version of this PDF that's much smaller and more efficient.

If you link your images on the server, LiveCycle Forms will store them in the PDF resource area when it renders the form. It also creates an index name and multiple copies of this image that will reference this one copy of the image stored in binary format. If you have a large image that's repeated four times, this method can decrease your file size by 75 percent.

Moving On

Now that you know all about Designer and PDF forms, it's time to learn about HTML forms. Part 3, "HTML Forms," will explore the new topic of using Designer to create HTML mobile forms.

HTML Forms

Now that you know all about LiveCycle Designer and PDF forms, it's time to learn how you can use Designer to create HTML forms. Although the LiveCycle Forms module has previously been able to render HTML forms, the new methodologies that began in LiveCycle ES4 are substantially more advanced. Previously, LiveCycle Forms supported only a small subset of Designer's features and functionality in its HTML rendering. However, the new features introduced in ES4 will render HTML forms that look and feel remarkably similar to the PDF forms you are familiar with. Part 3 will explore Adobe's new tools and techniques and show you best practices and examples of real-world HTML forms.

6

Introduction

I very much believe the Internet is indeed all it is cracked up to be.

— Jeff Bezos

Unlike PDF rendering, you need a LiveCycle Server to render your LiveCycle Designer forms as HTML. A LiveCycle Server transforms your Designer XDP form into an HTML form that can be displayed in a browser (**Figure 6.1**).

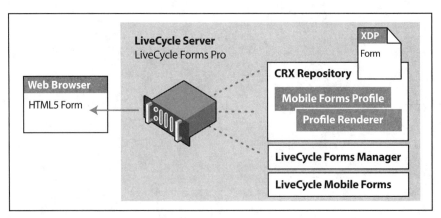

Figure 6.1 LiveCycle Forms Pro can render HTML5 forms from your Designer files.

This capability works only for XDP files (XFA forms) and won't work with other types of PDFs. The HTML that's generated is *HTML5*, the fifth revision of the HTML standard. The specific brand name for the LiveCycle Server that supports HTML rendering is *LiveCycle Forms Pro ES4*. This product includes all the following:

▪ CRX Content Repository: Adobe's content repository.

▪ LiveCycle Forms ES4: The main module.

▪ LiveCycle Mobile Forms: The module that supports the transformation of XDP forms into HTML5 forms.

▪ LiveCycle Forms Manager (not pictured): A browser-based application that simplifies and streamlines enterprise form management. You'll learn about this in Chapter 9, "LiveCycle Enterprise Suite."

As you'll see in this chapter, Adobe has done an amazing job mapping the XFA form structure and functionality to the HTML5 format. These new HTML forms work in all modern HTML5 browsers and don't require installing any additional client-side browser plug-ins. Adobe also refers to these forms as *mobile forms* because they work in iOS and Android browsers. Adobe HTML mobile forms support CSS (Cascading Style Sheets), JavaScript, and integration with existing web applications.

Previewing Your HTML Forms

You'll likely preview your HTML forms in many different browsers before you deploy them to users. In this section, you'll see two easy ways to preview your HTML forms as you develop them.

Previewing with Designer

So far, we've been previewing our Designer forms with the Preview PDF tab. We'll now preview our forms with the Preview HTML tab. However, in order for it to work, you must first configure your environment. Follow these steps to set up your Designer program for HTML Preview.

NOTE You can change these settings if you have your own LiveCycle Server. For instance, you can change the URL to point to your own server and change the other properties as you see fit. However, your server must be a LiveCycle Forms Pro ES4 or later server that supports HTML rendering.

1. Select Tools > Options > Server Options to view the Server Options panel (**Figure 6.2**).

2. Enter **http://www.smartdocdemo.com** as the Server URL.

3. Enter **8080** as the Port.

4. Enter **lc/content/xfaforms/profiles/default.html** as the HTML Preview Context. This reference points to a Mobile Forms profile on the server. You'll learn more about this profile later in the chapter.

5. Enter **lc/fm** as the Forms Manager Context. This is the location in the CRX repository where the Forms Manager components are stored.

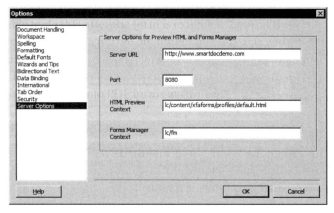

Figure 6.2 Designer's Server Options dialog box.

6. Click OK to save your settings.

7. Open the expenseReportCompleted.xdp form.

8. Select the Preview HTML tab in your Layout Editor.

   You are now viewing the HTML rendering of your form. Overall, it looks good and functions well. However, you'll see graphics that need improvement and functionality that has to be corrected. You'll get a chance to update and optimize this form for HTML rendering in Chapter 8, "Creating HTML Forms." Follow these steps to see features that are looking or working differently than they did in the PDF version.

9. Notice the display pattern in the Date Requested field in the top right of the form. The PDF rendering of this form displayed the current date, but the HTML rendering just shows a YYYY-MM-DD pattern.

10. Click the SmartDoc Client drop-down list and select Other. The Other Client text field does not display in the HTML rendering, but it did display in the PDF rendering.

11. Enter your first name and tab to the Last Name field and on to the Notes field. You'll find that these fields and the tabbing work just like they did in the PDF form.

12. Click the date field at the beginning of an expense row. You'll notice that the visual calendar control is also supported in HTML. The date field supports display patterns but not edit patterns.

13. Select a category from the Category drop-down list. List boxes and drop-down lists are fully supported in HTML forms.

14. Enter a description.

15. Enter a cost and you'll see that the Total at the end of the row updates automatically but the Sub Total and the Total of the report are not updated like they were in the PDF form. You'll also notice that the dollar sign ($) is missing in the HTML form.

16. Click the Add Expense button 20 times or until the page graphics overlap the page footer. This demonstrates one of the layout differences of HTML and PDF forms.

The HTML preview that you see in Designer's Preview HTML resembles a WebKit browser. WebKit is an open source layout engine software component designed to enable web browsers to render HTML pages. It is the engine behind many browsers in use today, including Apple's Safari and Google's Chrome.

Previewing with Mobile Forms IVS

If your company has LiveCycle Forms Pro ES4 or higher, you have Adobe's Mobile Forms IVS (Installation Verification Sample) application. This easy-to-use tool enables you to merge XML data into your form rendering to improve the thoroughness of your testing. Follow these steps to learn how:

1. Open your web browser and navigate to your Mobile Forms IVS application on your LiveCycle Server. The following is an example URL:

   ```
   http://<server address>:8080/mobileformsivs
   ```

2. Click the Browse button in the screen labeled Step 1 and locate the expenseReportHTMLCompleted.xdp file in your Samples folder. Click OK to close the Choose File To Upload dialog box.

3. Click the Upload File & List Existing Forms button to upload the XDP to your LiveCycle Server. You'll see your form in the Forms list box of the screen labeled Step 2.

4. Go back to the Step 1 screen and click the Browse button to upload an XML data file for testing.

5. Locate the expenseReportHTML.xml file in your Samples folder. Click OK to close the Choose File To Upload dialog box.

6. Select default in the Profile drop-down list. Your form will render with the default Mobile Forms profile on the server.

7. Select your form and your data file (**Figure 6.3**).

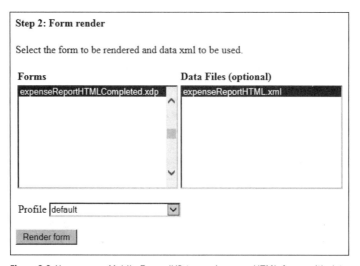

Figure 6.3 You can use Mobile Forms IVS to preview your HTML forms with data.

8. Click the Render Form button.

Your form will be rendered in a new browser window, and you can click the interactive and dynamic features to see how the form performs. If you're using an HTML5-compatible browser, you'll see that this rendering of the SmartDoc Expense Report is very similar to the PDF rendering you saw at the end of Chapter 3, "Creating the SmartDoc Expense Report."

NOTE *Adobe's Mobile Forms IVS is a sample application and should not be deployed to a production server.*

How It Works

The book's companion site contains links to Adobe documentation that explains the Mobile Forms Architecture in detail. This section will explain it at a higher level so that as a form developer, you can grasp the basics of how the technology works. By understanding the relevant basics, you'll know how to customize your HTML forms with a custom *Mobile Forms profile*.

As you saw in the two HTML preview examples, you reference a Mobile Forms profile when you render HTML mobile forms. This profile reference points to a location in the CRX Repository (**Figure 6.4**).

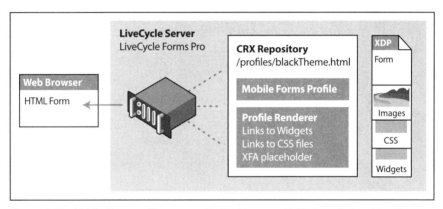

Figure 6.4 The Mobile Forms profile you use will affect how your HTML forms look and function.

The profile contains a series of name-value pairs, and one of the pairs points to a specific profile renderer. Here's an example:

```
sling:resourceType = /smartdoc/default
```

The profile renderer contains the following items that help LiveCycle Forms Pro properly transform your XFA form to an HTML presentation:

- JavaScript and widgets
- CSS
- An XFA placeholder for your Designer form

You can create a custom Mobile Forms profile in Adobe's CRX Content Repository that is included with LiveCycle Forms Pro ES4. You can access the development interface, called CRX DE Lite, at the following URL on your LiveCycle Server:

```
http://localhost:8080/lc/crx/de
```

A custom profile represents a customized version of the Mobile Form Render service. You can create a profile with custom CSS files for visually styling your HTML forms and custom widgets to alter the functionality of certain fields on your HTML mobile forms. Although creating a custom profile is beyond the scope of this book, there are links to further documentation on the book's companion site.

XFA to HTML Transformation

To illustrate this transformation, I'll show you how a standard Text Field object in Designer is transformed to an HTML text field. As you learned in Chapter 4, "PDF and Acrobat," the format of a Designer XFA form is well-structured XML. When you drag and drop a Text Field object from the Standard Object Library to a form, the following XML is added to your form:

```
<field name="myTextField" y="15.875mm" x="25.4mm" w="37mm"
➥ h="13.707mm">

   <ui>

      <textEdit>

         <border>

            <edge/>

         </border>

         <margin/>

      </textEdit>

   </ui>

   <font typeface="Arial"/>

   <margin topInset="1mm" bottomInset="1mm" leftInset="1mm"
➥ rightInset="1mm"/>

   <para vAlign="middle"/>

   <caption reserve="0.185306in" placement="bottom">

      <para vAlign="middle"/>

      <value>

         <text>myTextField</text>

      </value>

   </caption>

</field>
```

The complete transformation is complex and beyond the scope of this book. However, this simplified example will help you understand the new HTML structure so you can use custom profiles to change the look and functionality of your HTML forms.

Adobe LiveCycle Forms Pro transforms the XFA structure of our Text Field object into a parent `<div>` element that contains two child `<div>` elements. The first child `<div>` is for the input field and the second child `<div>` is for the caption (**Figure 6.5**). The XFA value field is represented by an HTML `<input>` element with a type attribute value of `"text"`. This will create a single-line text input field. The caption is rendered as an SVG element.

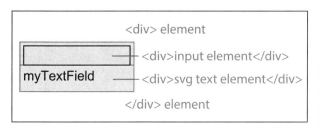

Figure 6.5 A simplified example to illustrate the HTML structure of Designer's Text Field objects.

The HTML code that LiveCycle Forms Pro creates for our Text Field object looks something like this:

```
<div class="field textfield myTextField">

   <div class="widget textfieldwidget textField">

      <input type="text">

   </div>

   <div class="caption">

      <svg>

         <text>myTextField</text>

      </svg>

   </div>

</div>
```

Each `<div>` element in the HTML is assigned one or more CSS class selectors. The class selectors for the parent `<div>` in our Text Field example are

▪ field

▪ textfield

▪ myTextField

You can modify the style properties of these classes to change the appearance of a group of form objects or an individual form object. You'll see examples of this in the next chapter.

Adobe Supported Browsers

Table 6.1 is a list of browsers that Adobe says support HTML Mobile Forms. We'll keep an updated link on the book's companion site.

Table 6.1 Supported Browsers

MICROSOFT WINDOWS	
BROWSER	**SUPPORTED VERSION**
Mozilla Firefox	13 and later
Google Chrome	19 and later
Microsoft Internet Explorer	9 and later
MAC	
BROWSER	**SUPPORTED VERSION**
Apple Safari	9 and later
Mozilla Firefox	Not Supported
Google Chrome	Not Supported
IPAD (IOS VERSION 5.1.1 AND LATER)	
BROWSER	**SUPPORTED VERSION**
Apple Safari	5.1
GOOGLE ANDROID TABLETS (ANDROID VERSION 4.0 AND LATER)	
BROWSER	**SUPPORTED VERSION**
Chrome for Android devices	Yes
Android default browser	No

NOTE This is the official list from the Adobe website. However, in our testing, the forms also worked in recent versions of Firefox and Chrome on the Macintosh platform.

CSS and SVG

LiveCycle Forms Pro uses many web standard technologies, including CSS and SVG.

CSS (Cascading Style Sheets) is a style sheet language used to style the visual aspects of HTML and XHTML documents. Many web programmers use CSS to separate the style properties of their web pages from the content of the pages. CSS uses selectors to match up a part of the HTML document to a style in the CSS file. One HTML form can be displayed with multiple different visual styles by using CSS files in a custom Mobile Forms profile.

SVG (Scalable Vector Graphics) are used by LiveCycle Forms Pro to render Draw elements and static text in HTML5 forms. SVG is one of the technologies that make it possible for the HTML rendering of your form to look remarkably like the PDF rendering. SVG is an XML-based vector image format used to display scalable vector images on the web.

Similarities and Differences

Although the LiveCycle Forms Pro technology is new, the way you create forms in Designer will seem familiar. Adobe has done a great job mapping the most important aspects of XFA forms to HTML. All the following features of smart forms are supported in LiveCycle Forms Pro:

- Dynamic forms that will grow or shrink based on data or user actions

- Dynamic subforms that support progressive disclosure

- Interactive fields with display patterns

- Form fragments and custom objects to increase the efficiency of your form creation and management

- Cross-filling of data to fields with global binding to simplify data entry

- Event-driven scripting to respond to user actions

However, even though the most useful and popular features are supported, there are some differences. This section will introduce you to some of the differences that will affect how you design and develop forms.

Different Host

HTML forms use a different host than PDF forms do. The host for HTML forms is the web browser and the host for PDF forms is either Acrobat or Reader. This will cause some common functions that work well in PDF forms to not function in HTML forms. Follow these steps to see an example:

1. Create a new form in Designer by selecting File > New to launch the New Form Assistant.

2. Select Use A Blank Form, click Next, and click Finish.

3. Drag and drop a Print Button from the Standard Object Library to your form.

4. Select Preview PDF to see how this works on a PDF form.

5. Click Print. Acrobat's Print dialog box will open.

6. Select Design View.

7. Select the Print Button, expand the Script Editor, and select the click event. You'll notice the following script:

```
xfa.host.print(1, "0", (xfa.host.numPages -1).toString(),
➡ 0, 0, 0, 0, 0);
```

8. Select Preview HTML.

9. Click Print. Nothing will happen because the script is calling a specific method of the Acrobat host with specific parameters.

10. Select Design View to update this script so it works for PDF and HTML forms.

11. Select the Print Button, expand the Script Editor, and select the click event. Update your script to add host detection and an if-else block that provides different scripts for the different hosts.

```
if(xfa.host.appType == "HTML 5"){

  window.print();

}else{

  xfa.host.print(1, "0", (xfa.host.numPages -1).toString(),
  ➡ 0, 0, 0, 0, 0);

}
```

The first line calls the appType property of the host. If the appType property is HTML 5, the window.print() method will execute. This will produce a web browser dialog box (**Figure 6.6**). If the appType property is something else, like Reader, the else block will execute and the traditional Acrobat print dialog box will open.

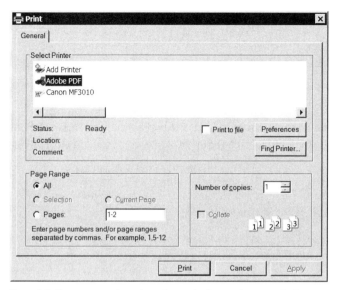

Figure 6.6 You can use a host detection script in your forms to display the appropriate Print dialog box to your users.

Dynamic Flow and Pagination

The pagination of a dynamic flowing form works differently in HTML forms. A dynamic PDF form will paginate based on the page size setting, but since an HTML form can be any length, a dynamic form will continue to expand lower on the same page. Follow these steps to see an example:

1. Open paginationExample.xdp from your Samples folder.

2. Select the expandingTextField object in the Hierarchy palette.

3. Select the Field tab of the Object palette. The Allow Multiple Lines property and the Allow Page Breaks Within Content property are both selected.

4. Select the Layout palette. The Expand To Fit property is selected, so this Text Field object will expand dynamically to accommodate all the text that is either input by the user or merged by a server process.

5. Select the page1 object in the Hierarchy palette and select the Subform tab of the Object palette. The Content property is set to Flowed, and Allow Page Breaks Within Content is selected. This is the parent subform for the expandingTextField object, so it will grow dynamically as its child object grows.

6. Select PreviewPDF to render this form as a PDF.

7. Open loremIpsum.txt from your Samples folder in Notepad or a similar text editing program.

8. Select all the text in the loremIpsum.txt file, copy it, and paste it into the text field in your PDF form.

9. Click on your form outside of the text field and scroll to the bottom of the form. You'll notice that there are two pages in your PDF form.

10. Select Preview HTML to render this form as HTML.

11. Select all the text in the loremIpsum.txt file, copy it, and paste it into the text field in your HTML form.

12. Click on your form outside the text field and scroll to the bottom of the form. You'll notice that there's only one page in your HTML form.

Layout and Graphics

The layout and graphics in your HTML forms will be remarkably similar to your PDF forms. There are some subtle differences, and the following tips will help you develop your Designer forms for HTML rendering. I recommend that you test all form designs in your target browsers with Adobe's Mobile Forms IVS application.

■ Use a web-safe font for your Designer forms that will render as HTML. LiveCycle Forms Pro doesn't embed fonts into the HTML rendering, and you should use a common font to ensure your layout will display accurately on your user's machine.

■ Make static Text objects and interactive Text Field objects larger than you typically would for a PDF form. This extra space will enable your text to properly display in browsers that have different kerning than you see in Designer or Acrobat. Kerning is the process of adjusting the space between individual letters.

■ Use form field properties that work well for either PDF or HTML forms. For instance, an Appearance property of Solid Box or Underlined will work for both types of forms but the Sunken Box property works only for PDF forms.

■ Set your Button Style property to Default for Radio Button objects to keep your HTML and PDF forms consistent.

- Set your Check Style property to Check for Check Box objects to keep your HTML and PDF forms consistent.

- Do not embed images in Designer. Instead, use a relative path to the image asset on your LiveCycle Server.

Patterns

You'll notice some similarities and differences when using patterns with your HTML forms. Many of the popular patterns are supported for display patterns, including the date and numeric field patterns listed in this section.

However, you will notice that edit patterns don't work in HTML forms like they do in PDF forms. In PDF forms, you'll see an edit pattern displayed when you're making a change to the field. You won't see this in HTML forms. In some cases, edit patterns may appear to be working in HTML forms. Follow these steps to see an example:

1. Open the socialSecurityNumber.xdp file from your Samples folder.

2. Select the Preview HTML tab.

3. Enter **123456789** in the field.

4. Click on the form outside the field. The display pattern will format your entry to display 123-45-6789.

5. Click the field to edit the number. You'll see your entry switch to all numbers (**Figure 6.7**). This looks like an edit pattern, but as you will see in step 10, the edit pattern for this form is blank.

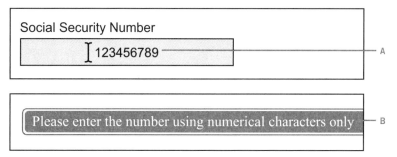

Figure 6.7 When you edit a U.S. Social Security Number object, the display pattern will be removed and you will see all numbers (A). The validation pattern message (B) will show if your entry does not match the validation pattern.

6. Select Design View to review the properties of the U.S. Social Security Number object.

7. Select the U.S. Social Security Number object and highlight the Field tab of the Object palette.

8. Click the Patterns button to open the Patterns dialog box.

9. Select the Display tab to see that the display pattern is text{999-99-9999}.

10. Select the Edit tab to see that the edit pattern is blank. The runtime display that you saw in step 5 was not defined by an edit pattern in this field.

11. Select the Validation tab to see that the validation pattern is text{999999999}. This pattern will define the validation pattern for the field.

12. Select the Value tab of the Object palette. Notice the validation pattern message in the bottom of this panel. This message will display to the user when an entry does not match the validation pattern.

13. Select the Preview HTML tab.

14. Enter **adobe** in the field.

15. Click on the form outside the field.

16. Click the field to edit the number. You'll see the validation pattern message appear (Figure 6.7).

HTML Date Field display patterns

The following date patterns are supported in HTML forms:

- date{M/D/YY}
- date{MMM D, YYYY}
- date{MMMM D, YYYY}
- date{M/D/YYYY}
- date{MM/DD/YY}
- date{MM/DD/YYYY}
- date{YY/MM/DD}
- date{YYYY-MM-DD}
- date{DD-MMM-YY}
- date{MMMM, YYYY}

HTML Number Field display patterns

All the numeric patterns in Designer's Patterns dialog box are supported, including these popular ones:

- num.integer{}
- num.decimal{}
- num.currency{}
- num.percent{}

Scripting and Events

HTML forms support the most commonly used XFA script constructs. You should test your forms in your target browser because, unlike PDF forms, HTML forms do not support all the XFA script constructs. You'll likely have issues with existing scripts that are host or page related because HTML forms use a different host and a different pagination model. Chapter 8 includes hands-on exercises where you'll update scripts so they work for both HTML and PDF forms.

Most of the important events for form developers are supported in HTML forms, including these:

- initialize
- click
- validate

- exit
- calculate
- change

 The book's companion site contains links to Adobe documentation with more details about scripting and events.

Moving On

Now that you understand the basics of HTML mobile forms, let's move on to some best practices for HTML forms.

7

Best Practices for HTML Forms

Coming together is a beginning; keeping together is progress; working together is success.

— Henry Ford

This chapter is a living and breathing document that is hosted on the book's companion site. As of this writing, SmartDoc Technologies has been working with Adobe for about a year on LiveCycle HTML forms. During that time, we've also worked on a number of mobile form projects for clients. This chapter contains the best practices that we've developed to date.

However, since LiveCycle HTML mobile forms is much newer than LiveCycle PDF forms, I expect these best practices to grow and evolve over time. The online version of this chapter will be updated periodically, and you are welcome to contribute to it.

Targeting

As you saw previously, it's always a good idea to know the type of viewer your form fillers are using. Chapter 5, "Best Practices for PDFs," detailed the issues involved with different versions of Acrobat, Reader, and other PDF viewers. In this section, you'll explore the added dimension of web browser targeting and support.

Testing with Different Browsers

If you preview your forms only in Designer, you'll see only one possible rendering of your forms. You can preview your forms in various browsers with Adobe's Mobile Forms IVS application, which you saw in the last chapter. Since Designer's preview is based on WebKit, you should also view and test your forms in the following two browsers, which don't use WebKit:

- Microsoft Internet Explorer
- Firefox

Internet Explorer uses the Trident layout engine, and Firefox uses the Gecko engine.

Form Development Strategy

Adobe LiveCycle technology offers great power and flexibility for form and document generation. Before you start a form development project, you should consider your form development strategy. This section profiles two useful strategies that you'll see demonstrated in the exercises of Chapter 8, "Creating HTML Forms."

One Master File Strategy

Since LiveCycle Forms Pro enables you to render HTML and various types of PDFs, you can follow a One Master File Strategy (**Figure 7.1**).

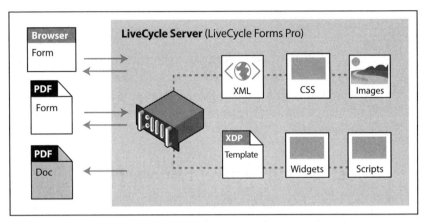

Figure 7.1 The One Master File Strategy makes form maintenance very easy.

This approach enables you to create one Designer XDP file and render it as HTML, interactive and dynamic PDF forms, and read-only PDF documents. A big advantage of this approach is that you need to maintain and update only one master template. To make this approach succeed, your master template needs to meet the following requirements:

■ You must use data patterns and scripting events that work for both PDF and HTML.

■ You must perform host detection and provide appropriate scripting for the different hosts.

You'll create a form that meets all these requirements in the next chapter. Although this strategy requires only one master XDP file, you can make the HTML form look different than the PDF form with a custom Mobile Forms profile.

Multiple Master File Strategy

If a One Master File Strategy is not appropriate, LiveCycle technology also supports a Multiple Master File Strategy (**Figure 7.2**).

In this strategy, you create a set of two or more master Designer files. Each file can have its own look and feel, but they'll all be bound to the same XML Schema file. Since they all share the same data structure, it's easy to move XML data from one form to another. The Address Change form in the next chapter is part of a Multiple Master File Strategy.

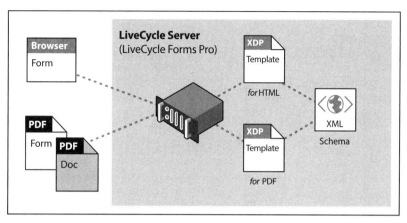

Figure 7.2 The Multiple Master File Strategy enables you to have two related documents that look very different from one another.

Form Graphics

This section will introduce you to some best practices for creating and maintaining your form graphics for HTML forms.

Form Fragments

As you learned in Part 2, "PDF Forms," fragments enable you to create a section of a form and reuse it across many different forms. When you update the fragment, all the forms that reference the fragment are also updated. The combination of form fragments with LiveCycle's ability to generate HTML forms enables your organization to greatly reduce the costs associated with form creation and management.

For instance, an insurance company typically manages hundreds of forms in many different file formats. Each form may have an HTML, PDF, and Microsoft Word version. Adobe LiveCycle Forms Pro enables an organization to streamline the creation and management of its forms and documents at the enterprise level (**Figure 7.3**).

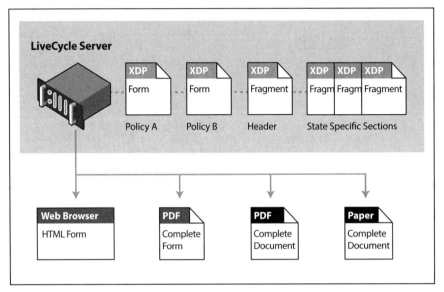

Figure 7.3 LiveCycle Server enables you to optimize your enterprise form management and develop master form components that can be used for many different business purposes.

Instead of creating and managing each form as a separate file, an organization can design a library of master form components. Figure 7.3 shows a LiveCycle Server system that meets all the following goals:

■ Policy documents are saved as separate XDP files. LiveCycle Server can combine these policy documents into a final insurance package.

■ The common header is saved as a separate form fragment that all policy documents reference.

■ State specific sections are saved as separate fragments so they can be updated at one time and referenced in many different policy documents.

■ These master LiveCycle forms can be used to generate any format your business requires, including HTML, PDF forms, and finalized PDF documents.

By organizing and rationalizing your form library and using LiveCycle Forms Pro, you'll realize the following business benefits:

■ **Reduced costs:** Form development and management will be faster, easier, and cheaper because redundant work will be eliminated.

■ **Greater consistency:** Your forms will look and function more consistently, which will improve the usability of your forms and the success of your form system.

- **Faster time to market:** You can quickly change a fragment based on a business update, and it will be deployed automatically to all forms once you publish it. You can change a fragment's content, layout, scripting, data bindings, and graphic style, and all forms that reference the fragment will be updated immediately.

Tables

If you're developing HTML forms in Designer, it's a good idea to keep your tables as simple as possible. Adobe advises that complex tables may have rendering issues in various web browsers.

In the first release of LiveCycle Forms Pro, there were a number of Designer's table features that were not supported in HTML forms. However, Adobe has been enhancing LiveCycle, and it now supports the following features in ES4 Service Pack 1:

- Adding sections to a table.
- Using the `colSpan` property in JavaScript.
- Using merged cells. Please note that even though merged cells will render in HTML, there are some inconsistencies in the thickness of the borders in tables with merged cells.

You should test your tables in various browsers with Adobe's Mobile Forms IVS application. In my testing, I noticed that row shading works for static forms (**Figure 7.4**) but doesn't work for dynamic forms.

Header	Header	Header	Header
Row 1			
Row 2			
Row 3			
Row 4			
Row 5			
Footer	Footer	Footer	Footer

Figure 7.4 Row shading works on a static table but doesn't currently work on a dynamic table in an HTML form.

Signatures

Traditional PDF digital signatures are not supported in HTML forms. However, Adobe has added a new XFA object called the Scribble Signature. This new object enables users to sign a mobile form with their finger or a stylus. If the form is being accessed by a mobile device, the object will also gather a timestamp and the geolocation of the user. The addition of this time and place information increases the validity of the signature. When a user taps on the Scribble Signature field, a signature dialog box will appear (**Figure 7.5**).

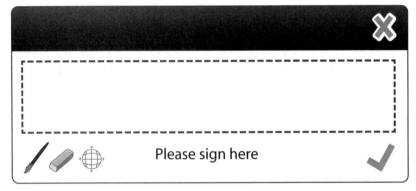

Figure 7.5 LiveCycle's new Signature Scribble object enables you to sign a form on a mobile tablet with your finger or a stylus.

Using Custom Profiles

As you saw in the last chapter, the Mobile Forms profile you use to render your HTML forms will affect how they look and function. In this section, you'll see a few examples of custom profiles. The first two custom profiles will illustrate how you can use CSS to change the visual aspects of your HTML forms. The last custom profile will show how you can use a custom widget to change the functional aspects of an HTML form field.

CSS

Chapter 5 showed how a standard Designer Text Field object will be rendered by LiveCycle Forms Pro as an HTML file that's similar to this structure:

```
<div class="field textfield myTextField">

    <div class="widget textfieldwidget textField">

        <input type="text">

    </div>

    <div class="caption">

        <svg>

            <text>myTextField</text>

        </svg>

    </div>

</div>
```

The first line includes three class selectors: field, textfield, and myTextField. You can apply Cascading Style Sheets to each one of these class selectors to set the visual style of your HTML forms. Of the three, the textfield class selector will be the one you use most in your form development. The following bullets will help you understand the hierarchy of these class selectors and how they relate to your form design:

- field: The field class selector will apply your CSS styles to all fields on the form, including check boxes, radio buttons, drop-down lists, and text fields. Because you'll likely want subtle differences in the styles you apply to these different form objects, you probably want to define only high-level attributes like a font setting to this class selector.

- textfield: The textfield class selector will apply your CSS styles to all text fields on the form so you can achieve a consistent form design and specify the unique graphic details of your text fields.

- myTextField: The myTextField class selector will apply your CSS styles to the specific text field named myTextField. You'll use this type of class selector only if you want a unique style applied to only one field on your form.

Because CSS affects the visual aspect of your forms, it's easiest to understand with a few visual examples applied to a simple form design.

Default profile

For this example, I created a form in Designer with two standard Text Field objects on a subform. I entered *value text* as each object's default text. If I render an HTML form with the default profile, LiveCycle Forms Pro will generate an HTML form that looks like **Figure 7.6**.

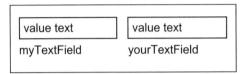

Figure 7.6 The example form rendered with the Adobe default profile.

The same Designer form can look very different if LiveCycle Forms Pro uses a custom profile.

Custom profile 1

The first custom profile includes a CSS file that specifically styles the first text field by referencing the myTextField class selector. This CSS file changes the font, font style, and font color of the text field (**Figure 7.7**).

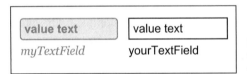

Figure 7.7 You can provide unique styles to a single form field by referencing that field's unique class selector.

```
.myTextField .widget {
    background-color: #d8e2f3;
    border-radius: 5px;
    border: 1px solid #007cc2;
}
.myTextField .widget input {
    color: #007cc2;
    font-weight: bold;
}
.myTextField .caption svg text {
    fill: #007cc2;
    font-style: italic;
```

```
    font-family: Georgia;

}
```

The first two blocks style the input field, and the last block styles the caption font.

Custom profile 2

The second custom profile includes a CSS file that references two other class selectors. The first class selector sets the background color of the subform, and the second class selector sets the visual properties of all the text fields (**Figure 7.8**).

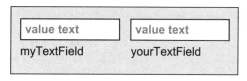

Figure 7.8 By using the textfield class selector, you can style all the text fields on a form.

```
.mySubform {

   background-color: #d8e2f3;

}
.textfield .widget {

   background-color: #ffffff;

}
.textfield .widget input {

   color: #007cc2;

   font-weight: bold;

}
```

You can use CSS files to maintain consistent fonts and font styles on your HTML forms even when the XDP file has different fonts and font styles.

Custom Widgets

Like style sheets, custom widgets also enable you to customize your HTML forms. Custom widgets are small applications that will override or enhance the default functionality of your form objects. You can create custom widgets in Adobe's CRX DE Lite interface using the framework provided by Adobe.

In this example, you'll see how a custom widget will improve the usability of your state drop-down lists for users of mobile tablets like the Apple iPad or Google Nexus. **Figure 7.9** shows a custom widget that changes the State drop-down list of the Address Change form.

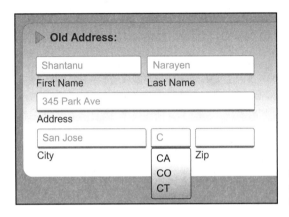

Figure 7.9 Custom widgets enable a rich data capture experience on mobile tablet.

The State drop-down list can take up a great deal of screen real estate on a mobile tablet. In this example, the form field uses a custom widget that supports auto-completion. When a user types the first letter of a state, all the states that begin with that letter will appear. Custom widgets support JavaScript and the JQuery libraries. Adobe provides out-of-the box widgets that you can review and extend.

Data Submission

As you learned in Chapter 5, a LiveCycle Server can receive and process data submissions from a PDF form. You can also create a LiveCycle Server process that receives and processes data from an HTML form. There are many business benefits to processing form data submissions. **Figure 7.10** shows how a LiveCycle Server can process your data and use it to update databases and enterprise systems, create workflows, and render and archive documents.

You create a LiveCycle process in LiveCycle WorkBench, which is part of Live-Cycle Enterprise Suite. You'll learn more about this in Chapter 9, "LiveCycle Enterprise Suite." To call the process from an HTML form, you'll add a REST endpoint. REST stands for Representational State Transfer and is sometimes spelled ReST. It uses the HTTP protocol and has many similarities with web services, including the following:

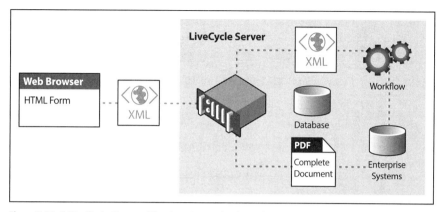

Figure 7.10 A LiveCycle Server will automate your business by processing form data and integrating it with your existing IT systems.

- It's platform independent.

- It's language independent.

- It can easily be used across firewalls.

To call the LiveCycle process from your form, you'll need the exact and complete URL for your process. You can retrieve this in the LiveCycle Workbench application (**Figure 7.11**).

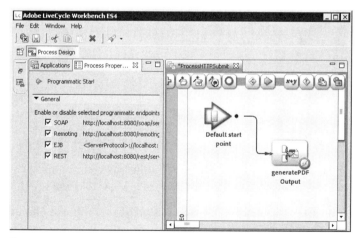

Figure 7.11 You can get the complete URL for a LiveCycle process by selecting the Default start point in LiveCycle Workbench.

The REST URL for your process will follow this format:

`http://[server]:8080/rest/services/[ServiceName]/[Operation]:[version]`

You can add a REST URL to two different button types in your Designer forms. Follow these steps to learn how to configure a standard Button object:

1. Open a new blank form in Designer by selecting File > New > Use A Blank Form.

2. Click Next in the New Form Assistant and click Finish to create your form.

3. Drag and drop a Button object from the Standard Object Library to your form.

4. Select the Field tab of the Object palette.

5. Set the Control Type to Submit. The Submit tab will appear.

6. Select the Submit tab and enter your REST URL in the Submit To URL field (**Figure 7.12**).

7. Click the Submit drop-down list and select XML Data (XML). This will result in your form data being submitted as XML when the button on your form is clicked.

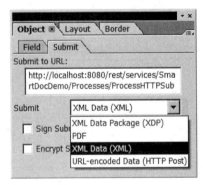

Figure 7.12 You can use a standard Button object as a submit button by setting its Control Type to Submit.

You can also use an HTTP Submit Button object to submit HTML form data to a REST URL. Follow these steps to learn how to configure this object:

8. Drag and drop an HTTP Submit Button object from the Standard Object Library to your form.

9. Select the Field tab of the Object palette.

10. Enter your REST URL in the URL field (**Figure 7.13**). Many other properties for this object already have default property settings, such as a caption, appearance, and highlighting, but you can change them if you want.

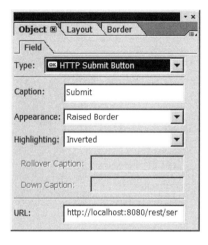

Figure 7.13 Designer includes an HTTP Submit Button that submits form data to a REST URL.

It's a best practice to validate your form data before you execute a form submission. You'll see an example of this in the next chapter.

Moving On

Now that you've learned how Designer is used to create HTML forms, it's time to exercise your knowledge by creating a few forms of your own.

8

Creating HTML Forms

The vision must be followed by the venture. It is not enough to stare up the steps—we must step up the stairs.

— Vance Havner

Now that you've learned more about HTML forms, it's time to put your knowledge to work. You'll create two HTML forms in this chapter to simulate two real-world projects. In the first exercise, you'll take an existing PDF form (the SmartDoc Expense Report) and update it for HTML. In the second exercise, you'll create a new HTML form in LiveCycle Designer from scratch.

Updating the SmartDoc Expense Report

As you saw in Chapter 6, "Introduction," you must take into account a number of issues when you render the existing SmartDoc Expense Report as an HTML form. There are graphics that need improvement and functionality that needs to be corrected. You'll see similar issues when you transition your legacy Designer forms to HTML.

In this chapter, you'll update the form so it looks and functions properly as either a PDF or an HTML form. This approach follows the One Master File Strategy and enables you to make updates once and deploy them as HTML forms, interactive and dynamic PDF forms, and read-only PDF documents.

Updating the Font

LiveCycle Forms Pro ES4 doesn't embed fonts into the HTML rendering of your XDP template, so it's a good idea to select a font that's likely to be resident on a viewer's machine. Although there's no guarantee that a font will be on a user's machine, it's a best practice to choose a web-safe font for your XDP forms that will render as HTML. An example of a web-safe sans serif font is Arial. Microsoft released Arial as part of their "Core fonts for the Web" initiative in 1996, and it's been popular ever since.

Follow these steps to change the sans serif font in your SmartDoc Expense Report so that it uses Arial instead of Myriad Pro:

1. Open the expenseReportCompleted.xdp file in Designer.

2. Save this file as **myExpenseReportHTML_1.xdp**.

3. Select File > Form Properties > Default Fonts. You'll see the Default Fonts panel you learned about in Chapter 1, "The Basics" (**Figure 8.1**).

4. Update the Typeface drop-down list in the Default Caption Font Properties section to Arial.

5. Click the Apply Properties To Existing Captions button.

6. In the Apply Default Caption Font Properties dialog box (**Figure 8.2**), be sure to select only the Typeface check box. You want to change only the typeface; you don't want all the form's text to have the same size and style.

7. Select the Apply To All Captions option and click OK to update the caption fonts on your form.

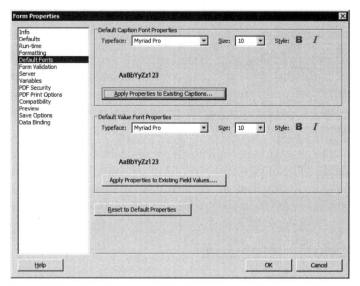

Figure 8.1 The Default Fonts panel of the Form Properties dialog box defines the default fonts for the current form. You can also use this panel to make a comprehensive font change to your form.

Figure 8.2 This dialog box gives you the option to change the typeface, size, and style of all the caption fonts on your form at one time.

8. Update the Typeface drop-down list in the Default Value Font Properties section to Arial.

9. Click the Apply Properties To Existing Field Values button.

10. In the Apply Default Value Font Properties dialog box, be sure to select only the Typeface check box.

11. Select the Apply To All Field Values option and click OK to update the value fonts on your form.

12. Click OK to close the Form Properties dialog box.

13. Save your file.

Designer will now display your form with the Arial font. Please note that you'll sometimes need to have layout adjustments when you make a comprehensive font change like this. The Arial font is visibly larger than Myriad Pro even at the same point size (**Figure 8.3**).

These are both the same point size.
Myriad Pro (11 point)

These are both the same point size.
Arial (11 point)

Figure 8.3 Even when you use the same point size, different fonts won't necessarily be the same visual size in your form.

Designer will show the Text Overflow Indicator in the bottom right of the Text Fields that need adjusting. You can make your font size smaller or your field size larger to correct your field for the larger Arial font and to remove these warning icons. Follow these steps to correct the layout issues on the master pages.

14. Select the Master Pages tab.

You might see the Text Overflow Indicator on the Text Field objects of masterPage1. If so, follow these steps to correct the issue.

15. Select the expensesTitle Text object and stretch the left side until you can see the *Expense Report* text (**Figure 8.4**, right).

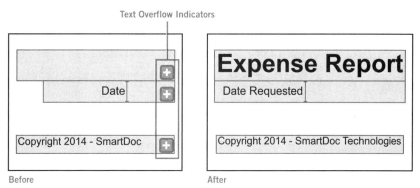

Figure 8.4 Designer's Text Overflow Indicators (left) show you the fields that need adjusting. You'll see the text after you expand your Text Fields (right).

16. Select the dateRequested Text object and stretch the left side until you can see the *Date Requested* text. You may also need to adjust the caption reserve by selecting the vertical bar in the middle of the field and sliding it to the right.

17. Select the copyrightFooter Text object at the bottom of the page and stretch the right side until you can see the *Copyright 2014 - SmartDoc Technologies* text.

18. Make the same adjustment to the copyrightFooter Text object at the bottom of masterPage2.

You've corrected the issues caused by the larger Arial font on the master pages. You can also make similar adjustments to the form objects on the page1 body subform.

Editing the XML Source

There's an alternate method of updating the fonts in a form that also works. This method involves editing the XML source directly by selecting the XML Source tab in the Layout Editor. Follow these steps to learn how to do a find and replace in the XML source of your form:

1. Select your XML Source tab. If you don't see this tab, select View > XML Source.

2. Select Edit > Replace or press Ctrl+H on your keyboard. The Replace dialog box will appear (**Figure 8.5**).

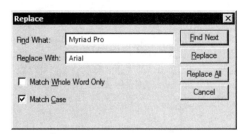

Figure 8.5 The Replace dialog box in the XML Source tab enables you to make many changes to your form at once.

Don't execute a change at this point because you already changed your fonts with Designer's interface in the previous exercise. Adobe recommends using the Designer interface to edit XDP files and not to edit the

XML source directly. If you do make edits in the XML Source tab, Designer will prompt you with a warning message when you leave the XML Source tab (**Figure 8.6**).

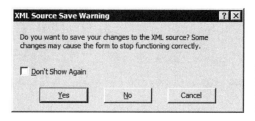

Figure 8.6 You can make edits directly in the XML source of your form. You'll be warned, but it will work if you do it correctly.

3. Save your file.

TIP If you had difficulty with the exercises in this section, you can compare your form to the expenseReportHTML_1.xdp file in your Samples folder. You can correct your file based on this sample or simply use this sample as a base for the next exercise.

Updating the Date Field

Date fields look and function differently in HTML forms. Follow these steps to analyze these differences and overcome them with JavaScript.

1. Select the Preview HTML tab in your Layout Editor.

2. Notice the display pattern in the Date Requested field in the top right of the form. The PDF rendering of this form displayed the current date in an MM/DD/YYYY pattern, but the HTML rendering just shows a YYYY-MM-DD pattern with no current date.

This YYYY-MM-DD display pattern is the default for Date Field objects in HTML preview. However, when a date is selected or a properly formatted date is provided in a script, the date field's display pattern is applied instead. In this case, you need to update the JavaScript so that a properly formatted date is provided when the HTML form is initialized. Follow these steps to update your form:

3. Select the Master Pages tab in your Layout Editor.

4. Select the dateRequested object, expand the Script Editor, and select the initialize event.

5. Replace the existing script with this one, which will work for both HTML and PDF forms:

```
if(this.rawValue == null && this.access == "open"){
  var oToday = new Date();
  var currYear = oToday.getFullYear();
  var currMonth = oToday.getMonth() + 1;
  if(currMonth <= 9){
    currMonth = "0" + currMonth;
  }
  var currDay = oToday.getDate();
  if(currDay <= 9){
    currDay = "0" + currDay;
  }
  var dateVal = currYear + "-" + currMonth + "-" + currDay;
  this.rawValue = dateVal;
  this.access = "protected";
}
```

6. Select the Field tab of the Object palette.

7. Click the Patterns button and select the Display tab. You'll see that the object's display pattern is date{MM/DD/YY}.

8. Click OK to close the Patterns dialog box.

9. Select Preview HTML to see today's date displayed in the Date Requested field.

10. Save your file as **myExpenseReportHTML_2.xdp**.

If you compare this new script to the old one, you'll notice a few significant changes. The changes have been made to create a dateVal variable in the format of YYYY-MM-DD regardless of the current date. Two if statements will format the currMonth and currDay variables to a two-digit number, and the concatenation of the dateVal variable uses a dash instead of a slash. This is a properly formatted date, and when this is sent to the HTML field, the display pattern will work properly and today's date will be displayed in an MM/DD/YY format.

TIP If you had difficulty with the exercises in this section, you can compare your form to the expenseReportHTML_2.xdp file in your Samples folder.

Host Detection and the Change Event

The SmartDoc Expense Report uses progressive disclosure to display the Other Client Name text field whenever a user selects Other in the SmartDoc Client drop-down. Currently this script resides in the change event of the drop-down list. Although the change event is supported in HTML forms, you need to update your script so that it can work for both PDF and HTML forms. Follow these steps to add a host detection script and other updates to your change event:

1. Select the clientName object in the employee subform.

2. Expand the Script Editor and select the change event from the Show Events drop-down list.

3. Replace the existing script with this one:

```
if(xfa.host.appType == "HTML 5"){

  if(this.rawValue == "Other"){

    otherClientName.presence = "visible";

  }else{

    otherClientName.presence = "hidden";

  }

}else{

  if(xfa.event.newText == "Other"){

    otherClientName.presence = "visible";

  }else{

    otherClientName.presence = "hidden";

  }

}
```

The host detection is performed in the first line of the script. The remainder of the script has two similar blocks of code with the following differences to support both PDF and HTML:

▪ The HTML block is checking for a value of "Other" in the rawValue property.

▪ The PDF block is checking for a value of "Other" in the xfa.event.newText property.

4. Select Preview PDF to see this work in a PDF form.

5. Click the SmartDoc Client drop-down list and select Other. You will see the Other Client Name field appear.

6. Select Preview HTML to see this work in an HTML form.

7. Click the SmartDoc Client drop-down list and select Other. You will see the Other Client Name field appear.

Updating the Patterns

The dollar sign ($) does not display in the decimal fields when the form is rendered as HTML. You can correct this issue by following these steps:

1. Select the cost field in the expenseRow subform.

2. Select the Field tab of the Object palette and click the Patterns button.

3. Select the Display tab if it isn't already selected.

4. Delete the num{$z,zzz,zzz.99} pattern from the Pattern field.

5. Select the num.currency{} in the Select Type list box.

6. Select OK to save your changes.

7. Apply this same display pattern change to the other Decimal Field objects on your form: total, subTotal, cashAdvance, and grandTotal.

8. Select Preview HTML to see this display pattern showing a dollar sign in front of the number (**Figure 8.7**).

9. Select Preview PDF to see that this pattern also works in a PDF form.

Description	Cost	# of	Total
▾ Airline flight to Boston	$455.00	1	$455.00
▾ Taxi ride to airport	$20.00	1	$20.00
▾ Dinner with client	$38.00	1	$38.00
▾ Hotel and breakfast	$238.00	1	$238.00
	Sub Total:		$751.00
	Less Cash Advance:		$.00
	TOTAL		$751.00

Figure 8.7 You can set display patterns in Designer so that your forms will render properly as HTML and PDF.

10. Save your file as **myExpenseReportHTML_3.xdp**.

TIP If you had difficulty with the exercises in this section, you can compare your form to the expenseReportHTML_3.xdp file in your Samples folder.

Updating the Sub Total Calculation

The script that calculates the sub total amount needs to be updated to work in the HTML form. As you'll recall from Chapter 3, "Creating the SmartDoc Expense Report," this script keeps a running total of the cost of all expense items as the user enters them. The existing script resolves all the expenseRow instances and assigns them to the myExpenses variable in the following line:

```
var myExpenses = expenseReport.page1.expenses.expensesWrapper.
➥ resolveNodes("expenseRow[*]");
```

To get this to work in HTML, you need to restructure your script because this line won't work. You can't currently pass a string parameter with a wildcard index ([*]) to the resolveNodes method. Follow these steps to update your script:

1. Select the subTotal field in the total subform.

2. Expand the Script Editor and select the calculate event.

3. Replace the existing script with this one:

```
var len = expenseReport.page1.expenses.expensesWrapper._expenseRow.
➥ count;


var sum = 0.0;
for (var i = 0; i < len; i++){
sum += expenseReport.page1.expenses.expensesWrapper.resolveNode
➥ ("expenseRow[" + i + "]").total.rawValue;
}


this.rawValue = sum;
```

   In the first line, the amount of expenseRow items is determined and assigned to the variable len. In the for loop, the script iterates through each expenseRow and adds the rawValue of each total field to the sum variable. The last line is the same as it was in the previous version.

4. Select Preview HTML to see this script in action.

5. Select Preview PDF to see that this script also works in a PDF form.

Updating the Layout

As you learned in Chapter 6, the dynamic flow and pagination work differently in HTML forms. PDF forms will paginate based on the page size setting, but since an HTML form can be any length, your Designer HTML form will continue to expand lower on the same page and won't paginate to a subsequent page (**Figure 8.8**).

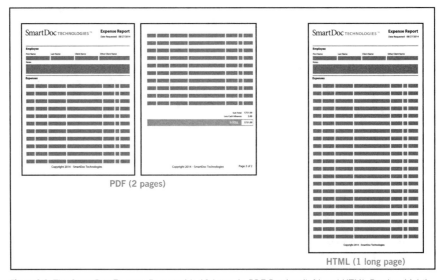

Figure 8.8 The SmartDoc Expense Report with 40 items in PDF Preview (left) and HTML Preview (right).

Follow these steps to analyze and correct the layout issues so that the form will render properly as a paginated PDF or a single-page HTML form:

1. Select the Preview HTML tab.

2. Click the Add Expense button to add 20 new expense rows. You'll eventually see the rows overlap with the footer of the page.

3. Select the Master Pages tab to update your layout.

4. Select copyrightFooter on the masterPage1 subform.

5. Select the Layout tab of the Object palette and update the Y coordinate to be **10.5625** inches.

6. Select the copyrightFooter field on the masterPage2 subform.

7. Select the Layout tab of the Object palette and update the Y coordinate to be **10.5625** inches.

8. Select the pages field on the masterPage2 subform.

9. Select the Layout tab of the Object palette and update the Y coordinate to be **10.5625** inches.

10. Save your file as **myExpenseReportHTML_4.xdp**.

You've successfully moved all the master page items away from the contentArea object. Doing so eliminates the overlapping issue in your HTML form. It's best to not put master page items in or have them touch the contentArea object.

TIP If you had difficulty with the exercises in this section, you can compare your form to the expenseReportHTML_4.xdp file in your Samples folder.

Dynamic Signature Fields

Since you're following a One Master File Strategy, you need to dynamically show the appropriate signature field object for your PDF and HTML forms. You can accomplish this by updating your form in the following ways:

- Adding a Signature Scribble object to your signature subform. This will support the HTML form, and the existing Signature Field object will support the PDF form.

- Adding a host detection script on the calculate event of the flag object on the signature subform to show the appropriate signature field based on the viewer application.

Follow these steps to update your form:

1. Expand the signature subform so there's room below the employeeSignature field for the new Signature Scribble object.

2. Drag and drop a Signature Scribble object from the Standard Object Library to the signature subform and place it below the current employeeSignature field.

3. Rename the Signature Scribble object **employeeSignatureScribble**.

4. Select the Layout tab of the Object palette and update the Width to **4** inches and the Height to **0.5** inches. You can make further design updates as you see fit to match the employeeSignature field.

5. Select the Field tab of the Object palette and update the caption to **Employee Signature Scribble**.

6. Select the signature subform. Change the Content property to Flowed in the Subform tab of the Object palette.

7. Drag and drop a Text Field object from the Standard Object Library to the signature subform.

8. Rename the Text Field **signatureFlag**.

9. Expand the Script Editor and select the calculate event.

10. Enter this script to detect the host:

```
if(xfa.host.appType == "HTML 5")

{

  expenseReport.page1.signature.employeeSignatureScribble.presence =
  ➥ "visible";

  expenseReport.page1.signature.employeeSignature.presence =
  ➥ "hidden";

}else

{

  expenseReport.page1.signature.employeeSignatureScribble.presence =
  ➥ "hidden";

  expenseReport.page1.signature.employeeSignature.presence =
  ➥ "visible";

}
```

11. With the signatureFlag field selected, click the Field tab of the Object palette.

12. Set the Presence property to Hidden (Exclude From Layout).

13. Select Preview HTML and you'll see the Signature Scribble object.

14. Select Preview PDF and you'll see the Signature Field object.

15. Save your file as **myExpenseReportHTML_5.xdp**.

TIP If you had difficulty with the exercises in this section, you can compare your form to the expenseReportHTML_5.xdp file in your Samples folder.

Your SmartDoc Expense Report will now look and function well as either a PDF or an HTML form. In the next section, you'll create an HTML form from scratch with Designer.

Creating the Address Change Form

In this exercise, you'll create a form to be rendered specifically as an HTML form for a mobile user with a tablet. In the next chapter, you will see an example of a document generation service that uses a companion form to generate the address change summary document. This is an example of a Multiple Master File Strategy, where you create a set containing more than one master file. Both master files will be bound to the same XML Schema, so they'll be related even though they'll look unique and serve different purposes for the user.

To help you along, I've included six master XDP files in the Samples folder that represent the completed results of each part of the exercise (**Figure 8.9**). If you find parts of this exercise to be formidable, compare your results to the step-by-step sample files. If you struggle with a step in the process, begin the next step with one of the completed files so you can continue the exercise.

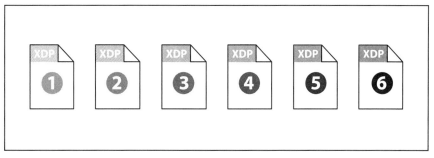

Figure 8.9 The Address Change exercise is saved as a series of steps and separate XDP files in your Samples folder.

Creating the Subforms

In this section, you'll create the form background and the individual subform. If this were a PDF form, you'd likely create the form background on a master page. However, since you're creating an HTML form, you'll create the background on the body page (page1). Doing so will enable you to change the color of the background with a CSS (Cascading Style Sheet) file later in the chapter.

The form background

1. Open the addressChange_Start.xdp file. This form has a layout width of 7.125 inches and a layout height of 5.3125, which makes it ideal for the Apple iPad.

2. Select page1 in the Hierarchy palette and highlight the Border palette on the right.

3. Click the Background Fill Style drop-down list and select Linear – To Bottom.

4. Click the Fill Color (Start) drop-down list and select More Colors.

5. Click Define Custom Colors.

6. Enter RGB (Red – Green – Blue) values of **0, 124, 194** in the individual fields. Click Add To Custom Colors. You'll see the Blue color in your Custom colors palette.

7. Enter the other colors (see **Table 8.1**) in the same way.

Table 8.1 Color Palette

COLOR NAME	RGB COLORS
Dark Blue	0, 78, 195
Light Blue	227, 234, 246
Dark Gray	70, 70, 70
Light Gray	125, 125, 125

8. Select your custom Blue, the first color you entered, and click OK.

9. Click the Fill Color (End) drop-down list and select More Colors.

10. Select your Dark Blue and click OK.

11. Drag and drop the addressChangeHeader object from the SmartDoc Object Library to the upper left of your form. Your Layout palette should show that your AnchorX and AnchorY values are both 0.25in.

The individual subform

12. Right-click page1 in the Hierarchy palette and select Insert Subform. Name this subform **individual**.

13. Select the Layout palette and update the following properties of the individual subform: AnchorX = **0.25** inches, AnchorY = **2.0625** inches, Width = **6.625** inches, and Height = **1.9375** inches.

14. Select the Border palette and update the following properties of the individual subform: Edges = Edit Together, Border drop-down = Solid, Border Width = **0.0069** inches, Border Color = **RGB(225,225,225)**, Corners = **Round corner**, Radius = **0.15** inches, Background Fill Style = **Solid**, and Background Fill Color = **RGB(225,225,225)**.

15. Right-click on individual in the Hierarchy palette and select Insert Subform. Name this subform **oldAddress**.

16. Select the Layout palette and update the following properties of the oldAddress subform: AnchorX = **0.25** inches, AnchorY = **2.0625** inches, Width = **3.3125** inches, Height = **1.9375** inches, Left Margin = **0.125** inches, Top Margin = **0.125** inches, Right Margin = **0.125** inches, and Bottom Margin = **0.125** inches.

17. Drag and drop the following form objects from your SmartDoc Object Library to the oldAddress subform: one arrow, one sectionHeader, five addressChangeFields, and one addressChangeState. These objects all use the Arial font, so your forms will display correctly on your users' machines.

18. Double-click the sectionHeader object and enter **Old Address** as the section header copy.

19. Enter the names and captions shown in **Table 8.2** for the remaining form objects. You can change the caption properties in the Field tab of the Object palette.

Table 8.2 Form Object Names and Captions (oldAddress Subform)

FORM OBJECT	NAME IN HIERARCHY	CAPTION
arrow	arrow	none
sectionHeader	oldAddressHeader	none
addressChangeField	firstName	First Name
addressChangeField	lastName	Last Name
addressChangeField	address	Address
addressChangeField	city	City
addressChangeField	zipCode	Zip Code
addressChangeState	state	State

20. Arrange the form objects in the oldAddress subform to match **Figure 8.10**.

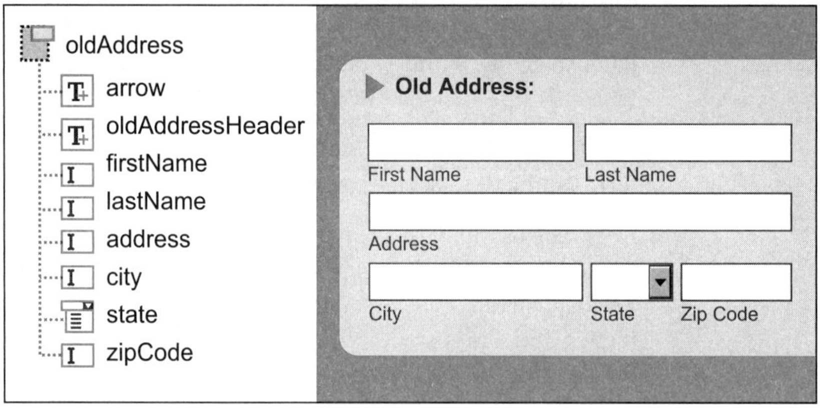

Figure 8.10 The oldAddress subform showing the form objects with their proper names in the hierarchy (left) and their proper positions in the layout (right).

21. Select the oldAddress subform in the hierarchy and select Edit > Duplicate to add oldAddress[1] to the individual subform. Rename the newly created subform **newAddress**.

22. Select the Layout palette and update the following properties of the newAddress subform: AnchorX = **3.5625** inches, AnchorY = **2.0625** inches, Width = **3.3125** inches, Height = **1.9375** inches, Left Margin = **0.125** inches, Top Margin = **0.125** inches, Right Margin = **0.125** inches, and Bottom Margin = **0.125** inches.

23. Select oldAddressHeader within the newAddress subform and rename it **newAddressHeader**.

24. Change the newAddressHeader text to **New Address**.

25. Save your file as **myAddressChange_1.xdp**.

TIP If you had difficulty with the exercises in this section, you can compare your form to the addressChange_1.xdp file in your Samples folder.

You've finished the layout for the individual subform. You'll now use this subform as the basis for the family and business subforms.

The business and family subforms

26. Select the individual subform in the hierarchy and select Edit > Duplicate to add individual[1] to page1. Rename the newly created subform **business**.

27. Select the individual subform in the hierarchy and highlight the Subform panel on the Object palette.

28. Set the Presence property to Hidden (Exclude From Layout).

29. Select the Layout palette and update the following properties of the business subform: AnchorX = **0.25** inches, AnchorY = **2.0625** inches, Width = **6.625** inches, and Height = **1.9375** inches.

30. Delete the lastName objects from the oldAddress and newAddress subforms on the business subform.

31. Rename the firstName object on the oldAddress subform to **businessName**.

32. Update the caption of the businessName object to **Business Name**.

33. Repeat the last two steps for the newAddress subform on the business subform.

34. Arrange the form objects to match the layout in **Figure 8.11**.

Figure 8.11 The business oldAddress subform showing the form objects with their proper names in the Hierarchy (left) and their proper positions in the layout (right).

35. Select the business subform in the Hierarchy palette and highlight the Subform panel on the Object palette.

36. Set the Presence property to Hidden (Exclude From Layout).

37. Select the individual subform in the hierarchy and highlight the Subform panel on the Object palette.

38. Set the Presence property to Visible.

39. Select the individual subform in the Hierarchy palette and select Edit > Duplicate to add individual[1] to page1. Rename the newly created subform **family**.

40. Select the individual subform in the hierarchy and highlight the Subform panel on the Object palette.

41. Set the Presence property to Hidden (Exclude From Layout).

42. Select the Layout palette and update the following properties of the family subform: AnchorX = **0.25** inches, AnchorY = **2.0625** inches, Width = **6.625** inches, and Height = **1.9375** inches.

43. Drag and drop a sectionHeader object from the SmartDoc Custom Object library to the oldAddress subform on the family subform.

44. Rename this object **headOfHousehold**.

45. Change the headOfHousehold text to **For the Head of the Household**.

46. Select the Font palette and remove the bold style and add an italic style.

47. Repeat steps 43 to 46 for the newAddress subform on the family subform.

48. Arrange the form objects to match the layout in **Figure 8.12**.

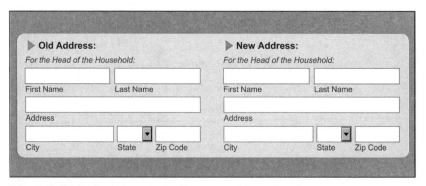

Figure 8.12 The family subform showing the new headOfHousehold Text object.

49. Save your file as **myAddressChange_2.xdp**.

TIP If you had difficulty with the exercises in this section, you can compare your form to the addressChange_2.xdp file in your Samples folder.

The approval subform

The approval has an email address, a signature field, and a submit button. Follow these steps to learn more about this subform:

50. Drag and drop the approvalSection object from the SmartDoc Object Library to the bottom of your form (**Figure 8.13**).

51. Select the Layout palette and update the following properties of the approval subform: AnchorX = **0.25** inches and AnchorY = **4.125** inches.

52. Select the signature field in the Hierarchy palette. This is the new Adobe Scribble Signature form object.

53. Select the validateButton object in the Hierarchy palette.

54. Expand the Script Editor and select the click event. The script calls a method in a script object that you'll add later in the exercise. You could also add your data submission script here. For instance, you can call the execute method of an HTTPSubmitButton with this script.

    ```
    HTTPSubmitButton.execEvent("click");
    ```

55. Save your file as **myAddressChange_3.xdp**.

Figure 8.13 The approval subform with Adobe's new Signature Scribble form object.

TIP If you had difficulty with the exercises in this section, you can compare your form to the addressChange_3.xdp file in your Samples folder.

Creating a Data Connection

After you've finished styling your form, you can bind the fields to the schema by following these steps. You'll use a combination of absolute binding for the parent subform and relative binding for the child form fields.

1. Choose File > New Data Connection to launch the New Data Connection wizard.

2. Enter **addressChange** for the name of your connection, select the XML Schema option, and click Next.

3. Browse to addressChange.xsd in the Samples folder. Ensure that address-Change is the root element.

4. Select the Embed XML Schema option. Click Finish to create your connection.

5. Click Yes in the pop-up message that asks if you want to clear the Use Name data bindings. You'll now see your data connection in the Data View palette on the left.

6. Click the Hierarchy palette and select the typeOfMove object in the header subform.

7. Click the Binding tab of the Object palette and select the Data Binding drop-down list (**Figure 8.14**). Select Use "addressChange" > typeOfMove to bind the field to the typeOfMove node in the schema. The Binding Properties dialog box will appear.

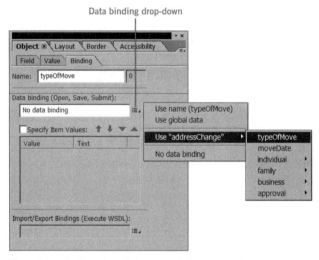

Figure 8.14 Binding a form field to a node in the XML Schema.

8. Select Don't Update Any Related Properties and click OK. The Data Binding field will update with the value of $.typeOfMove to indicate your binding is successful.

9. Repeat steps 6 through 8 and bind these fields to their corresponding schema nodes:

   ▪ **startChangeDate:** $.moveDate

   ▪ **individual:** $.individual

   ▪ **individual.oldAddress:** $.oldAddress

   ▪ **individual.oldAddress.firstName:** $record.individual.firstName

   ▪ **individual.oldAddress.lastName:** $record.individual.lastName

- **individual.oldAddress.address:** $.address
- **individual.oldAddress.city:** $.city
- **individual.oldAddress.state:** $.state
- **individual.oldAddress.zip:** $.zip
- **individual.newAddress:** $.newAddress
- **individual.newAddress.firstName:** $record.individual.firstName
- **individual.newAddress.lastName:** $record.individual.lastName
- **individual.newAddress.address:** $.address
- **individual.newAddress.city:** $.city
- **individual.newAddress.state:** $.state
- **individual.newAddress.zip:** $.zip

10. Use the same technique to bind the fields in the family subform to the appropriate nodes in the schema.

- **family:** $.family
- **family.oldAddress:** $.oldAddress
- **family.oldAddress.firstName:** $record. family.headOfHouseholdFirstName
- **family.oldAddress.lastName:** $record. family.headOfHouseholdLastName
- **family.oldAddress.address:** $.address
- **family.oldAddress.city:** $.city
- **family.oldAddress.state:** $.state
- **family.oldAddress.zip:** $.zip
- **family.newAddress:** $.newAddress
- **family.newAddress.firstName:** $record. family.headOfHouseholdFirstName
- **family.newAddress.lastName:** $record. family.headOfHouseholdLastName
- **family.newAddress.address:** $.address
- **family.newAddress.city:** $.city
- **family.newAddress.state:** $.state
- **family.newAddress.zip:** $.zip

11. Use the same technique to bind the fields in the business subform to the appropriate nodes in the schema.

   ■ **business:** $.business

   ■ **business.oldAddress:** $.oldAddress

   ■ **business.oldAddress.businessName:** $record.business.businessName

   ■ **business.oldAddress.address:** $.address

   ■ **business.oldAddress.city:** $.city

   ■ **business.oldAddress.state:** $.state

   ■ **business.oldAddress.zip:** $.zip

   ■ **business.newAddress:** $.newAddress

   ■ **business.newAddress.businessName:** $record.business.businessName

   ■ **business.newAddress.address:** $.address

   ■ **business.newAddress.city:** $.city

   ■ **business.newAddress.state:** $.state

   ■ **business.newAddress.zip:** $.zip

12. The final field to bind is the emailAddress on the approval subform.

   ■ **approval:** $.approval

   ■ **emailAddress:** $.emailAddress

13. Save your file as **myAddressChange_4.xdp.**

TIP If you had difficulty with the exercises in this section, you can compare your form to the addressChange_4.xdp file in your Samples folder.

Creating a Dynamic Subform

You've created three different subforms and bound their form fields to your XML Schema. In this exercise, you'll add script to dynamically show the appropriate subform based on the user's selection. Follow these steps to add script to the change event of the typeOfMove object:

1. Select the typeOfMove Drop-down object and expand the Script Editor.

2. Select the change event and enter this code:

```
if(typeOfMove.rawValue == "An Individual"){


  type.txtIndividual.presence = "visible";
  type.txtFamily.presence = "hidden";
  type.txtBusiness.presence = "hidden";
  page1.individual.presence = "visible";
  page1.family.presence = "hidden";
  page1.business.presence = "hidden";


}else if(typeOfMove.rawValue == "A Family"){


  type.txtIndividual.presence = "hidden";
  type.txtFamily.presence = "visible";
  type.txtBusiness.presence = "hidden";
  page1.individual.presence = "hidden";
  page1.family.presence = "visible";
  page1.business.presence = "hidden";


}else if(typeOfMove.rawValue == "A Business"){


  type.txtIndividual.presence = "hidden";
  type.txtFamily.presence = "hidden";
  type.txtBusiness.presence = "visible";
  page1.individual.presence = "hidden";
  page1.family.presence = "hidden";
  page1.business.presence = "visible";
}
```

3. Make sure JavaScript is selected as the Language and Client is selected as the Run At property.

When a user clicks the typeOfMove object at runtime and makes a change, the change event is fired. The script will evaluate the rawValue property of the typeOfMove object and display the appropriate text and subform for the user.

4. Save your file as **myAddressChange_5.xdp**.

TIP If you had difficulty with the exercises in this section, you can compare your form to the addressChange_5.xdp file in your Samples folder.

Creating the Scripts and the Script Object

You'll add a script object to your form in this exercise. This will be similar to the script objects you added to your PDF forms in Part 2, "PDF Forms." However, since you're creating an HTML form, you need to use the form properties that are supported in HTML forms. Previously, your validation script highlighted the background of a text field in yellow to indicate missing information. Since you're using HTML forms, you now need to outline the text field to provide a similar indication to the user. This outline is typically done with red, but we will use blue in this exercise for illustration purposes. This section shows you how to create the script object.

Creating the script object

Open the addressChangeCompleted.xdp file from the Samples folder along with your working file and follow these steps to create a script object on your working file:

1. Select the topmost node (addressChange) of your form in the Hierarchy palette.

2. Right-click this node and choose Insert Script Object. Designer inserts a script object at the bottom of your form hierarchy.

3. Right-click this new script object and select Rename Object. Enter **validation** as the new name.

4. Select Window > addressChangeCompleted.xdp to switch to the completed file.

5. Select the validation script object at the bottom of the Hierarchy palette and expand the Script Editor. Click the Show Events drop-down list and select `All Events`.

6. Select all the JavaScript in this script object and be sure to select only the JavaScript below this comment line:

    `// Copy all the JavaScript below this line.`

7. Right-click and select Copy.

8. Select Window and switch back to your working file.

9. Select the validation script object at the bottom of the Hierarchy palette and expand the Script Editor.

10. Right-click in the Script Editor and select Paste to put all the JavaScript into your script object.

Your script object now has various functions to validate your form data. The following list matches a validation goal with the function to call:

▪ To validate required fields, call `function requiredFields()`

▪ To validate zip codes, call `function USZipCode(fld, type)`

▪ To validate email addresses, call `function email(fld)`

You'll call these functions in the next exercise.

Referencing functions in script objects

Once the functions are defined in your script object, it's easy to call them from your form object. In this exercise, you'll provide form field validation for the zipCode and emailAddress fields. You'll also add form validation for all required fields.

11. Select the zipCode object in the individual > oldAddress subform.

12. Expand the Script Editor and select the `exit` event in the Show Events drop-down list.

13. Enter this script in the Script Editor:

    `validation.USZipCode(this,0);`

14. Repeat steps 12 and 13 for all zip code fields on the form.

15. Select the emailAddress object in the approval subform.

16. Expand the Script Editor and select the `exit` event in the Show Events drop-down list.

17. Enter this script in the Script Editor:

```
validation.email(this);
```

18. Select the validateButton object in your approval subform.

19. Expand the Script Editor and select the `click` event in the Show Events drop-down list.

20. Review this script in the Script Editor:

```
if(validation.requiredFields()){


    xfa.host.messageBox("Your form data will now be submitted.",
    ➥ "Data Submit", 1,0);


    // HTTPSubmitButton.execEvent("click");
}
```

The required fields form validation is called when the user clicks the Submit button. The first line of this script calls the `validation.requiredFields()` function. If data is missing, the script within the script object will outline the fields in blue (**Figure 8.15**) and the remainder of the script in the `click` event of validateButton will be ignored.

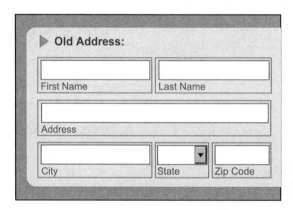

Figure 8.15 Required fields will be outlined if their data is missing.

If there's no missing data, the `validation.requiredFields()` method evaluates to true and the script block that follows this call will execute. In this case, a simple message box is shown to the user. In a production form, you could also put code here to submit the form's data.

21. Save your file as **myAddressChange_6.xdp**.

TIP If you had difficulty with the exercises in this section, you can compare your form to the addressChangeCompleted.xdp file in your Samples folder.

Testing Your Form

Now that you've finished developing these features, you can test them by following these steps:

1. Open the addressChangeCompleted.xdp form or your myAddress-Change_6.xdp form.

2. Select Preview HTML.

3. Before filling out any information, click the Submit button at the bottom of the form. Since you have required fields that are missing data, you'll see a warning message (**Figure 8.16**).

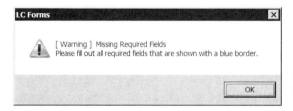

Figure 8.16 The Missing Required Fields warning message.

4. Click OK. Your required fields with missing data will be outlined in blue.

5. Select a date by clicking the date field in the header subform.

6. Enter your first name and last name in the Old Address section. Notice that these values cross-fill to the New Address section. This works because you bound both first name fields to the same schema node and both last name fields to the same schema node.

7. Complete the remainder of the form.

8. Click the Submit button. You'll see a message box indicating that all required fields are complete and the form submission will be called. Please note: If you don't have a LiveCycle Server and if you haven't properly configured the URLs in the submit buttons of the approval form, there will be no actual data submission.

NOTE The script object uses the xfa.host.setFocus method. As of this writing, this method wasn't supported for date fields in HTML forms.

Using CSS

As you learned in previous chapters, you can modify the appearance of your form elements with CSS. Follow these steps to see an example:

1. Open the addressChangeCompleted.xdp form or your myAddressChange_6.xdp form in Designer.

2. Select the page1 object in the Hierarchy palette and select the Border palette.

3. Change the Background Fill property to None. You must make this change so the background color can be assigned with the CSS file.

4. Select Tools > Options > Server Options.

5. Change the HTML Preview Context from the default.html file to **blackTheme.html**. Here's the entire line:

   lc/content/xfaforms/profiles/blackTheme.html

6. Click OK to save your new setting.

7. Select Preview HTML to see how your form looks with these new colors. You'll now see light gray subforms on a black background (**Figure 8.17**).

Figure 8.17 You can use CSS to control the color of your HTML forms.

NOTE If you have issues with this exercise, make sure you are using the most current version of LiveCycle Designer ES4.

In addition to the background colors, the following other items are customized by the Cascading Style Sheet.

■ The value font color for the Text Field objects is set to black.

■ The Text Field objects have a rounded corner.

■ The Text Field objects have a thick gray underline.

■ **Figure 8.18** shows a detailed view of these items on your HTML form.

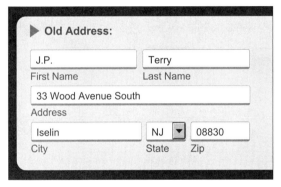

Figure 8.18 The Text Field objects are customized with rounded corners and a thick gray underline.

NOTE After you finish this example, you should change the HTML Preview Context back to the default profile. The complete path is lc/content/xfaforms/profiles/default.html.

If you have a LiveCycle Server, you can also use Mobile Forms IVS to preview your forms with CSS.

Using Mobile Forms IVS

As you learned in Chapter 6, the Mobile Forms IVS application is an easy-to-use tool that enables you to preview your forms in various browsers. If you have a LiveCycle Server with this capability, you can test your HTML form and Cascading Style Sheet across the different browsers of your client base. Follow these steps to learn how:

1. Open your web browser and navigate to your Mobile Forms IVS application on your LiveCycle Server. The following is a sample URL:

```
http://<server address>:8080/mobileformsivs
```

2. Click the Browse button in Step 1 and locate the addressChangeCompleted.xdp file. Click OK to close the Choose File To Upload dialog box.

3. Click the Upload File & List Existing Forms button to upload the XDP to your LiveCycle Server. You'll see your form in the Forms list box in the Step 2 screen.

4. With your form selected, click Custom in the Profile drop-down list.

5. Enter the name of your Cascading Style Sheet in the text field to the right. **Figure 8.19** shows a reference to a Cascading Style Sheet titled blackTheme.

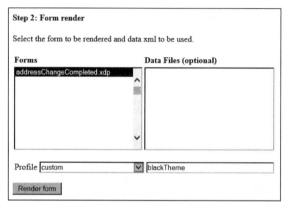

Figure 8.19 Step 2 of the Mobile Forms IVS application enables you to specify a custom Cascading Style Sheet for your HTML form preview.

6. Click Render Form. A new browser window will open with the addressChangeCompleted form rendered using the blacktheme.

You can make more colorful profiles. We used the simple blue and black examples to match the two printing colors of this book.

Moving On

You've now mastered the Designer tool and learned all the details of PDF and HTML forms. The last part of the book, Part 4, "Automating Business," will show you how to use your forms and documents to automate your business and streamline your organization's workflow.

Automating Business

Now that you've learned how to develop forms, you'll see how these forms can be integrated with your enterprise systems and workflows. This last part of the book shows how your forms and documents will be used to automate your business or organization.

CHAPTER 9: LiveCycle Enterprise Suite

CHAPTER 10: Going Mobile

9

LiveCycle Enterprise Suite

The first rule of any technology used in a business is that automation applied to an efficient operation will magnify the efficiency. The second is that automation applied to an inefficient operation will magnify the inefficiency.

—Bill Gates

Although the focus of this book is LiveCycle Designer, it's important for all form developers to know about the LiveCycle Server products. As mentioned in the introduction, Adobe offers many important and complementary LiveCycle products and services as *LiveCycle Enterprise Suite*. These products and services can be used to achieve all the following goals:

- Integrating your Designer forms and documents with your enterprise systems and databases

- Automating and streamlining your form-based workflows

- Facilitating a transition from a manual paper-based process to an automated paperless process with automatic document processing and generation

Introduction

LiveCycle Enterprise Suite (ES) is a Java J2EE-based server software system that runs on most major J2EE application servers and most major server operating systems. LiveCycle ES is designed to seamlessly integrate with existing enterprise systems, including directories, databases, document management systems, and email servers. LiveCycle implements a service-oriented architecture and provides its functionality through loosely coupled services.

The LiveCycle suite is organized into three major parts: the foundation, the solution components, and the development tools (**Figure 9.1**).

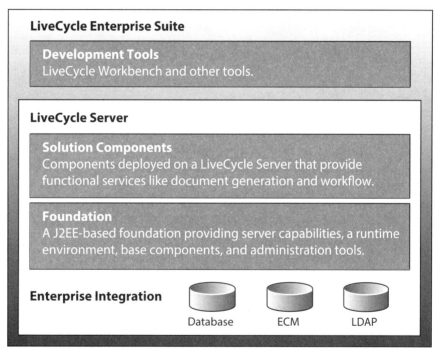

Figure 9.1 The three major components of LiveCycle ES.

Foundation

The foundation contains the required server functionality for the solution components and applications and is provided with all licensed configurations of LiveCycle ES. The major parts of the foundation are the common runtime environment, the base components, and the administration tools.

Common runtime environment

The common runtime environment is used by all LiveCycle modules and applications to support these activities:

- Process coordination and service management to link solution components into a process.

- User management to create a database of users or to integrate with an existing LDAP (Lightweight Directory Access Protocol) system such as Microsoft Active Directory. LiveCycle's user management provides authentication and authorization services for the LiveCycle solutions that you develop.

- Event management to use events during the design and development phase and in your workflow process at runtime. LiveCycle ES supports asynchronous events, exception events, and timer events.

Base components

Multiple base components are included in the LiveCycle foundation. These components make it easy to integrate your LiveCycle applications with your existing IT infrastructure. The following are a few of the base components that provide services for your LiveCycle applications:

- An LDAP component to query your LDAP server

- An Email component to integrate with an email server

- An FTP (File Transfer Protocol) component to integrate with an FTP server

- A JDBC (Java Database Connectivity) component to integrate with a database

- File Utility components to read and write files and organize the storage of your files

Administration tools

The third major section of the foundation is the administration tools. You can access these tools with the LiveCycle Administration Console—a web-based application that enables you to configure and manage many aspects of your LiveCycle system and applications (**Figure 9.2**).

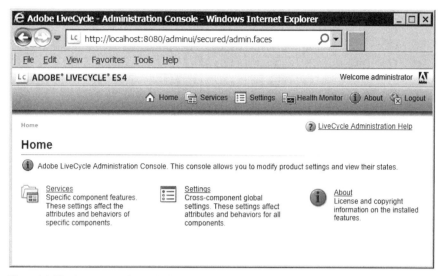

Figure 9.2 The home page of the LiveCycle Administration Console can be accessed with a web browser.

The Administration Console includes

■ Administration tools for the major Adobe Solutions components.

■ Configuration tools for user groups, roles, and permissions.

■ Configuration and deployment tools for applications.

■ Configuration tools for process and service endpoints.

■ Administration tools for installation and configuration of LiveCycle archive files.

■ Troubleshooting tools for monitoring processes and solving problems. For instance, you can use these tools to retry or terminate a stalled process.

Solution Components

Solution components provide the server-side functionality that you'll use in your LiveCycle applications. Solution components include one or more services that perform business tasks related to the component. Services expose their functionality through operations. You can drag these operations onto your process diagram in LiveCycle Workbench, and these operations will be included in your process. LiveCycle Workbench is described in "Development Tools."

Because these solution components and services are modular, you can combine them in many ways to provide the server-based functionality of your LiveCycle application. You can purchase solution components from Adobe or develop your own.

Adobe solution components

Depending on your needs, you can buy one or more solution components. **Figure 9.3** shows the Reader Extensions solution component with its services and operations.

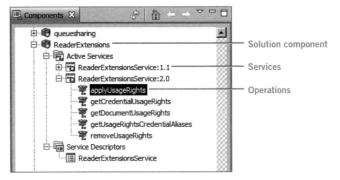

Figure 9.3 The Reader Extensions solution component, as shown in Workbench.

Adobe markets their solution components as *modules*. The following is a short list of popular Adobe LiveCycle modules that you can license for your enterprise:

- Adobe LiveCycle Forms Standard and Pro
- Adobe LiveCycle Reader Extensions
- Adobe LiveCycle Process Management
- Adobe LiveCycle Output
- Adobe LiveCycle PDF Generator
- Adobe LiveCycle Rights Management
- Adobe LiveCycle Digital Signatures
- Adobe LiveCycle ECM Connectors

NOTE Adobe offers optimized packages of modules along with their industry-leading AEM (Adobe Experience Manager) software. One package is called AEM document services, and it includes LiveCycle Forms Pro, Reader Extensions, and PDF Generator. Another package is called AEM document security, and it includes LiveCycle Rights Management.

Custom solution components

You can also develop your own LiveCycle solution components with Java. These components can be deployed to the LiveCycle runtime environment and accessed as services just like standard Adobe components. You may want to develop a custom component to integrate standard LiveCycle components with the specific requirements of your environment. You may also want to develop a custom component to provide a common service that is not provided by the standard Adobe modules. For instance, my company once developed a component for a client that read Microsoft Word and Excel files to integrate their contents with Adobe LiveCycle document generation. There is more information about developing custom components on the book's companion site.

Development Tools

You can call LiveCycle services from many different types of applications, including Microsoft.NET and Java applications. Adobe also provides an integrated LiveCycle development environment called LiveCycle Workbench.

Workbench is an Eclipse-based IDE (integrated development environment) that enables developers to create LiveCycle applications. It includes an integrated repository for collaborative development and simplifies deployment via an archive file that contains all the assets associated with the application. Workbench provides a visual process design environment that enables you to drag and drop services from the Adobe modules and set their properties using palettes and dialog boxes. There are also process development tools that enable you to combine these services into a new process (**Figure 9.4**). Once your process is complete, you can easily deploy it to your LiveCycle Server as a service.

Workbench runs on a local Windows-based computer. However, to run Workbench, you need access to a LiveCycle Server. You'll be asked to connect to a server when you log in to Workbench.

In addition to Workbench, Adobe provides the LiveCycle SDK (Software Developer Kit) and the SDK help system. LiveCycle Designer is also considered a development tool that's part of the LiveCycle Enterprise Suite.

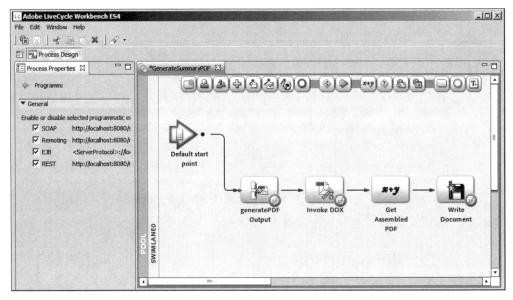

Figure 9.4 LiveCycle Workbench showing the LiveCycle process that is described later in this chapter (right) and the endpoints for the process (left).

Endpoints

LiveCycle Server supports many endpoints for your services. You already saw a few examples of LiveCycle service endpoints when you configured your forms to submit data to a LiveCycle service. Enterprise applications can interact with your LiveCycle services through any of these endpoints:

- **SOAP:** A SOAP (Simple Object Access Protocol) endpoint enables your service to be called as a web service.

- **Remoting:** A Remoting endpoint enables your service to be called from an Adobe Flex application.

- **EJB:** An EJB endpoint enables your service to be called from a Java application, and this method is estimated to be 30 percent more efficient than using web services.

- **REST:** A REST (Representational State Transfer) endpoint enables your service to be called directly from a web page, an HTML form, or a PDF form. This is the endpoint you used in the previous chapters to submit your form data. REST uses the HTTP protocol and has many similarities with web services.

You can get the complete URL for your LiveCycle service endpoint in the LiveCycle Workbench application (Figure 9.4). Double-click the start point icon in your process diagram and the URLs for the endpoints will appear in the Process Properties panel. These are the endpoints that Workbench creates automatically for your service. You can also add the following endpoints to your service:

- **Watched Folder:** A Watched Folder endpoint enables your service to be invoked when a file is dropped into a watched folder.

- **Email:** An Email endpoint enables your service to be invoked by an email message.

- **Task Manager:** A Task Manager endpoint enables your service to be invoked by a user of the Adobe Workspace application.

Document Generation

You can use the services provided by the LiveCycle modules to develop an automated document generation process. This process will use a REST endpoint to receive data from the Address Change form you created in Chapter 8, "Creating HTML Forms." It will be a simple process because it leverages the functionality in LiveCycle's Output and Assembler Services. **Figure 9.5** shows how this process will generate a custom PDF document when a user completes the Address Change form.

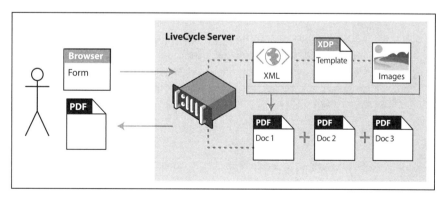

Figure 9.5 This process leverages LiveCycle's Output, Assembler, and foundation services to create a custom PDF that documents the user's address change.

The document that's generated is customized for the user and is a composite of the following documents:

■ **Doc 1:** The first document is a one-page PDF file that contains the user's personal address change information. This document is created by the LiveCycle Output service by merging the XML data with an XDP template and images. The rendered file is a flattened PDF file. LiveCycle Output is an example of a LiveCycle solution component that you can license from Adobe.

■ **Doc 2:** The second document is a two-page PDF file that contains a helpful Moving Checklist to assist the user with the planning of their address change.

■ **Doc 3:** The third document is a four-page PDF file that contains energy savings information for a new homeowner.

These three documents are assembled by the LiveCycle Assembler service into one composite PDF file. Assembler is another LiveCycle solution component that you can license from Adobe. The LiveCycle process that generates this new document is represented by the process diagram in **Figure 9.6**.

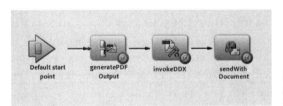

Figure 9.6 You can create process diagrams with LiveCycle Workbench.

Each of the four steps in the process is represented by an icon. The process starts with the Default start point and moves sequentially through each step until the PDF is emailed to the user in the last step. Let's examine each step further.

The Start Point

This is the REST endpoint of the process. You configured your Address Change form to submit data to this endpoint. It's called a start point because your process will start when this endpoint receives an XML data submission. The XML will be saved as an input variable named inputData. The REST endpoint URL will follow this format:

http://server_name:8080/rest/services/[ServiceName]/[Operation]:[version]

Generate PDF Output

The next step in the process is to generate the customized summary page. The generatePDFOutput activity will call the LiveCycle Output service with the following two parameters:

- The inputData process variable

- A reference to the addressChangeSummary.xdp file

The LiveCycle Output service will generate a one-page PDF file with the user's address change information. Although a flattened PDF is generated, address-ChangeSummary.xdp is a dynamic template. It will show or hide the subforms that are relevant for the user based on the XML data submission. For instance, if the user completed an address change for a business, the business-related subforms and information will be rendered on this PDF.

Invoke DDX

The next step in the process is to assemble the customized summary PDF with the supporting documents. The invokeDDX activity will call the LiveCycle Assembler service with the following two parameters:

- A reference to the DDX (Document Description XML) file

- An Input Document Map with references to the three PDF files to assemble

The DDX file provides instructions to LiveCycle Assembler and is listed here:

```
<DDX xmlns="http://ns.adobe.com/DDX/1.0/">

   <PDF result="resultPDF">

     <PDF source="summaryPDF"/>

     <PDF source="printPDF1"/>

     <PDF source="printPDF2"/>

   </PDF>

   <?ddx-source-hint name="summaryPDF"?>

   <?ddx-source-hint name="printPDF1"?>

   <?ddx-source-hint name="printPDF2"?>

</DDX>
```

The Input Document Map provides references to the source documents as listed here:

```
summaryPDF = /process_data/@outputPDF
```

```
printPDF1 = /process_data/@movingChecklist
```

```
printPDF2 = /process_data/@energySavers
```

You can also use DDX to add page numbering to your composite document. Using this approach, as opposed to page numbering at the individual document level, offers the following advantages:

- You can number the entire composite document from beginning to end.

- The location, size, and font style of your page numbering will be consistent even when many different source documents are used in the assembly.

The following is a DDX example that creates page numbering in the footer of the assembled document:

```
<Footer>
  <Center>
    <StyledText>
      <p font-size="10pt" font-family="Arial" color="#000000">
        Page
        <_PageNumber/>
        of
        <_LastPageNumber/>
      </p>
    </StyledText>
  </Center>
</Footer>
```

Send with Document

The last step in the process sends an email with the attached composite PDF. The sendWithDocument service is part of the LiveCycle foundation, and it sends an email with a single attachment. The service is called with the following parameters:

■ An email address for the recipient

■ An email address for the sender

■ An email subject and message

■ The attachment name

■ A reference to the attachment file

The previous LiveCycle process example demonstrates how LiveCycle Enterprise Suite makes it easy to automate a document generation process to respond to a form submission. In the next section, you'll learn about other LiveCycle modules and tools to streamline enterprise form management.

Enterprise Form Management

Adobe offers a number of modules and tools to enable organizations to manage and deploy their forms, including the following:

■ **Adobe AEM and the Forms Portal:** Adobe is a leader in web content management, and its industry-leading software is called the Adobe Experience Manager (AEM). This web content management solution also delivers capabilities for digital asset management, dynamic media delivery, and social communities across all digital channels. AEM can be combined with Adobe's Forms Portal Solution and Adobe's LiveCycle Forms Pro ES4 to provide an easy-to-use forms portal for organizations.

■ **LiveCycle ECM Connectors ES4:** These LiveCycle modules enable you to connect your LiveCycle design assets and applications with enterprise content management systems, including Microsoft SharePoint, IBM FileNet, and the EMC Documentum ECM system.

■ **Adobe Forms Manager:** An easy-to-use web-based tool that enables organizations to deploy and manage their enterprise forms library.

Because Forms Manager comes packaged with LiveCycle Forms Pro ES4, this section will show you how to use it to manage and deploy your Designer forms.

Previously, LiveCycle forms were deployed and managed with Workbench. The new Forms Manager enables nonprogrammers to edit, deploy, and manage production form files, including XDPs, PDFs, and images. LiveCycle Forms Pro ES4 keeps everything synchronized by replicating data in the repositories that support Workbench and Forms Manager (**Figure 9.7**).

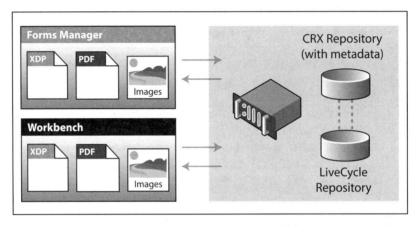

Figure 9.7 LiveCycle ES4 includes two ways to deploy and manage your forms: the traditional Workbench and the new Forms Manager.

If a Workbench user updates a form or related asset, Forms Manager is updated automatically. The reverse is also true. This enables you to streamline the management, reuse, and publishing of your form assets, including form fragments. Nonprogrammers can easily locate the correct form assets by browsing or searching the Forms Manager metadata.

All users can easily understand how form assets relate to one another. For instance, if you select a form fragment, Forms Manager will show you all the XDPs that currently use the fragment. **Figure 9.8** shows the Forms Manager tool in use at my company. We use the common header.xdp form fragment on three of our internal forms. We can look up the header.xdp fragment in our Forms Manager program and Forms Manager will display the three forms that are currently referencing this fragment.

Figure 9.8 Forms Manager enables you to easily see which forms are referencing a particular form fragment file. You can use the Download link to download an asset to your local machine for editing.

Using Forms Manager

If your company has LiveCycle Forms Pro ES4 or higher, you have Adobe's Forms Manager application. This easy-to-use tool enables you to download a form, edit it in Designer, and upload it to your production server. Follow these steps to learn how:

1. Open your web browser and navigate to Forms Manager on your LiveCycle Server. The following is an example URL:

   http://<server address>:8080/lc/fm

2. Log in as **administrator**. The password is likely **password** unless it has been changed on your server.

   The Forms Manager will display all LiveCycle applications that contain forms or image assets. If you do not have any LiveCycle applications, Forms Manager will display a *DefaultApplication* to get you started.

3. Double-click the application that contains the forms you want to edit. I'm using my internal SmartDoc application, but you can use any of the applications on your server.

4. Double-click the application version number. Forms Manager will display the XDP forms in your application (**Figure 9.9**).

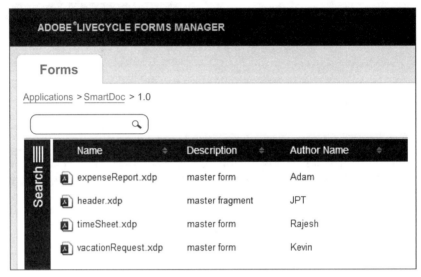

Figure 9.9 Forms Manager displays all the forms in a LiveCycle application along with important metadata associated with the form.

5. Double-click the form you want to edit. I'll edit the expenseReport.xdp form on my internal server. The form's detail page will appear.

6. Click the Download link on the left side (Figure 9.8). You'll see a Download Forms dialog box (**Figure 9.10**). Click Save to download a copy of the form to your local machine for editing.

Figure 9.10 You can download and save an XDP form to your local machine for updating. The path and filename for your file will be different than the pathname shown here.

7. Unzip the ZIP file that contains your XDP file.

8. Open the XDP file in Designer.

    You can now make the updates and corrections that you desire. These updates won't affect the form on your LiveCycle Server, because you're working on a copy of the form on your local machine. When you're finished with your edits, follow these steps to upload your new form to your LiveCycle Server.

9. Go back to Forms Manager and navigate to the parent folder of your forms.

10. Select the parent folder, and you'll see the Upload button in the upper right of the screen (**Figure 9.11**).

Figure 9.11 The Forms Manager Upload button.

11. Click the Upload button and the Upload Forms dialog box will appear. You can upload one XDP or a ZIP file containing multiple XDPs.

12. Click Browse to locate your updated XDP file on your local machine.

13. Click Upload to upload your XDP file to the server. The Uploading Assets dialog box will appear. This dialog box shows you which files will be added and which files will be overwritten.

14. Click Upload in the Uploading Assets dialog box.

15. Double-click the parent folder to view your forms.

16. Double-click the form you just uploaded. The form's detail page will appear.

17. Select Preview and the Preview Form dialog box will appear.

18. Select either HTML or PDF. I will select PDF for my expenseReport.xdp form.

    You can also browse for a sample XML data file for your preview.

19. Click the Preview button, and Forms Manager will preview your form in a new browser window (**Figure 9.12**). If you don't see your form, make sure your browser is not set to block pop-ups.

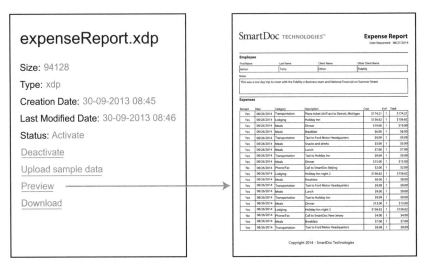

Figure 9.12 You can use Forms Manager to preview your forms in either HTML or PDF.

As you can see, Forms Manager can also be used to preview your forms with data. You can use Forms Manager to test your forms in different target browsers.

Moving On

You now understand how LiveCycle's server modules are used to automate your workflows and manage your enterprise forms. You also know how Forms Manager is used to manage hundreds or thousands of enterprise forms.

In the last chapter, you'll see how these tools and services are used to support mobile forms. You'll also compare and contrast the LiveCycle mobile form development approach to the traditional approach of developing native mobile apps.

10

Going Mobile

When I'm drivin' free, the world's my home, when I'm mobile.

—The Who

As you saw in the previous chapter, there are a number of LiveCycle modules that support and complement the forms you create in LiveCycle Designer. In this chapter, you'll learn about the LiveCycle Process Management module. This module enables you to create streamlined and automated business workflows. Your workflows can include people, systems, forms, documents, and business rules.

LiveCycle Process Management ES4 enables you to go mobile by extending your workflows and forms to mobile devices. Mobile users can complete forms and workflow tasks even when they are offline. You'll see an example of this with Adobe's Mobile Workspace app. This chapter will also compare and contrast the Adobe LiveCycle solution for mobile apps with a traditional approach to mobile app development.

LiveCycle Process Management

The LiveCycle Process Management module enables you to create automated workflows to streamline a business process. You create a workflow process in LiveCycle Workbench by dragging and dropping activity icons and creating routes between the activities (**Figure 10.1**).

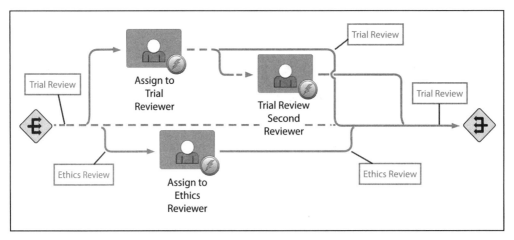

Figure 10.1 An illustration of a process management diagram in Workbench.

A process management diagram typically includes task assignments for users. These tasks assignments are represented by the head and shoulders icons in Figure 10.1. When users are assigned tasks in a Workbench process, the process immediately switches from a short-lived process to a long-lived process because the process will go into a holding pattern until the user completes his task. Users use the web-based LiveCycle Workspace program to review and execute LiveCycle tasks.

In addition to automating workflow processes, LiveCycle Process Management includes management tools that are beyond the scope of this book. There are tools to monitor work queues, backlogs, and track key performance indicators (KPIs). You can find more information about the management tools on the book's companion site.

Workspace

When a workflow process is deployed, it becomes a LiveCycle service and user tasks will be assigned to individual users or to groups of users. These tasks can be reviewed and completed in the LiveCycle Workspace program, for which there are currently three versions:

- **The legacy version:** The traditional version of Workspace is based on Adobe's Flex programming language, and it runs in the Adobe Flash Player. Your browser will need the Flash plug-in installed to use this version.

- **The new HTML version:** Beginning with LiveCycle Process Management ES4, Adobe released a new HTML-based Workspace (**Figure 10.2**). Unlike the Flex version, this version is modular because it is based on JavaScript components that can be customized and used in other web applications.

- **The mobile version:** This version is available for the Apple iPad and is described in the next section.

Figure 10.2 The new HTML version of Workspace can be integrated with other web applications.

Workspace has two main sections for working with tasks. The first section is called *Start Process* (Figure 10.2), which enables you to begin a new Workspace process.

Clicking the Start Process icon takes you to a screen that lists all the LiveCycle processes and forms you can access. Typically, a user clicks this icon and selects a form to start a process. When the form is completed, the user submits the form to the next step in the process. This form is then routed to someone else's To-do list or to another LiveCycle process. This instance of the form will no longer appear in the user's Start Process section.

The second section is named *To-do* (Figure 10.2), and it displays a list of the LiveCycle tasks that have been assigned to you. For instance, if you're a manager and one of your employees submits an expense report, it will appear in your To-do list. You'll see the tasks specifically assigned to you and the tasks assigned to the groups you are a part of. If a task is assigned to a group, you can claim it and move it to your personal queue.

Mobile Workspace

The LiveCycle Process Management module also includes the Mobile Workspace app (**Figure 10.3**). This app enables fieldworkers to complete forms and tasks with an Apple iPad.

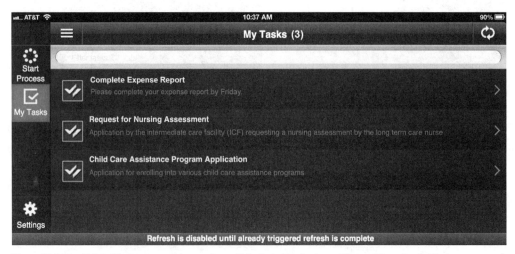

Figure 10.3 The Mobile Workspace enables you to participate in LiveCycle workflows with an Apple iPad.

Since this is a mobile app, it also enables you to take advantage of many of your device's features. You can record location information with your tasks and attach photos, videos, and electronic signatures.

Offline HTML forms

The Mobile Workspace app enables you to complete interactive and dynamic Designer forms whether you are online or offline. **Figure 10.4** shows the SmartDoc Expense Report that you created in Chapter 8, "Creating HTML Forms," in the Mobile Workspace app.

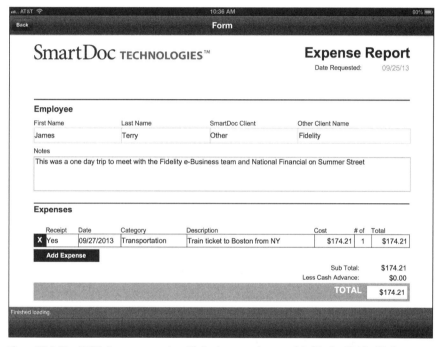

Figure 10.4 The HTML forms you create with Designer can be completed in the Mobile Workspace app even when you're disconnected from the Internet.

If you complete a form offline, the Mobile Workspace application will submit the form or the form's data automatically when you reconnect to the Internet.

Customizing the Mobile Workspace app

Adobe enables you to customize the look and feel of the Mobile Workspace app with HTML and CSS. The complete source code for the Mobile Workspace app is available, and it includes HTML and CSS files that control the visual properties of the app.

Mobile Strategies

This section will compare and contrast different approaches for mobile form app development. To make the comparison easy and understandable, we'll use the SmartDoc Expense Report as an example in each of the strategies.

Going Native

The most obvious and traditional approach for mobile app development is to develop a native app. Although there are many types of mobile devices, most native app development is created for Apple's iOS environment or Google's Android environment. This section will describe each development environment and then summarize the advantages of going native.

Apple's iOS

You develop a native iOS application with Apple's Xcode IDE. Xcode uses the Objective-C language, and it includes many visual tools for app development, testing, and deployment. This approach enables you to take advantage of Apple's design patterns, native user interface controls, and operating system functionality. You can develop very powerful and lightweight form management apps with Xcode for the iOS platform.

To see an example of a native iPad form application that relates to the examples in this book, download the free "SmartDoc Expense Report" from the Apple App Store. This native app makes it easy to create business expense reports while you are on the road with your Apple iPad (**Figure 10.5**).

Figure 10.5 An illustration of the native SmartDoc Expense Report app for iPad. You can download this free app on your iPad from the Apple App Store.

NOTE Since Adobe's Mobile Workspace is an iPad application, you'll use Apple's Xcode IDE to open and edit the source code. You can use Xcode to customize, compile, and deploy your Workspace app.

Google's Android

You take a similar approach when developing a native Android application, but you use different tools. Google provides the Android Development Toolkit (ADT) that works with the Eclipse IDE. Google's ADT uses the Java language, and it includes many visual tools for app development, testing, and deployment.

Like the native iOS approach, this approach enables you to take advantage of everything that Google and their partners have already built. Google provides instructions on how to implement their design strategies and user interface guidelines so you can develop an app that seems familiar to existing Android users. Android makes it easy to integrate applications through its structure of intents. An *intent* acts as a glue between activities in your application and activities that exist outside your app. You can develop a native form app that integrates with a user's other apps, including email, calendars, and web browsers.

The native advantage

Even though they use different tools, developing native applications on either iOS or Android offers similar advantages. You can expect the following advantages for your form app if you take the native development approach:

- **Integration:** Native apps are easy to integrate with the functionality of the mobile device and operating system. Apple and Google offer powerful features like voice activation, cloud-based services, location services, and push notifications. Native apps are also able to integrate with your device's camera for photographs or video.

- **Usability:** Native apps can be easy to use if they take advantage of the standard UI elements that Apple or Google recommends. If you follow this approach, people will intuitively understand your app the first time they use it. To see an example of an app that uses standard iOS UI elements, download the "SmartDoc Expense Report for iPhone" from the Apple App Store (**Figure 10.6**). This native app uses standard UI elements that were available in iOS version 6 and earlier.

Figure 10.6 An illustration of the native SmartDoc Expense Report for iPhone. You can download this free app on your iPhone from the Apple App Store.

- **Optimized for touch:** Native apps support direct manipulation through many different gestures, including touch, double touch, swipe, long press, drag, and pinch.

- **Excellent IDEs:** iOS and Android both have excellent and full-featured integrated development environments for app development, testing, and deployment.

■ **Proven UI design standards:** Apple and Google both provide UI design standards for their mobile operating systems. These standards enable you to make highly functional and aesthetically pleasing apps.

Using a native form app

You can experience the advantages of a native form application by following these steps and reviewing the SmartDoc Expense Report app on your Apple iPad:

1. Go to the App Store on your Apple iPad.

2. Search for **SmartDoc Expense Report**.

3. Tap the SmartDoc Expense Report icon in the iPad Apps panel. The app's detail page will appear.

4. Tap the Free button below the app's icon. The button will change to "Install App."

5. Tap the Install App button.

6. Enter your Apple password and tap OK. The app will install on your iPad.

7. With your iPad in a horizontal or landscape position, tap the app's icon to launch the app. The app launches with one default expense report.

8. Rotate your iPad to see how the expense report form adjusts to the new vertical or portrait format. This is an example of a usability advantage. The form is presented in the orientation that the user prefers.

9. Rotate your iPad back to horizontal or landscape position.

10. Tap New Report and the New Report popover will appear.

11. Enter **My Report** as the Report Name and tap Done. A new report will be created.

12. Tap an empty row in the report. The row will be highlighted in blue and the Add Expense popover will appear. This is an example of direct manipulation. Native apps are optimized for touch and make it easy for users to understand how to complete a form.

13. Select Meals as the category for your expense. Tap the Done button.

14. Tap the Enter A Description text field. The keyboard will appear. If you have an iPad with Siri, you can tap the Siri button on your keyboard and use your voice to enter a description (**Figure 10.7**). Otherwise, you'll need to type your description. This is an example of an integration advantage. Native apps are easy to integrate with the functionality of the mobile device and operating system.

Figure 10.7 An iPad keyboard showing the Siri button. A native app can be integrated with the functionality of the device.

15. Enter an amount for your expense.

16. Tap Done to enter it in your report.

17. Tap the Settings button in the top-left of the app. The Settings popover will appear.

18. Tap Currency Formats.

The currencies are displayed in an iOS Picker control. This is an example of a native iOS user interface control. Apple and Google have created ideal user interface controls for mobile apps, and you can use these controls in your native applications.

The LiveCycle Advantage

Inasmuch as a native mobile app offers advantages, the Adobe LiveCycle approach is ideal for developing and managing a forms and workflow-based mobile application. LiveCycle technology and products are powerful, comprehensive, and practical.

■ **Powerful:** As you have seen in the last two chapters, LiveCycle technology and products offer powerful solutions for enterprise integration, document generation, enterprise form management, and workflow management. The new LiveCycle Enterprise Suite ES4 enables you to extend these powerful features to mobile users. Adobe's Mobile Workspace iOS source code empowers you to realize native app advantages while building on the robust and proven features of the LiveCycle platform. Adobe's new Scribble Signature object demonstrates how Adobe can update XFA objects to make it as ideal for mobile forms as it has been for PDF forms over the past 10 years.

■ **Comprehensive:** As you have seen throughout this book, LiveCycle technology and products offer comprehensive solutions for business forms, workflow, and documents. You can develop one system, and even one XDP file, for all your business needs. LiveCycle's extensive products and solutions support desktop-based PC users, mobile users, and even people who prefer paper. Your LiveCycle system is ideal for your legacy and future requirements.

■ **Practical:** The most important LiveCycle advantage is that it's practical. Form authors can create forms and graphic designers can design documents without becoming programmers. Forms and documents are independent and decoupled from the application and the data. In the real world, this is the only approach that works. The presentation, data, and application are all integrated, but each can be developed and managed by different people in your organization. This supports a practical division of labor and enables everyone to focus on their expertise and responsibility, knowing that the parts will work together seamlessly.

It's LiveCycle Designer that makes this all possible. Designer's easy-to-use visual tools enable you to create forms and documents for desktop and mobile workflow applications. You can create dynamic smart forms with embedded business logic or simple interactive forms for data gathering. You can integrate your forms with data and enterprise applications. You can deploy them as PDF and HTML. And you can automate your business.

Moving On

You now know what LiveCycle Designer is, how to create smart forms, and why this is important for your organization. Forms are everywhere today. It's our job to make them easy for our users to complete and powerful enough to meet our business requirements. You'll find more information and useful Adobe links on the book's companion site. Please feel free to write me about your LiveCycle Designer success at jp@smartdoctech.com. Thank you for reading.

Index

U

Universally unique identifiers (UUIDs), 165
Use Global Data, data binding approaches, 18
Use Name, data binding approaches, 18
UUIDs (universally unique identifiers), 165

V

Validation
  adding form validation, 223–225
  regular expressions for, 60–61
  scripts for, 31
Validation script object
  creating and referencing script objects, 102–103
  Hierarchy palette and, 223
  referencing functions in, 104
Variables
  form variables, 39–40
  naming, 39
  script variables, 39–40
  types of, 38
Vision disability, accessibility and, 150, 153

W

Warnings tab, Report palette
  Missing Required Fields warning, 225
  overview of, 68–69
  Target Version setting and, 132
Watched folder, Workbench endpoints, 237
Web browsers
  Adobe supported, 176
  default PDF viewers, 129–130
  testing HTML forms in, 185
  testing tables in, 189
Web services
  calling, 83–84
  connecting to WSDL file, 80–83
  extending Reader to call, 122–123
  overview of, 80
  REST (Representational State Transfer) compared with, 194–197
Web-safe fonts, 180, 199
Widgets, customizing for HTML forms, 193–194
Windows OSs
  Acrobat support, 120
  browser support, 176
Workbench
  creating LiveCycle process in, 194–195
  development tools in LiveCycle Enterprise Suite, 235–236

endpoints, 237
  forms deployment and, 242
  process management in, 248
Workspace
  customizing, 24
  illustration of interface, 4
  Layout Editor and, 4–5
  left-side palettes for organizing forms, 5–6
  LiveCycle Workspace program, 249–250
  Mobile Workspace app, 250–252
  Process Management module and, 248
  right-side palettes for creating/editing form objects, 7
  Script Editor and, 5
WSDL file, 80–83

X

Xcode, developing iOS apps with, 252
XDP files
  Master File Strategy for development and, 186
  master form fragment saved as, 138
  optimizing caching of resource files, 162–163
  options for saving forms, 8
  policy documents saved as, 188
  transforming into HTML forms, 169
XDP forms, web-safe fonts for, 199
XFA (XML Forms Architecture) PDF
  accessibility features, 151
  Adobe Reader support, 119
  comparing with HTML forms, 177
  dynamic forms, 111–112
  overview of, 109
  static forms, 110
  third-party viewers and, 129
  transforming to HTML, 174–176
  version support in Acrobat and Designer, 132–133
XFS files, 8
XML files
  Multiple Master File Strategy for development and, 186
  optimizing performance with, 159–161
  options for saving forms, 8
XML Forms Architecture (XFA) PDF. See XFA (XML Forms Architecture) PDF
XML schema, binding blank form to, 21–23
XML source
  changing fonts by editing, 202–203
  Layout Editor tabs, 5